THE BEST OF WILL ROGERS

THE BEST OF WILL ROGERS

by Bryan B. Sterling

Foreword by
WILL ROGERS, JR.

M. EVANS & COMPANY, INC.
NEW YORK

M. Evans and Company, Inc.
216 East 49th Street
New York, New York, 10017

Manufactured in the United States of America

ISBN 0-87131-913-6

9 8 7 6 5 4 3

Dear Reader:

You are looking at a new edition of The Best of Will Rogers. You may ask—and quite rightly so—how can one call something "new" that has been "The Best" for two decades? Well, this book was originally compiled and printed in 1979 to celebrate the one-hundredth anniversary of Will Rogers' birth. Though three different presses have issued innumerable reprints, not a single word was ever changed, nor indeed is there any change from the original text in this edition. So you ask: "Well, if that is so, what then is new about it?" Let me explain.

When first published, this book received the most positive reviews and almost a half million copies have been sold since. Over the years a surprisingly large number of readers took time to write complimentary letters, but to our astonishment there was a single recurrent regret, mostly from younger readers: "We would have liked to see more photographs of the man our parents told us so much about."

And that is the answer to what makes this a new edition. The current publisher, M. Evans and Company, listened to the letter writers and ordered that the number of pictures be increased by 50 photographs, some never before seen in print. We all feel that this will enrich the enjoyment of reading this book. When you can see more of the man who literally eclipsed his era, you can better understand his unparalleled influence. These additional pictures of Will Rogers will definitely increase the appreciation of the man whose philosophy and wit are the most widely quoted of all Americans.

A question which comes up sooner or later in many letters and invariably in almost every interview is the puzzle as to what attracted a native Austrian to explore the life and work of Will Rogers. Reporters automatically believe that since there is obviously a chasm between our backgrounds, there cannot be an understanding. But that is one of the secrets of Will Rogers: his insight and power of observation addresses the human conditions where there exist no national or language frontiers.

I must confess that I knew absolutely nothing about Will Rogers when I crossed the border from Canada into the United States in 1950. While Mr. Rogers had traveled to Vienna, my home town, I was too young at the time to know about it. In fact, I must further admit that on my first sightseeing drive across the United States, I stopped in Claremore, Oklahoma—Will Rogers' adopted home town—just long enough to buy a cup of coffee before driving on along Route 66 to Tulsa without visiting the local memorial his native state had built to its most famous son.

Since then, fate has seen to it that this unjustifiable deficiency in my scholastic indoctrination be remedied. I have spent the past forty-odd years reading every available word by, and about, this most remarkable American. With my equally absorbed wife, Frances, by my side, and two children converted to our engrossment in tow, we have traveled from sea to shining sea and from the northern to the southern border in search of information about Will Rogers. We have interviewed the high and the mighty, and those who were neither. We learned details in Hollywood, California, and had them corroborated in Alaska; we learned something about a unicycle in Teaneck, New Jersey, and had it confirmed in Bakersfield, California. John Ford, the famous director, would tell us that Will was on the motion picture set ahead of him in the morning, while an airplane mechanic in Fairbanks, Alaska, would tell us about Wiley Post's hybrid plane having only a single fuel gauge while using seven gasoline tanks; Rose Okpeaha Leavitt in Barrow, Alaska, would recount to us how her father took a kayak to paddle to Barrow after seeing the crash, but had to beach it because ice floes threatened to upset it. In a public library in London, England, we found at last the details of Will Rogers' benefit performance in Ireland after a devastating fire in Drumcollier decimated the village. Over the years we separated facts from anecdotes, the truth from continuously repeated fabrication. We befriended Will's sons and daughter, his fellow actors and his acquaintances—we found no foes.

Much has changed since I first found Will Rogers. I had come upon him at a time when I truly thought I was one of very few people in America who knew about him. I was amazed just how much I had to learn. Book reviewers and a reading public were way ahead of me; they all knew Will Rogers, the humanitarian, the performer, the philosopher, the wit, the chronicler of an age. His were the eyes of a kindly and wise uncle who looked at his world, and with a smile and his Oklahoma twang would try to nudge his fellow citizens to do the right thing. All right, sometimes it was a little more than a nudge, it was a push. He used the power of humor to achieve what criticism could never have done.

But always remember that this man was no ordinary comedian, no funny man who made people laugh but forget the next moment what it was that had been so amusing. He was far more than that. He saw the stark flaws without accusation. He could throw velvet-tipped harpoons at sacred cows, unerringly hitting his mark, making his point, yet never leaving a scar. He saw his country's foibles, its leaders' errors, the Mississippi floods, the stock market crash, the tragedy of the great Depression, the Dust Bowl calamity, the hunger of children and parents, and was the first to offer help and his own money.

Even more has happened since Will Rogers' death in a plane crash in 1935. There have been wars, genocide, catastrophe upon annihilation, unemployment, economic and political upheaval. Yet through it all, you will find that Will Rogers' wise views of his fellow man are just as true today as they were when he first coined them.

And that is why even this edition has not a single word changed in its text., for this book truly contains The Best of Will Rogers.

Bryan B. Sterling
New York City, November 4, 1999

"I contend that nothing could be written about America during the 1918–1935 period without including Will Rogers, because he spoke on the events as they happened, day by day. Reading Will Rogers gives one the best history of America during this crucial period, told in that inimitable Rogers manner, sparked with spontaneous wit and wisdom, and set down in a style that all can understand and enjoy."

> Paula McSpadden Love
> (1901–1973)
> Curator, Will Rogers Memorial
> (1938–1973)

My first impulse was to dedicate this book to our friend Robert W. Love, manager of the Will Rogers Memorial at Claremore, Oklahoma, from 1938–1975. With his wife, the late Paula McSpadden Love, he established the policy of integrity and friendliness at the memorial, making it representative of the spirit of Will Rogers.

But my wife, Frances, who is my right arm, my extra pair of eyes, and often my backbone, suggested that we dedicate this book to the next generation, to Suzanna and Mark, the two Will Rogers fans we raised, and to Raymond and Lois, their respective mates, who became converts.

> B.B.S.
> New York City, 1979

CONTENTS

FOREWORD

by Will Rogers, Jr.

BRYAN STERLING KNOWS THE WRITINGS of Will Rogers probably better than any other person. For years he has been editing these writings in a reprinting of the Will Rogers daily column. This gives him an authoritative position from which to select "The Best of Will Rogers."

From 1926 to his death in 1935, Will Rogers wrote a daily column. Only a few paragraphs long, it was usually printed in a box with the title "Will Rogers Says." Appearing on the front page of over four hundred newspapers, it was easily the most read column of its day.

I thought, as most people thought (and probably Dad did, too), that its appeal was its timeliness. People would read the headline first, and what Will Rogers said about that headline, immediately thereafter. It was the instant insight, the instant gag that, I felt, gave the column its popularity and political power.

So when Bryan Sterling proposed a reprinting, I tried to discourage him. It was my memory that while many of Will Rogers's remarks were lasting, most of them simply referred to long lost happenings. There was not enough material.

I was wrong. In fact I am surprised to see how relevant to current events are so many of the comments in this book. This, it seems to me, is because so many of the things we think of as referring to today's news are actually a human condition. Party politics, investigations, political pomposities, all have a way of repeating themselves. Bryan Sterling had the eye to see this, and his selection, sharpened by his years of editorship, makes this very much *The Best of Will Rogers*.

There is one side of the man, however, that will not be in this book. Will Rogers could not write about how the country regarded him. It is hard, even today, to express the hold Will Rogers had on so many millions of Americans in his lifetime.

He was called "typically American," and in many ways he did have the family background and traits we like to think of as distinctive to our country. He was both Indian and cowboy, serious writer and comedian, movie star and political analyst.

In his lifetime the whole country knew who Will Rogers was and what he was. They respected him and his judgment. So read, not just for the gags, but for the kindly, tolerant, understanding, constructive attitude behind them. For that was the real Will Rogers.

It's a great country but you can't live in it for nothing.

Will Rogers.

INTRODUCTION

IN DECEMBER 1922, WILL ROGERS wrote the first of 667 weekly articles, which he continued until his death in 1935. In addition, between 1925 and 1927 he wrote 511 columns called "The Worst Story I've Heard Today"; and beginning in 1926 until his death in 1935 he also wrote 2,861 daily squibs, now called "The Daily Telegrams." There were also syndicated articles covering Democratic and Republican national conventions and feature articles for the *Saturday Evening Post, Life, The Theatre, New York American, New McClure, American,* and *Photoplay.* One must further mention the introductions to over half a dozen books, ranging from two books about western artist Charles Russell to biographies of Eddie Cantor and Annie Oakley.

Every one of the above articles has been preserved; so, too, have been the transcripts of Will Rogers's sixty-nine radio broadcasts. The most conservative estimate places the combined total at well over 2 million words. If Will Rogers had done nothing else, the average would be over 150,000 words a year—every year—truly a phenomenal record. But during that same period, 1922–1935, Will created new material not only for the *Ziegfeld Follies* of 1922 and 1924 but also for lectures in almost four hundred cities and towns across America, with original material specifically prepared for each community. He had to write, and update, his part in the Broadway show *Three Cheers,* in which Rogers never adhered to the original script. In the twenties Rogers wrote the continuity for at least two dozen of his silent films. There were literally hundreds of charity performances and after-dinner speeches, from which only a relatively small number of notes have been found. And lastly,

1

Will Rogers made twenty-one sound films; for each of these he completely reworded his own part.

The Best of Will Rogers has been selected from all this wealth of material. Any such selection would have to be subjective, but it was made with a view to topicality and variety. Unfortunately it could be quite possible that a reader's favorite quotation seems to be missing. If that be so, please blame the selector, not Will Rogers. For as Rogers wrote:

The great trouble is that you are apt to hit on some subject that does not appeal to certain people. For instance, if I write a learned article on chewing gum, I find that I lose my readers who are toothless. Then, when I write on politics, I find that the honest people are not interested. Then, if I write on some presidential candidate, I find that there are so many of them that few readers know the one I am writing about. When I write an article on bathing beaches, I find that I lose the interest of most of my readers that are not interested in bathing, either by tub or beach. Why, once I wrote an editorial for High Brows and I found that a High Brow is a man that wouldn't read anything that was not written by himself. So I am going to work along the same lines as a newspaper—I'm just going to touch on each subject!

And that was attempted here—just to touch on each subject.

BIOGRAPHY

WILEY POST NEVER REALLY LIKED THE NEW PLANE. "I wish we were flying the *Winnie Mae*" he confided to friends. But Will Rogers felt secure with Wiley at the controls: "No danger with this guy," he wired his wife.

When Will Rogers had heard that his friend and fellow Oklahoman planned to fly to Alaska, Will decided to go along. "I never have been to that Alaska!"

But the monoplane, the *Winnie Mae*, had served her purpose. She had helped Wiley Post to become one of America's foremost fliers. It was with the *Winnie Mae* that Wiley had established a number of outstanding records, including two around-the-world flights. Another long-distance flight would just be too much for her.

Will contributed $25,000 and Wiley bought a secondhand Lockheed Orion, Model 9 E. A brand new 550 horsepower Pratt & Whitney engine was installed. Post also replaced the wings, the propeller, the fuel tanks, and exchanged the wheels for pontoons. Thus refitted, the plane no longer resembled the original design: the engine was too powerful for the relatively small plane; the oversized pontoons made the plane nose-heavy and difficult to handle.

Will Rogers suggested they call the plane *Post's Toasty*, but the plane was never officially named. In his articles Will does refer to it as *The Little Red Bus*. The two men were now ready for their flight to Alaska, and possibly onward to Europe, via Siberia.

On August 7, 1935, Will and Wiley left Seattle, Washington. Ignoring reports of storms on their route, they took off for Juneau,

Alaska. They covered the distance of 875 nautical miles in eight and a quarter hours. When the plane set down on Gastineau Channel, crowds lined up to see the two famous men taxi to the dock. Steady rainfall the next day delayed their departure plan. Will Rogers bought a pair of rubbers and a raincoat and went out to talk to old friends and meet new ones.

A number of short side trips were made as the continuing inclement weather permitted. By August 15 Will Rogers and Wiley Post were in Fairbanks, eager for the 500-mile flight to Point Barrow. During the early hours of the day, fog and low clouds made a take-off unthinkable. In the afternoon the clouds parted for a while. Rogers and Post decided to risk the relatively short hop to their next destination. Friends, more experienced and familiar with Alaskan weather, tried to persuade the two men to postpone the flight to another day. But Wiley was impatient. He had sat around long enough. It was time to go.

Taking advantage of the temporary break in the overcast, the small plane took off on its way toward the small lake, fifty miles distant, where the tanks could be topped with fuel. From there the heading was toward the mountains of the Brooks Range, and the little community of Barrow, beyond.

Ground visibility was almost nonexistent. Clouds obscured the mountains, which in turn prevented Post from flying under the cover. But Wiley was undaunted; he had been in difficult situations before. He set his course and flew on instruments.

It was near eight o'clock in the evening when the two men felt that they were approaching Barrow. Somewhere below them was the small outpost, but where? If Wiley's calculations were correct, they must have cleared the mountains and would now be over the coastal plain. They could go lower to look around.

The plane began to descend through the clouds. A sudden break in the ground fog revealed an inlet with a small group of Eskimos camped nearby. It was decided to land and to ask for directions. The small plane circled for the approach. Will Rogers moved to the rear of the fuselage, to counterbalance its nose-heaviness.

The end of the man was only minutes away. The beginning lay fifty-five years in the past.

The Indian Territory (now Oklahoma) in the late 1870s was peaceful and quiet. The Civil War was over, and the tribes of the

Great Plains were seemingly resigned to a life in the territory. Towns and villages began to spring up beside the railroads.

Before the war Clement Vann Rogers had come to the Cooweescoowee District, so called after the Indian name of John Ross, the famous Cherokee leader. On Rabb's Creek, Rogers had laid out his ranch and built his house. Here he had brought his bride, Mary America; here, too, their first child, Elizabeth, was born. As a cattleman and trader Clem Rogers had prospered and acquired a sizeable fortune when the Civil War broke out. Clem sent his wife and daughter to Texas for safety and joined the cause of the Confederacy as a cavalry officer.

Four years later, the war over, Clem returned. His cattle had been driven off; the house was in ruins. Little Elizabeth had died, and Sallie, Robert, and Maud were born before Clem brought his wife to a new two-story house, now built on the Verdigris River. Clem went to work to restore his fortune. In the years that followed three more children enlarged the family, though two of them died in infancy.

On Tuesday, November 4, 1879, William Penn Adair Rogers was born in the log annex of the "White House on the Verdigris," as the Rogers home was known. Will later told the story: "Just before my birth my mother had them remove her into the log part of the house. She wanted me to be born in a log house. She had read the life of Lincoln. So I got the log house end of it OK. All I need now is the other qualifications."

Of Irish, Welsh, English, either German or Dutch, and Cherokee ancestry on both his parents' sides, William Penn Adair Rogers was listed on the official Cherokee rolls as No.: 11384. At home the boy was simply called *Willie*. Clem Rogers wanted the boy to follow in his footsteps and someday take over the ranch. Mary America Rogers was a gentle, kind, and thoughtful woman, who quietly wished for her son to become a preacher. But Willie, unaware of his parents' ambitions for him, was never happier than when he rode his pony or practiced the rope tricks taught him by the hired hands around the ranch.

Life began in earnest for Willie when he was sent to attend his first school. The days in the one-room schoolhouse were misery for the boy who had spent all his time outdoors. He would volunteer to run errands or fetch water rather than be confined to the classroom. Most of his fellow pupils were full-blooded Indians. As Will put it later: "I had just enough *white* in me to make my honesty questionable."

He was really joking, because he was well liked—at least by the students, if not by the teachers. When the year closed, Will decided that school was not for him. He tried to persuade his father to let him stay at home. But "he sent me to about every school in that part of the country. In some of them I·would last three or four months. I got just as far as McGuffey's *Fourth Reader*, when the teacher wouldn't seem to be running the school right, and rather than have the school stop, I would generally leave."

When Will was ten years old, his mother died. He was sent to live with his older sister Sallie and her husband, Tom McSpadden. It was from their home near Chelsea that Will continued to go to school. For when Will Rogers talked about his battles with formal education, he was partly joking. His dislike of schools was real, but his progress was steady. In 1897 he was sent to Boonville, Missouri, to attend the Kemper Military School. "I spent two years there," he later wrote, "one year in the fourth grade, and one year in the guardhouse. One was as bad as the other." The end came when he and the commandant didn't see eye to eye on school matters. Will, being "an accommodating boy," left. He was through with schools for life!

Back home, his father gave him some cattle and a spread and suggested that he try ranching on his own. It kept Will busy for a while, but he much preferred racing horses, roping anything that moved, or going to dances and parties. He tried singing tenor in a quartet. "I have what is called a fresh voice. It's got volume without control; it's got resonance without reason. It's got tone without tune. I got a voice that's got everything but a satisfied listener."

It was here at Oologah, now a small town, that Will met Betty Blake. He was almost twenty-one. Betty had come from her native Arkansas to visit her sister Cora, who was married to the local station agent, Will Marshall. Will fell in love with Betty immediately and courted her shyly and tenderly for the next eight years. Many months would go by without either hearing from the other. For Will had left Oologah and was on his way around the world.

A restlessness that would drive him all of his days had to be obeyed. The horizon was always a barrier to be scaled; there were always other people to meet and to talk to; there were always new things to see and learn.

Will wanted to go to the Argentine to see the gauchos. He arrived in South America via England, but found it difficult to get work. Finally he was offered a job on a ship bound for South Africa. He was to "chaperone mules and she-cows." The thirty-two-day trip proved a horrible experience. Will was seasick almost the entire trip and could do little work, but "they couldn't fire me."

From Durban, Natal, Will helped drive the herd one hundred fifty miles inland, worked for a while on the ranch, but soon became restless again and left. To earn a living, he saddle broke horses for the British Army, then signed up for a cattle drive to Johannesburg. There he met the man who gave him his first introduction to show business, and Will was "ruined for life, as far as actual work was concerned."

The man was Texas Jack, owner and principal star of a Wild West show. Will's preoccupation and constant practice with the lariat paid off. He could do all the tricks Texas Jack performed nightly and had an additional array of spectacular stunts. He was immediately hired as the new roping star of the show at the liberal salary of $20 a week. He was billed as the "Cherokee Kid." Will learned a lot about showmanship from Texas Jack: "It was him who gave me the idea for my original stage act with a pony . . . and from him I learned the great secret of show business—I learned when to get off!"

From South Africa, Will went to Australia and joined the Wirth Brothers' Circus. When the company moved to New Zealand, Will went along. At the end of the tour Will had just enough money left to book a third-class passage back to America. He reached San Francisco broke and traveled the rest of the way by freight train. Will had been gone three years and he had circled the world; he had shown that he could earn his own way, but he was not yet ready to settle down.

When Colonel Zach Mulhall formed a Wild West group to perform at the St. Louis World's Fair in 1904, Will joined him. He also went with the Colonel the following year to perform in New York's Madison Square Garden as an additional event in conjunction with the annual Horse Fair. When the Colonel left to return home, Will stayed behind. He was determined to break into vaudeville. Remembering Texas Jack's advice, he had practiced roping a pony on stage. He made the rounds until finally the manager of Keith's Union Square Theatre hired him for a single performance. The audience liked the unusual act, and Will was booked for the balance of the week. From there Will was booked to appear at Hammerstein's Theatre, where he proved such a remarkable hit that he was asked to stay for the rest of the summer.

An extended tour of European capitals followed. In London, Will appeared before King Edward VII. He enjoyed Paris, but he loved Berlin. Since he was still corresponding with Betty Blake, Will sent her clippings and reports. He also tried to make Betty jealous by writing what a simply wonderful time he was having in the night spots of Europe.

As Will Rogers had planned the act, it was "dumb." Will would simply perform his rope tricks, either by himself or by having a horse and rider gallop across the stage. Without saying a word he would rope both, or any part of either. While the audience liked what they saw Will do with such seeming ease, they did not realize the art involved. A fellow performer finally suggested that Will better introduce and explain each trick. The shyness of the Westerner came across the footlights and improved the act. Will then prepared a few ad libs that he used if he missed a trick, which was very rare indeed. "Swinging a rope is all right," he would say as he retrieved his lariat, "provided your neck ain't in it!" Or on another occasion: "Well, I got all my feet through—but one!" Roars of laughter greeted these little asides, and Will began missing his throws on purpose, so he could use his special gags. As the weeks went by he would add comments about other acts on the same program. Since he usually looked down at the rope he was preparing for the next trick, audiences thought these remarks were ad-libbed. Actually they had been well prepared.

As Will changed his act slowly from being a silent performer to one who made audiences laugh, he kept looking for new material. Soon, references to other performers were not enough, and he began to joke about topics he felt would be of interest to theatre patrons. People came to see the act as much to listen to the man as for the rope tricks. Even Betty finally listened and on November

25, 1908, they were married. Their honeymoon started with a two-week booking in New York and continued all along the Orpheum circuit. The marriage proved to be ideal, for Betty was not only his wife, and mother of his children, but his advisor, his critic, and in many ways even his mother. Will needed someone to love, someone who gave stability to his life, someone who was there when he needed her, yet would not stand in his way or compete with him. In all honesty Will could say on their twenty-fifth wedding anniversary: "The day I roped Betty, I did the star performance of my life."

Early in 1912 Will opened in his first regular Broadway show, *The Wall Street Girl*, staring Blanche Ring. Will received rave notices and the show played a year. After it closed Will went back to vaudeville. Another child was expected, and since he had to be on tour, Betty and Will Jr., born in 1911, moved to Arkansas. Mary Amelia, named after her two grandmothers, was born in 1913.

The following year Will wired Betty to leave the children in the good care of her mother and to meet him in Atlantic City, New Jersey. When Betty arrived expecting problems, Will surprised her with tickets for a trip to Europe. Betty had to buy clothes and accessories in a hurry. Will had no engagements planned in Europe, but since he had been there before, he was known. Within a few days he was booked at the Empire Theatre in London, at $400 per week. While Will was busy in a show, Betty and some of her friends went to the Continent to see the sights and, naturally, to do some shopping.

Will felt uneasy about the political situation in Europe. Despite protestations from their friends that there would be no war, Will left the show and booked passage for their return to the United States. Before the German ship, the *Imperator*, docked in New York, war had been declared in Europe.

Again Will returned to vaudeville. He was now getting quite discouraged. His career had not advanced as he had hoped. He seriously considered returning to Oklahoma and life on a ranch.

Fred Stone, the famous star of many Broadway hits and one of Will's closest friends, persuaded him to stay. Will rented a house in Amityville, Long Island, across the road from Fred's home. Here the family spent the summer of 1915; here James Blake

Rogers, the third child, was born; here, too, occurred an accident that could well have ended Will Rogers's career.

One exceptionally hot morning Fred Stone, his brother-in-law Rex Beach, the famous novelist, and Will decided to go swimming. Not realizing that the tide was out, Will dived into the now shallow water. His head hit a submerged rock. Will was dragged from the ocean semiconscious; his right arm was paralyzed. Practicing hour after hour with total concentration and determination, Will taught himself to perform his entire act with his left arm. During the first few weeks following the accident, he also increased the verbal part of his routine.

In time Will regained the full use of his right arm, but by then he was completely ambidextrous and could perform his rope tricks with equal ease with either arm. Will did not miss a single show because of the accident.

Once again Broadway tempted. Will appeared in two short-lived shows. In *Hands Up* he received good personal notices, but the musical did not. In Ned Wayburn's *Town Topics* Will had an even shorter run. Again he returned to vaudeville.

Gene Buck, Florenz Ziegfeld's right-hand man, came to Will's rescue. Buck had seen a performance of *Hands Up* and felt that this unusual cowboy would bring a new brand of humor to the *Midnight Frolic*. Ziegfeld had two productions: the *Follies*, in the New Amsterdam Theatre, and the *Midnight Frolic*, upstairs on the theatre roof, which had been transformed into an ultrafashionable nightclub. The *Follies* were a regular revue, while the *Frolic* began at midnight and catered to the late crowd. It was the most lavish nightclub production ever attempted, having well over fifty members in its cast.

Ziegfeld, who did not particularly like comics or humorists, was not convinced that some cowboy could add anything to his extravagant presentation. Buck finally persuaded Ziegfeld to give Will a chance.

One problem arose immediately. In vaudeville a performer could perfect one act and play it again and again, without a single change, all along the circuit. Audiences would change nightly. But with the *Midnight Frolic* audiences consisted of many repeaters, and new material was essential—not weekly, or even monthly, but nightly! Betty came up with the solution. Will, she suggested, should talk about the day's news. Will's longtime habit of reading all available newspapers from front page to back page provided all the background he needed.

Nightly he kidded public figures, their actions or inactions, the events of the moment. Because of the war in Europe, Americans suddenly became aware of the importance of the times and the men who were forging their present and their future. With his good-natured humor Will talked sense to the audience while he made them laugh. He was sure that the war would eventually involve America, and he joked about her unpreparedness: "We are the only nation in the world that waits till they get into a war before we start getting ready for it."

At a special performance for President Wilson he continued that thought: "There is some talk of getting a machine gun—if we can borrow one." When Will saw that the President led the laughter, he pushed further: "We're going to have an army of 250,000 men," he started to spin his rope, "Mister Ford makes 300,000 cars a year," another whirl of the lasso, "I think, Mr. President, we ought to at least have a man to every car."

In January 1916 came a call from Florenz Ziegfeld: could Will perform in the *Follies* as well as the *Frolic*—starting at once? Will did not hesitate; he agreed. That evening he used the material he had prepared for the midnight show. Around eleven o'clock he sent out for the latest editions of the morning newspapers and prepared an entirely different act for the *Frolic*. This remained the routine as long as Will Rogers starred in both Ziegfeld productions.

Acclaimed by the critics, Will Rogers became Ziegfeld's greatest star. His words were repeated by those who heard them, and even President Wilson quoted him. Will Rogers became an important voice.

The importance of Will Rogers can best be judged by Ziegfeld's dramatic concession in the following letter:

My Dear Bill:

I tried everywhere to get you on the telephone today before leaving for Easthampton, but it was impossible to find you.

Gene Buck tells me he had a long talk with you and we are to see the new skit Tuesday at 3 P.M.

Gene also told me you insisted on being away three matinees during the Polo Games—that your heart and soul are set upon seeing those games. You know Bill, there isn't anything in the world I would not do for you, but you must realize we have an enormous organization, enormous expenses, and with the productions necessary now for the *Follies*, it takes a year to get our production back. To give matinees without you in them *would be absolutely impossible.*

There is only one thing to do. Of course it is going to entail a great loss, because unquestionably our matinees will be greatly hurt. There is only one solution—give the matinee on Friday instead of Saturday, and on Monday instead of Wednesday. Mr. Holzman will see you about this, and I think we can get a good story through the dramatic column so we will be able to have them; owing to your desire to see the Games I agreed to this, so you know in what high esteem I hold you.

What the result will be Bill, we will only have to wait to determine, but I want to please you in every way I possibly can. I would like to talk with you, so if you can call me at 115 M Easthampton when you get this, I will be glad to talk with you.

Very sincerely yours,

[signed] Flo

Will was not overly impressed with the letter or the unparalleled matinee arrangements. He crossed out the typing with a soft pencil, wrote the word *over* in brackets at the bottom of the page, and used the reverse side to make notes for a biography.

America went to war. At first Will Rogers was hesitant about continuing his special type of humor, but he found that people were eager to hear him put the news into his own individual perspective. His oft-quoted chide that "the airplane program turned out more air than planes" resulted in a Senate investigation. His comment that "the guy who makes the bullets was paid $5 a day, and the man who stopped them got $15 a month" was an indictment that he strengthened by adding, "Of course, stopping bullets comes under the heading of unskilled labor!"

When Will spoke the political and industrial leaders listened. The cowboy from Oologah—or Claremore, as he preferred to be known as he felt that only an Indian could pronounce Oologah—became their friend and adviser; he met the great and the near great, but he remained what he had been, sincere and unaffected: "I joked about every prominent man of my time, but I never met a man I didn't like." Will was one of the largest individual contributors to the Red Cross and to the Salvation Army. Indigent actors could always count on his liberal help, and he was proud of being asked to participate at a benefit, much as if he had just been invited to the White House. When disaster struck anywhere, be it flood or earthquake, Will would be there to help—usually beating the Red Cross to the site.

Peace came and the soldiers returned. "If we really want to honor our Boys," Will asked innocently, "why don't we let *them* sit in the reviewing stands and have the people march by?"

It was also in 1918 that Will made his first motion picture, *Laughing Bill Hyde*, written by Rex Beach. When Will saw the finished film he was aghast. "I am the world's worst actor!" he said, crestfallen. He was all the more surprised when Sam Goldwyn offered him a two-year contract at more than triple the income he earned in the *Follies*. There was one stipulation: Will would have to move to California. After years in New York City the wide open spaces of the West Coast were tempting. The family had now grown to three boys—Fred Stone Rogers was born in 1918—and a girl. Will and Betty felt that California would offer more of the life they themselves had known; it would certainly be good for the children. It was therefore decided to leave the East and see what the movies would bring. Will went on ahead and rented a large house on Van Ness Avenue. The family followed, bringing everything they had on Long Island, including the ponies.

Once settled in Los Angeles, tragedy struck. During a nation-wide diphtheria epidemic the three boys became sick. Twenty-month-old Freddie could not be saved. Will grieved over the loss of his little boy for the rest of his life, but never again did he mention him. Stoically he refused to display his innermost sorrow publicly.

Before going to work at the Goldwyn Studio, Will published *The Cowboy Philosopher on the Peace Conference*, and *The Cowboy Philosopher on Prohibition*, two collections of quips he had used on those subjects during his stay with the Ziegfeld Follies.

During the two years of his association with Goldwyn, Will made twelve films. When the contract expired the studio did not exercise its option. Will knew what was wrong with the motion pictures he had made. Several won awards and some made lists of special merit, but they were not the great financial successes Goldwyn had hoped they would be.

Will tried to produce his own pictures. Of these *The Ropin' Fool* is truly outstanding. Here Will Rogers preserved a permanent record of his unmatched roping skill. Using slow-motion photography, Will captured the movements of white ropes. The loops seem alive as they unerringly seek their targets. Incredible tricks are performed with such seeming ease, proof of the many hours Will practiced every day throughout his life.

But Will learned that there was more to film making than just putting a story on celluloid. Financial problems arose, especially with regard to distribution. Will was forced to mortgage his home, borrow against his insurance policies, and liquidate most of his assets. When all this was still not enough, he signed a contract with Hal Roach to star in a dozen two-reel comedies. Still deprived of his voice—the films were still silent—the comedy films reduced everything to slapstick and sight gags. Will could not count the number of times he had to lose his trousers while being chased. This was not what he wanted to do. Will left the family in California and went back to New York to star once again in the *Ziegfeld Follies*.

In 1922, in addition to his appearance on Broadway, Will embarked on two new phases in his career. He began to write a series of weekly articles for the McNaught Syndicate. These proved immensely popular and he continued them until 1935. He also broadcast his first monologue from Pittsburgh, Pennsylvania. This was the forerunner of Will's weekly radio talks. He was also in demand as an after-dinner speaker.

One would assume that Will Rogers's waking hours were filled to capacity. He appeared nightly in the *Follies*, he wrote weekly articles, read stacks of newspapers, practiced roping for hours, and addressed innumerable functions. This would have taxed any ordinary man, but Will was not an ordinary man. His habits were uncomplicated, his demands few. He rarely slept more than four or five hours at night. He might take short naps during the day, if an opportunity presented itself. Five minutes in a chair, or in a car, and he would be as refreshed as another man after eight hours sleep. He could eat anywhere, for his tastes were simple. A bowl of chili or beans, reminiscent of the days on the ranch, would be his favorite dish. His taste in clothing was equally unpretentious— a plain white shirt and a simple suit. When he traveled he would often take his bath while he sent a bellboy to buy another set of underwear, socks, and a shirt. Will never stayed long enough in any place to send the laundry out. It was simpler to abandon used clothing than to carry the soiled articles along. Unencumbered by the tasks that occupy other men, Will had more time to concentrate on those matters that were important to him.

In 1924 he began to take on even more work. He published the *Illiterate Digest*, a summary of earlier articles. He also began preparations to leave New York City and to embark on a nationwide lecture tour the following year.

In 1925 on his way to California, Will stopped at the "National Joke Factory" (Congress) in Washington. He was to be guest speaker at the annual Gridiron Dinner. There he met General Billy Mitchell, who invited Will to join him on a flight the following day. Will accepted. Though he had been aloft in a plane before, it was this flight that made Will a firm believer in the future of aviation. When the plan landed, Billy Mitchell told Will, "You have been with me on the last flight I will make as a Brigadier General. Tonight at twelve o'clock I am to be demoted to a Colonel, and sent to a faraway post, where, instead of having the entire Air Force at my command, there will be seven planes." Will took up Mitchell's cause for a strong United States Air Force and advocated it for the rest of his life.

Will's decision to tour America on a lecture circuit was really not unusual. He had been asked to speak in almost every city, but his commitments in either New York or California had never allowed him to go "meetin' the regular Bird." Now Will was free to go and speak in hundreds of cities and towns, as well as address conventions. "I faced men," Will wrote, "who made every known and unknown commodity that the American people could very well get along without. I even got so low one time that I talked to real estate men." He told them what no other speaker would have dared, and the closer to the truth he came, the better they liked it. "Loan Sharks and Interest Hounds" was his opening salutation to the National Bankers' Convention. "The Robbing Hoods of

America" were the advertising men, and when he spoke to the automobile dealers he called them "The Old-Time Horse-Trading Gyps with White Collars On."

Will contracted to write a series of articles for the *Saturday Evening Post* from Europe. He pretended that he was really going as the "self-appointed unofficial ambassador" and that his articles were reports to President Coolidge. These "confidential" communications were gems of insight and observation, truth and humor. These reports were later published in book form as *Letters of a Self-Made Diplomat to His President*.

Feeling that certain thoughts should be expressed immediately, Will started still another feature. It was a short daily telegram called "Will Rogers Says." It appeared in well over four hundred daily newspapers all across the country and was one of the first items read over American breakfast tables.

Will's penetrating descriptions of conditions in Europe were far more profound than anything the American public had ever read. "Will Rogers' analysis of affairs abroad was not only more interesting but proved to be more accurate than anything I had heard," wrote Franklin Delano Roosevelt later.

On this trip Will had a camera crew following him, filming his visits to a number of countries. These films were later released as travelogues and were trend setting in this field.

After covering Europe, Will decided to fly to Russia. Unlike others of his time, he was not ready to dismiss that huge country as simply being "in the grips of an experiment." Will always had to see for himself. He returned with a far deeper understanding of Communism than most of his contemporaries. "To me," he wrote, "Communism is one-third practice and two-thirds explanation . . . but these people are going somewhere and we better watch out while they are on their way!"

Back in London, Will stepped into a faltering revue Charles Cochran had produced. Called England's Ziegfeld, Cochran was an old friend, and Will was happy to help him. With Will in the cast the show was sold out nightly. Wrote England's foremost critic, James Agate: "A superior power had seen fit to fling into the world, for once, a truly fine specimen—fine in body, fine in soul, fine in intellect."

Will eventually had to leave the show to honor a commitment to make a motion picture with Dorothy Gish (*Tip Toes*). Charles Cochran offered Will a signed blank check. Will just tore it up.

When Will finally returned to California, a surprise awaited him. During his absence he had been elected Mayor of Beverly Hills, and a large crowd came out to greet him at the station. Will addressed the reception committee: "It don't speak well for your town when this many of you haven't got anything to do but come to meet me." He was proud to have been chosen by his friends and neighbors and signed his daily columns as *His Honor, Mayor Rogers*.

Ether and Me was written after Will's famous gallstone operation. He wrote it, he said, to pay the doctor bills. He had suffered slight attacks before, but the first serious pain struck him in Bluefield, West Virginia. Despite the severity of the attack, Will continued his tour, which was about to close. When he reached California, Betty sent for the doctor. After a thorough examination it was decided to operate. Will prepared his daily and weekly columns to cover the time he expected to be in the hospital.

After the operation Will's condition was far more serious than had been anticipated, and for a time it was doubtful that he would survive. The hospital issued frequent bulletins of his condition, and the news media reported them as if he were a head of state. Thousands of letters and telegrams flooded his hospital room.

In the summer of 1927 the National Press Club in Washington, D.C., "elected" Will Rogers congressman-at-large and invited him to a formal installation dinner. After he was "officially" commissioned by Senator Ashurst of Arizona, Will delivered his inauguration speech: "I certainly regret the disgrace that's been thrust on me here tonight. . . . I certainly have lived, or tried to live, my life so that I would never become a congressman, and I am just as ashamed of the fact I have failed as you are. And to have the commission presented by a senator is adding insult to injury."

One of Will's first "official" acts as congressman-at-large was on the international level. Relations with Mexico had deteriorated, in fact were approaching the breaking point. As Will put it: "Up to now our calling card to Mexico or Central America had been a gunboat or valentines shaped like marines. . . . We always had their good will and oil and coffee and minerals at heart. Is it any wonder that some of these nations weren't exactly crazy about us?"

President Coolidge had appointed Dwight Morrow as the

ambassador to Mexico, hoping that this able man would help re-
cement relations. One of Morrow's first acts was to invite Will
Rogers and Charles Lindbergh to Mexico City. Just a few months
earlier Lindbergh had electrified the entire world with his daring
solo crossing of the Atlantic. By asking Rogers, America's foremost private citizen, and Lindbergh, the world's current hero, to
come to Mexico, Morrow created precisely the feeling toward the
United States he had hoped for. Will joked with President Calles
as he would have with President Coolidge or, for that matter, with
any other man. The Mexican appreciated the obviously genuine
friendship Will exuded. This, in turn, gave Morrow the opening to
discuss diplomacy on a far more personal basis. Will's visit to
Mexico was an unqualified success, and Lindbergh's natural charm
and youthful openness completely captivated his Mexican hosts.

In January 1928 Will was master of ceremonies on an important
"first" in radio history—a national coast-to-coast hookup. Will was
to broadcast from his home in California, Fred Stone would be in
Chicago, Paul Whiteman in New York, and Al Jolson in New
Orleans.

With millions listening Will announced that he had a great
surprise for his listeners. The next voice they heard seemed to be
the voice of President Coolidge giving a most humorous State of
the Nation speech. It was incredible that the dignified Mr.
Coolidge would say such things, but it was his voice—or was it?
Few people knew of Will's uncanny ability to imitate voices. Often
Will would amuse friends with his imitations of important
politicians and movie stars. Will explained after the broadcast:
"The idea that anyone could imagine that it was him uttering this
nonsense—it struck me that it would be an insult to anyone's sense
of humor to announce that it was not him." Will immediately sent
a letter to the President explaining the incident. President Coolidge
returned a handwritten note saying that Will should not give it a
moment's worry.

Will planned to attend the two national conventions that
summer to report on the "national follies." The Republicans met in
Kansas City, Missouri. Will, now traveling by air whenever he
could, took a plane from Los Angeles. Landing at Las Vegas,
Nevada, his plane broke a wheel and turned over. Stunned, Will
changed planes. Later, taking off near Cheyenne, Wyoming, he

crashed again. Undismayed, Will took still another plane that finally brought him to Kansas City.

The airplane was still in its infancy, and accidents, both minor and major, were part of the growing-up process. Dorothy Stone, Fred's daughter, and a Broadway star in her own right, recalls one morning at the family house when "Uncle" Will arrived, ashen and disheveled. He had flown into town and his plane had crashed on landing. Could Will clean up before going to his own home so that Betty needn't know about the accident.

It was a plane mishap that brought Will back to Broadway. Fred Stone had been taking flying lessons, and when his plane crashed in Connecticut his broken body was rushed to the hospital, where doctors worked desperately to save his life. Their verdict finally was that Fred Stone would live, but his legs were too severely crushed for him to ever walk or dance again. Will raced to his friend's bedside to comfort him. He reassured him that he would be back on the stage, greater than he had been in his original hit *The Red Mill*. When Will left his injured friend he had succeeded in buoying up Fred's spirits. He had given him hope. A few minutes later Dorothy Stone walked into the hospital corridor and found Will, his head resting against the wall, sobbing over the tragedy that had befallen his best friend.

Before the accident Fred Stone had been in rehearsal for the Broadway musical *Three Cheers*. Dorothy Stone was to costar. Will now offered to take his disabled friend's place.

Dillingham, the producer, was delighted. Will Rogers' offer promised to save the show, for if anyone could help the audience forget the absence of Fred Stone's artistry, it would be Will Rogers. This act of friendship touched America, and especially Broadway, where acts of sentiment are rare. Few people ever knew that Will Rogers had to cancel a fully booked lecture tour that would have grossed close to half a million dollars. Will repaid all expenses incurred by the promoters and insisted on paying each theater for lost profits that they expected from his appearance.

Three Cheers was not a good show, the critics agreed, but Will Rogers made it a hit. Though he had rehearsed, he made no effort to learn his lines. Will simply carried the script in his hip pocket and consulted it periodically. Mostly he would make up his own lines. He would deviate from the plot and do what he had done in the *Follies*. Dorothy Stone's talent and charm were a perfect foil for Will. Together they presented a show unlike any New York had ever seen, or would ever see again. The audiences loved it.

After a performance, Will, who used no makeup, was the first to leave the theatre. Usually there were a number of indigent actors and beggars waiting at the stage door. Will was prepared: he had a roll of dollar bills that he distributed. Soon the rumor of this windfall spread around town, and a crowd would gather nightly to take part in the bountiful handout. The crowd grew so large that eventually police had to be on hand nightly to help the other actors get to their cars.

There is just one footnote to this episode. Fred Stone recovered almost completely. He not only walked again but danced in many Broadway performances.

During the presidential campaign of 1928 between Republican Herbert Hoover and Democrat Al Smith, the humor magazine *Life* nominated Will Rogers as its candidate on the *Bunkless* ticket. Will entered into the jest by paraphrasing Calvin Coolidge's famous statement: "I chews to run!" Will waged his campaign solely in the pages of *Life* magazine, his only campaign promise being that if elected he would resign. This mock campaign, simply a series of articles commenting on the actual campaign going on, was endorsed by Henry Ford, Nicholas Murray Butler, Judge Ben B. Lindsey, Charles Dana Gibson, Reverend Francis J. Duffy, Glenn H. Curtiss, Harold Lloyd, William Allen White, Grantland Rice, Ring Lardner, General William Mitchell, and Babe Ruth, among many others.

On November 2, 1928, election day, *Life* declared Will Rogers the winner on the vote by the great silent majority, and called Will "Unofficial President of the United States."

The twenties had less than ten weeks to roar when the house of stock certificates collapsed. Will had warned: "You will try to show us that we are prosperous, because we have more. I will show you where we are not prosperous, because we haven't paid for it yet." The time to pay had arrived, and America was to pay dearly.

Will Rogers changed his tone. He realized that what the country needed most was confidence. "Of course," he kidded, "I haven't been buying any stock myself. I wanted to give the other fellow a chance to have confidence first." Will traveled throughout the

Birth room of Will Rogers. Note the hand-hewed walnut and oak logs.

Will and Betty at a picnic.

Jimmy and Mary playing at the pool side of their Beverly Hills home.

Betty Rogers with (l to r) Jimmy, Bill and Mary.

Will Rogers with his son Jimmy and daughter Mary.

Will between his sister Maud Lane and his aunt Juliette Schrimsher.

Betty, Bill, Jimmy, and Mary go riding at the Beverly Hills home.

The Rogers ranch house in Pacific Palisades, California.

Will's study at Pacific Palisades, California.

Will Rogers types his daily column.

Will Rogers as teenager about town.

Will Rogers models latest 1910 bathing suit fashion.

Will Rogers and Lois Josephine in "Town Topics." 1915.

Charlie Chaplin drops in on the Goldwyn set of Will Rogers' *An Unwillling Hero* and gets a roping lesson. 1921.

Will as Ichabod Crane in a scene from *The Headless Horseman.* 1922

Will amid the 1924 Ziegfeld Follies girls.

Irene Rich with Will in
They Had to See Paris.
1929.

With the young Maureen O'
Sullivan in a scene from *So
This is London*. 1930.

Will Rogers and Joel
McCrea, in scene from
Lightnin'. 1930.

Will and Myrna Loy, in *A Connecticut Yankee*. 1931.

Advertising poster for *State Fair*. 1933.

Advertising poster for *David Harum*. 1934.

Will with actor Mickey Rooney, in *The County Chairman*. 1935.

Will with Billy Burke (Mrs. Florenz Ziegfeld, Jr.) in *Doubting Thomas*. 1935

Actors between takes (l to r): Will Rogers, William Harrigan, Lew Ayres, and Paul Kelley. 1935.

Will in *Old Kentucky*. 1935.

(left to right)
W.C. Fields, Wiley Post, and
Will at Premiere of Fields'
film *David Copperfield*. 1935.

Janet Gaynor, Will and Shirley Temple,
the three stars of Fox Film Corporation.

Rogers and Bill "Bojangles" Robinson in a dance lesson from *In Old Kentucky.*

(above) Will reduced to domestic chores in *Down to Earth.*

(below) Will as Sage in Ziegfeld Follies' sketch.

Vice-President John Nance Garner with Will at Uvalde, Texas.

Will Rogers and Mrs. Eleanor Roosevelt.

Will presents a dime to John D. Rockefeller. Betty is at far right.

Will Rogers introduces Franklin D. Roosevelt to Los Angeles Coliseum crowd, during FDR's first presidential campaign. 1932.

Will on Central relief tour after Nicaraguan earthquake,
March 1931.

(above) Star polo player Will is off after the ball.

(below) Vaudeville days; Buck McKee on Teddy, and Will.

The Rogers family Polo team. left to right, Jimmy, Mary, Bill and Will.

Wiley Post with Will in Alaska.

Will watches the polo game with
friend Spencer Tracy.

Will Rogers and his artist
friend Charles M. Russell.

Will Rogers and
Billy Mitchell, 1925.

Will and Wiley examine a paddle to
be put aboard the hybrid plane.

Will winces as he and Charles A.
Lindbergh watch a bull fight in
Mexico City, 1927.

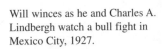

Will Rogers and Col. Charles A. Lindbergh on first flight of the San Diego passenger plane service, Sept. 22, 1927.

The launching of SS Will Rogers, Fairfield. Maryland., November 8th, 1942.

In Boston's Children's Hospital, with Babe Ruth and wife.

Will visits with Robert R. Morton, Principal, Tuskeegee Normal and Industrial Institute, Montgomery, Alabama.

(l to r) Pilot Johnny Champion, Mary, Fred Stone, Jimmy, Will, Betty and Bill, at Pacific Palisades.

For his aid after its 1931 earthquake Nicaragua honors Will Rogers with this 5 stamp set, March 31, 1939.

country, raising morale, contributing huge sums to relief, and playing benefits. Though his sentiments were with the Democrats, Will quickly came to the defense of President Hoover: "You'd think Hoover got up one morning, looked out the window, and said, 'This looks like a nice day for ruining the country, I think I'll do it today.'"

The impact of the depression reached into every corner of the American economy. Yet the years that followed were most lucrative for Will Rogers. Motion pictures had discovered sound, and in 1929 Will made his first talking picture, *They Had to See Paris*. It created an immediate demand for more Will Rogers pictures. Will, playing himself, became a top movie star, and by 1933 he was the top male box-office attraction.

In 1930 Will signed a contract with E. R. Squibb & Sons to go on a coast-to-coast radio network for fourteen Sunday talks. They would last fifteen minutes each, and he would receive a salary of over seventy thousand dollars. Will Rogers never even saw the check. He stipulated that the entire amount be divided between his two favorite charities, the Red Cross and the Salvation Army. His reasoning was simple: "The most unemployed or the hungriest man in America has in some way contributed. . . . A few years ago we were so afraid that the poor people were liable to take a drink, and now we have fixed it so that they can't even get something to eat."

Millions of Americans would find excuses not to attend their houses of worship on a Sunday morning, but to miss Will Rogers' radio talk on a Sunday evening was unthinkable. And yet his "little jokes and digs" were more penetrating, more thought provoking and inspiring than most sermons. Will spoke *with* America and *for* America. His casual opening "All I know is what I read in the papers" was so disarming that his follow-up discussion of the news made it all the more discerning.

Will did not preach or lecture in the accepted way. With a twinkle in his eyes, an infectious grin, his Oklahoma drawl, and chewing gum, he would use his perceptive humor to make Americans laugh—at themselves. And each would think he had, all by himself, discovered the deeper hidden meaning. Instead of pointing an accusing finger at his countrymen for their mental and moral laziness, Will just chuckled: "The trouble with us Americans is we are not running-minded; we are kinder riding-minded. I reckon some folks figure it a compliment to be called 'broad-minded.' Back home, broad-minded is just another way of saying a feller is too lazy to form an opinion."

Those who had remained untouched by his daily telegrams, his weekly articles, his lecture tours, his stage performances, his films, were now lassoed by his radio talks.

Will's astute observations, his ability to put into words what his generation knew to be right, raised him to a level of influence unparalleled in the history of America. Since he was unencumbered by political ties, his observations and reproaches were not open to charges of partisanship. His talks were always in the language of the people, accurately understanding their thoughts and fears; he was their man and they listened. Such powers in the hands of a lesser man could have been dangerous. But Will Rogers never changed, neither did he ever abuse the trust. He simply went on doing what he had always done better than anyone else: serving as the official conscience of his country.

Lightnin', made in 1930, featured as a juvenile lead a handsome newcomer just out of the ranks of the extras. His name was Joel McCrea. According to McCrea, Will helped him that first day of shooting. The scene was to take place in a buggy, the two men sitting side by side. Will had some lines, then McCrea was to answer. As they were running through the dialogue McCrea couldn't hear his cue. Finally Will turned to him and said: "You know, Joe," Will would call him Joe from then onward, "I fix up my own dialogue. Sometimes I make it better, sometimes I don't. But when I think I've said enough, I'll poke you. Then it's your turn." The two men became good friends, and to this day Joel McCrea maintains that he owes everything to Will Rogers' help.

Will was in New York, his picture commitments fulfilled, when he suddenly made up his mind to go to London to attend the Disarmament Conference. Will's decision came so suddenly that he did not even have time enough to buy a suitcase. He carried his packages of clothing aboard ship, right in the bags in which he had just purchased them.

The intent of the conference was to reduce armament of the major nations and thus insure peace. Will took one look at the delegates and expressed his doubt by paraphrasing President Wilson: "It looks like open Covenants secretly arrived at."

Will was barely back home when he decided to take a closer look at the Far East. When Will Rogers had a thought it had to be executed at once. Something had to be going on at all times. Rest or relaxation to Will Rogers was simply a different activity. He could never sit still for any length of time. He had to be in motion.

Will took the S.S. *Empress of Russia* and arrived in Japan on December 6, 1931. He toured Japan and visited Korea, then on to China where he was presented to the Emperor. From Malaya, Will traveled by plane to Iraq, Palestine, and Egypt. In London he met Betty, and together they attended the Geneva Disarmament Conference. Will had been through the agony of observing it before, in London. With eternal hope he took another look. His conclusion: "There is nothing to prevent their succeeding—but human nature."

Betty and Will returned to America. Will was now under contract to Fox Film Corporation and was their biggest star. Films like *A Connecticut Yankee, State Fair, David Harum,* and *Steamboat 'Round the Bend* are classics of a budding film industry. Much of what is seen and heard in those films is purely Will Rogers'. He rarely left dialogue as he found it, and he constantly added "business" and gags neither the writer nor the director ever imagined.

This was the era of the glamorous dressing rooms on motion-picture sets. To keep a star happy, the studio would build what was called a dressing room, but actually consisted of living room, bedroom, kitchen, bathroom, *and* dressing room. The importance of a star was generally assessed by the size and type of "dressing room" the studio was willing to build. When Will Rogers signed with Fox Film Corporation, the studio built an entire desert home for him, complete with cactus garden. It was to be a great surprise for Will Rogers, but Will never went near the place. He parked his car close to the camera and stretched out in the back seat, or sat in it to type his column.

After having made a number of films for Fox, Will went to see Winfield Sheehan, the head of the studio. "Winny," he said, "I'd like to choose my own films from now on. I know what I can do, and I wouldn't choose the wrong story."

Sheehan tried to be tactful with his biggest star: "Will, let me think it over." The next day a truck pulled up at Will's Santa Monica ranch. On it were almost every script, book, and treatment

Fox owned or had optioned. The driver handed Will a note typed on pink interoffice stationery: "Dear Will, please read these and let me know which ones you would like to do. If you can't find anything in this lot, I will send you another load. [signed] Winfield."

Will just marked a big cross over the memo and wrote on the other side: "You win! You pick 'em. [signed] Will." The truck was never unloaded.

Will Rogers was the least temperamental star Fox ever had. He would help another star as much as he would the smallest bit player. If a picture came in ahead of schedule, Will would feel sorry for the extras and bit players and pay their lost salaries out of his own pocket.

Just as soon as he had finished one picture, Will liked to start a new one. He wanted no time off in between. That way he would work continuously for several months at a time, and then he would take the rest of the year off and do the things he wanted to do. Now this was 1932, an election year, and Will wanted to be at the conventions. That year both parties met in Chicago. The Republicans renominated Herbert Hoover.

Then the Democrats took over. On the first ballot Oklahoma nominated Will Rogers as the favorite-son candidate, with all twenty-two votes going to him. "I made the mistake," he kidded afterward, "of going to sleep, and when I woke, my votes had been stolen. I not only lost my twenty-two delegates but I woke up without even as much as an alternate." The Democrats chose Franklin D. Roosevelt.

Early in 1933 Will signed with Gulf Oil to broadcast seven talks coast to coast. When he had fulfilled his contract he told reporters that he had decided not to broadcast again. Shortly after the news reached the papers, a most unusual petition was delivered to Will. It asked Will Rogers that he reconsider his decision to abandon radio. It was signed by every member of the United States Senate, as well as the secretary and the sergeant-at-arms. Will was touched: "The next fellow that knocks the Senate will have to answer to me . . . that's my privilege and nobody else's." Will did return to radio, again for Gulf Oil.

Will had his obligations to Fox Film Corporation, but whenever time allowed he could be found in Washington at the "National

Joke Factory." Increased air service made it easier for Will to travel. He had special permission from the Department of Commerce to fly on any aircraft—passenger, freight, or mail. It was the least the government could do for its unofficial president.

There was still one form of show business—outside grand opera—Will had not attempted, the legitimate theatre. Now, in 1934, he agreed to star in the West Coast production of Eugene O'Neill's play *Ah! Wilderness*. It would be the first time Will would have to study a script without changing a single word, the first time he would have to sustain a role—no cuts, no retakes. On opening night the applause that greeted his first appearance lasted several minutes. The critics were unanimous in their praise, and the limited engagement had to be extended.

Only once during the entire run did Will Rogers deviate from the script. During an afternoon polo game Will's horse was forced against a guardrail and tripped, spilling its rider. Will lay stunned for a moment, then got up unaided. Betty thought that Will should cancel that evening's performance and rest. Will would not hear of it. He finally agreed to let his son Jimmy drive him to the theatre. The curtain went up on time. But during the play the dialogue between Will Rogers as Nat Miller, and Anne Shoemaker, as his wife, suddenly stopped. Will hesitated, then began to talk about current politics. Anne Shoemaker entered into the spirit of the monologue. She asked questions, replied to Will's statements, and slowly guided the conversation back to the script. Will picked up his cue, and the play proceeded without further incident. The audience was completely unaware that the obvious deviation had not been planned. Jimmy drove his father back home after the performance. The next day Will could remember nothing that took place the previous evening. The fall from the horse had been more serious than anyone had suspected.

During the summer of 1934 the family planned to take a tour around the world. Only Mary wanted to stay behind and act in summer stock in Maine. On July 22, Betty, Will, Will, Jr., and Jim sailed from San Francisco aboard the S.S. *Malolo* for Hawaii. They were gone more than two months and Will showed them some of the places he had visited before.

In the months that followed, Will was busy. There were more films to be made, weekly radio broadcasts to be prepared, the daily

ROGERS FAMILY TREE

ROBERT ROGERS   m. 1810   LUCY (BETTY) CORDERY
b. 1790   b. 1790

[2 Sisters]

ROBERT J. ROGERS
b. 16 Jul. 1815
d. 4 Jul. 1842

[2 Brothers]

John, b. 1817
(m. Hetty Mosley,
Catherine Vann)

James, b. 1819*

Catherine, b. 1811
(m. Alexander McDaniel)

Nannie
(m. Alexander Jordon)

Avery Vann, b. 1770
(m. Margaret McSwain)

m. 1835

SALLY VANN (11th child)
b. 28 Jan. 1818
d. 28 May 1882

CLEMENT VANN ROGERS
b. 11 Jan. 1839
d. 29 Oct. 1911

[1 Sister]

Margaret Lavinia,
b. 12 May 1836
(m. Allison W. Timberlake)

m. 1858

MARY AMERICA
SCHRIMSHER

b. 9 Oct. 1839
d. 28 May 1890

Matthew Martin
Schrimsher
1806–1865
m. 1831
Elizabeth Hunt
Gunter
1804–1877

[5 Sisters]

[2 Brothers]

Elizabeth, b. 1861*

Robert Martin, 1866–1883*

Homer, b. 1878*

Sallie Clementine, 1863–1943
(m. 1885, John Thomas McSpadden)

Maud Ethel, 1869–1925
(m. 1891, C. L. Lane)

May, 1873–1909
(m. Matt Yocum, Frank Stine)

Zoe, b. 1876*

WILL ROGERS
b. 4 Nov. 1879
d. 15 Aug. 1935

James W. Blake
1845–1882
(m. ca. 1866)
Amelia J. Crowder
1845/6–1922

m. 25 Nov. 1908
BETTY BLAKE
1879–1944

Will, Jr. (1911–)   Mary (1913–)   James (1915–)   Fred (1918–1920)*

*died without issue.

telegrams and weekly articles. There was roping and riding, polo, speeches to be made, visits to Washington; there was very little time for the family. Will Rogers' unique talents had made him a part of America; he now belonged to all. His family had to share him with the rest of the country.

In the spring of 1935 a reporter asked Will Rogers: "You have done all you ever wanted to do, seen all there is to see. Is there anything else?" Will thought for a moment, then he replied: "I never have been to that Alaska." When he heard that his friend and fellow Oklahoman planned to fly to Alaska, Will decided to go along.

Now the two men were preparing to set the plane down on the narrow inlet. The red pontoons reached for the safety of the water. Wiley Post landed the plane smoothly and coasted as close to shore as he dared. A submerged rock could easily tear the pontoons. He cut the engine and opened the door. Clair Okpeasha, one of the Eskimos camping nearby, came to the water's edge. Wiley called to him: "Where is Barrow?" Will came to the door to hear the answer. "Fifteen miles!" the Eskimo shouted back and stretched his arm in a northerly direction.

The door of the plane closed. Will moved again toward the rear as Wiley started the engine. The plane taxied away from shore. The time was 8:18 P.M. Wiley revved the engine, and the plane began to move along the surface. Finally it lifted off steeply. At a height of fifty feet, the engine sputtered and the plane banked sharply.

Clair Okpeasha still stood by the inlet's edge when the plane hit the water and turned over. He waded out as far as he could and shouted.

His was the only voice piercing the Arctic silence.

There was no answer.

THE BEST OF WILL ROGERS

1 CONGRESS

PROBABLY THE MOST FREQUENT TOPIC of Will Rogers' comments was Congress or, as he called its members, "our hired help." Collectively, Will claimed, "they do vex the very devil out of me, and all of us, at times. The President," Will continued, "this is the way he works 'em: he never scolds 'em; he knows they are just children at heart. So when he wants something done he just coaxes 'em, and first thing you know they have voted 'yes.' Well, I can't do that; in fact, there is few that can. I am not that even tempered. I have to cuss 'em a little sometimes. I like 'em maybe as much as the President, maybe more." And he did—individually.

Will knew most senators and congressmen personally, and many were his friends. On his frequent trips to Washington, D.C., he would always make it a point to go up to Capitol Hill. He would call on Speaker Nicholas Longworth and later on Vice President John N. Garner. Both were very good friends of his and Will would use their respective offices as his temporary headquarters. The men would get together and talk about national and international events. Then, leaving his hat and coat, Will would make the rounds, sitting first in the visitors gallery in the House of Representatives, then in the Senate. Many times he would be spotted by a legislator, and he would be officially greeted from the floor. Lunch was usually taken in the Senate dining room. And no matter who was sitting with Will Rogers, before the meal was partway finished, a group had collected around the table. Everybody wanted to be seen with Will Rogers, to get his opinion on pending legislation or on conditions around the country. Will knew more about the pulse of America than any poll taken at that time.

One senator Will kidded often was Huey Long, the Kingfish, self-made Grand Sachem of Louisiana. Even though it was known that Long was not one of Rogers' favorite lawmakers, Huey would want to sit with Will Rogers.

Will referred to Congress as the "National Joke Factory," for here was where most of his material came from. "People ask me," he would explain, "where I get my jokes. Why, I just watch Congress and report the facts; I don't even have to exaggerate." He could peek behind all the vote trading, the party politics, the shenanigans, the lobbying, and he could laugh at the seriousness with which the lawmakers pretended to conduct the nation's business. To him it was just so much sham, but he enjoyed the front-row seat he had. He summed it up best when he wrote:

I have written on nothing but politics for years. It was always about national and international affairs. I have been in almost every country in the last few years. I have talked with prominent men in those countries, our ambassadors or ministers, and I would have to be pretty dumb not to soak up some information. Now I read politics, talk politics, know personally almost every prominent politician, like 'em, and they are my friends, but I can't help it if I have seen enough of it to know there is *some* baloney in it. I am going to keep on the same as I have in the past. I am going to call 'em like I see 'em. If I don't see things your way, why should I? I hope I never get so old that I can't peek behind the scenes and see the amount of politics that's mixed in this medicine before it's dished out as *pure statesmanship.*

One wonders what Will would have said had he lived to see his oldest son, Will, Jr., elected to Congress from the Sixteenth District in California.

Congress is so strange . . . a man gets up to speak and says nothing . . . nobody listens . . . and then everybody disagrees.

The bad part about our whole structure of paying our congressmen is that we name a sum and give 'em all the same, regardless of ability. No other business in the world has a fixed sum to pay all their employees the same salary. If some efficiency expert would work out a scheme where each one would be paid according to his ability, we would save a lot of money.

Being a U.S. senator looks to be about the best graft, as there is no one to watch them. I guess the people figure that the class of men they send to the senate would get caught if they took anything, whether they had anyone watching them, or not.

All our senators and congressmen are away from Washington now. This is the season of the year when they do the least damage to their country. They are scattering all over the nation. Some are going to Europe, some even to Turkey. A senator or a congressman will go anywhere in the world, just to keep from going back home and facing his people.

Congress meets tomorrow morning. Let us all pray: Oh Lord, give us strength to bear that which is about to be inflicted upon us. Be merciful with them, oh Lord, for they know not what they're doing. Amen.

If we could just send the same bunch of men to Washington for the good of the nation, and not for political reasons, we could have the most perfect government in the world.

This new senator says he is going to use "common sense" in the senate. That's what they all say when they start in. But then, if nobody don't understand you, why, you naturally have to switch.

The House of Representatives was in session. What I mean by being in session is that a tax bill was up for debate, and they were arguing on "Better Golf Courses for the Medium-Salaried Man." I suppose, if a World Court bill had been up, they would have been talking on "Shall America Park Oblong or Parallel?"

We all joke about congress but we can't improve on them. Have you noticed that no matter whom we elect, he is just as bad as the one he replaces?

★

I read where they are going to limit debate in the senate. It used to be that a man could talk all day, but now, as soon as he tells all he knows, he has to sit down.

Most of these birds will just be getting up and nodding now. Why, some of them won't be able to answer roll call.

Now we are a rich nation—on paper—and our officials should be the best paid in the world. But the principal bad feature is that it will make more men want to hold office, and once a man holds a public office, he is absolutely no good for honest work.

I see where they introduced a bill to raise senators' and congressmen's salaries. Most of the legislators run away and wouldn't vote on the salary raise. They ran on a "Fearless Ticket," not afraid to come out on anything, and then they run away from this. I'm going to hold a meeting and vote myself a higher salary.

Looks like with congress charging more, the people are getting harder to displease than they used to be.

Congress met and adjourned right away. One more day's salary for six hundred went up the taxpayers' flue. When do the taxpayers adjourn on pay?

The President's message comes tomorrow. That's another day lost.

I just blew down to our Capital to find out if the Boys we send there are with us or against us. I thought I'll get an early start and see a lot about the workings of our government. I grabbed a taxi up to the Capitol—and there is nobody ahead of me up there, but the statues. I looked at the old argument factory and then strolled over to the House Office Building. If there is ever another pay raise, let's see that it goes where it is deserved— to the secretaries.

We cuss Congress, and we joke about 'em, but they are all good fellows at heart—and if they wasent in congress, why, they would be doing something else against us that might be even worse.

We have a lot of senators in there that have been elected on nothing but a slogan. But what have they cost us after they got in? You take a fellow that has never juggled with real jack, and he don't know the value of it; a billion and a million sound so much alike that he thinks all the difference is just in the spelling.

Now these fellows in Washington wouldn't be so serious and particular if they only had to vote on what they thought was good for the majority of the people in the U.S. That would be a cinch. But what makes it hard for them is every time a bill comes up they have things to decide that have nothing to do with the merit of the bill. The principal thing is of course: What will this do for me personally back home?

Politics and self-preservation must come first, never mind the majority of the people in the U.S. A legislator's thoughts are naturally on his next term more than on his country.

The "Ways and Means Committee" is a committee that's supposed to find the Ways to divide up the Means.

If we didn't have to stop to play politics, any administration could almost make a Garden of Eden out of us. We could transfer Congress over to run Standard Oil or General Motors, and they would have both things bankrupt in two years. No other business in the world could afford to carry such deadwood. But if they are smart enough to make us feed 'em, why, then we are the fools, not them.

About all I can say about the United States Senate is that it opens with a prayer, and closes with an investigation.

In Washington, yesterday, everybody I tried to talk to was a presidential candidate. Both Houses spent all last week arguing politics. Did you ever figure it out? They are the only people that are paid to do one job, and do every other one there is, but that. If businessmen strayed as far from their actual business, we would have the prosperity of India.

Congress has promised the country that it will adjourn next Tuesday. Let's hope we can depend on it. If they do, it will be the first promise they have kept this season.

Some senate committee is all excited over finding a man that is working for Senator Bingham and at the same time drawing a salary from somebody else. Why, that's how everybody in America that makes anything, does it. Nobody can live on one salary any more.

After all, what does a senator do about his law cases?

Never blame a legislative body for not doing something. When they do nothing, they don't hurt anybody. When they do something is when they become dangerous.

This country has come to feel the same when congress is in session as we do when the baby gets hold of a hammer. It's just a question of how much damage he can do before we take it away from him.

★

I received a wire from a congressman friend of mine who wants a copy of some fool thing I have written that pertains to the bill that they are kidding about in congress. He wants to read it into the Congressional Record.

I feel pretty good about that. That's the biggest praise that a humorist can have, is to get your stuff into the Congressional Record. Just think, my name will be right alongside all those other big humorists.

★

The senate just sits and waits till they find out what the president wants, so they know how to vote against him. Be a good joke on 'em if he didn't let 'em know what he wants. That's the way Mr. Coolidge used to do it. He would keep 'em guessing so long that they voted his way accidentally part of the time.

★

Any program that has to pass by that senate is just like a rat having to pass a cat convention; it's sure to be pounced on, and the more meritorious the scheme is, the less chance it has of passing.

★

A senator learns to "swap" his vote at the same age a calf learns which end of its mother is the dining room.

★

The week's biggest laugh and the year's biggest guffaw came from the United States senate during the oil-lobby hearings when they discovered that senators were trading oil votes for sugar votes. Now they say they were surprised and practically dumbfounded that such vote-trading conditions existed.

Yes, just about as surprising to everyone that knows politics as it would be to discover that the president was born in the United States, was over 35 years old, and white.

★

The senate passed a bill appropriating 15 million for food, but the house of representatives has not approved it. They must think it would encourage hunger.

★

The house of representatives turned down the 15 million dollar food bill and passed 15 million dollars to improve entrances to National Parks. You can get a road anywhere you want out of the government, but you can't get a sandwich. In two years there won't be a Poor Farm that won't have a concrete road leading up to it.

The most assuring news of the past couple of weeks was the adjourning of congress. Boy, I tell you, all we have to do is make it for 'em, and they sure do distribute it.

It's not really intent on the government's part that they don't do better, it's ignorance.

Whether congress ever meets again, or not, I don't care. I hope they don't, but it would be just about like 'em to meet—they got no regard for the people's welfare.

I see where there is a bill up in congress now to amend the Constitution. It means that the men who drew up this thing years ago didn't know much, and we are just now getting a bunch of real fellows who can take the old parchment and fix it up like it should have been all these years. And I guess, when they get the Constitution all fixed up, they'll start in on the Ten Commandments, just as soon as they'll find somebody in Washington who has read them.

In Washington, one man could do what ten of them do. There could be only a quarter or a third as many congressmen or senators, and we would pick better ones then. But it's the system that we have always used, and there is no use getting all overcome with perspiration over it. Things kinder run themselves, anyhow.

Diary of the United States senate trying to find 2 billion dollars that it already had spent, but didn't have:

Monday—Soak the rich.
Tuesday—Begin hearing from the rich.
Tuesday afternoon—Decide to give the rich a chance to get richer.
Wednesday—Tax Wall Street sales.
Thursday—Get word from Wall Street: lay off us or you will get no campaign contributions.
Thursday afternoon—Decide "we are wrong on Wall Street."
Friday—Soak the little fellow.
Saturday—Find out there is no little fellow. He has been soaked till he drowned.
Sunday—Meditate.

Next week, same procedure, only more talk and less results.

★

Today congress went to work. What are you laughing at? Honest, they went to work. Well, they did come in and sat down.

★

Coolidge said in his autobiography: "If the Senate has any weakness, it's because the people send men lacking in ability and character, but this is not the fault of the senate; it can't choose its members; it has to work with what is sent to it."

Now there is the opinion of a man that listened to 'em for two years and argued with 'em for six.

★

People have often wondered what really costs the people of the United States more money—the man in Washington with a vote and the right to pass a bill, or the guy that has a gun and can get money with that.

Statistics have proven, I think, that congress has got more money out of the people than those other fellows have.

★

To show you that we get along better without 'em, since congress adjourned business has jumped up like it's been shot. If congress had adjourned before they had met, I expect we'd have been the most prosperous nation in the world.

★

Funny thing about being a U.S. senator, the only thing the law says you have to be is 30 years old. Not another single requirement.

They just figure that a man that old got nobody to blame but himself if he gets caught in there.

★

Congress got all the committees made up now, and they are composed of two Democrats to each Republican; so what a pleasant year that poor fellow will be in for.

★

The U.S. senate may not be the most refined deliberative body in existence, but they got the most unique rules: any member can call anybody in the world anything he can think of, and they can't sue him or fight him. Yes, sir, our Constitution protects aliens, drunks, and U.S. senators.

★

Did I ever tell you I had my stuff in the Congressional Record? This senator read my offering and another senator said: "I object to the remarks of a professional jokemaker being put into the Congressional Record."

Well, he had me wrong. Compared to them I'm an amateur. My jokes don't hurt anyone. You can take 'em or leave 'em. They don't do any harm. But with Congress, every time they make a joke, it's a law. And every time they make a law, it's a joke.

When a senator or congressman, or even a man of great ability, comes to Washington with a plan, send him to Russia. That's the home of plans. They eat and drink and sleep plans. Everything in Russia is run by plans, everything here is run by accident.

You know how congress is, they will vote for anything if the thing they vote for will turn around and vote for them. Politics ain't nothing but reciprocity.

There is nothing in the world as alike as two senators. No matter how different their politics, how different the parts of the country they come from, they all look alike, think alike, and want alike.

Senators are a never-ending source of amusement, amazement, and discouragement.

The trouble with senators is that the ones that ought to get out, don't.

FILIBUSTER

The senate filibustered. We pay for wisdom and get wind.

Washington, D.C., newspaper says: Congress is deadlocked and can't act. I think that is the greatest blessing that could befall this country.

Senator Heflin held up all senate business yesterday for five hours. That is a record for narrow views.

During one filibuster one senator threatened to read the Bible into the Record, and I guess he would have done it, if somebody in the Capitol had had a Bible.

They are having what is called a filibuster in the senate. It means that a man can get up and talk hours at a time, just to keep some bill from coming to a vote. Imagine a ballplayer standing at bat and not letting the other side play. Why, they would murder him.

If a distinguished foreigner was to be taken into the senate, and not told
what the institution was, and he heard a man rambling on, talking for
hours, he would probably say: "You have lovely quarters here for your
insane, but have you no warden to see they don't talk themselves to
death?"

LOBBYISTS

A president only tells congress what they should do. Lobbyists tell 'em
what they will do.

Can't Congress do anything that's not on a lobbyist's list? They can, but
they never have.

Why don't these lobbyists run for the senate? Would you get out of the
driver's seat and go down and pull with the other horses?

A lobbyist is a person that is supposed to help a politician make up his
mind—not only help him but pay him.

If we have senators and congressmen in Washington that can't protect
themselves against these lobbyists, we don't need to change our lobbies,
we need to change our representatives.

If you could just get these lobbyists out of Washington, D.C., it would
be as good as almost any city.

WASHINGTON, D.C.

History does not record as terrible a place as Washington is now. It is
under government control, and if we can't do anything with it, what kind
of example are we setting for other cities?

I came to the county seat of Cuckooland yesterday and spent the day
prowling around the old "Fun Factory," watching the hired help trying
to fool the boss and make him think they were doing something.

They will tell you how George Washington's farsightedness is ex-
emplified in the width of Pennsylvania Avenue, that he knew that some
day merry Fords and frolicsome Chevrolets would be flitting hither and
thither.

As a matter of fact, the width of the Avenue was determined to give senators and congressmen room to stagger to their lodgings without bumping into a building.

★

Washington, D.C., has an underground tunnel running from the government offices to the Capitol. That's so when senators and congressmen receive their checks every month, they can get to their homes, without someone arresting them for robbery.

2 AMERICA

WILL LOVED AMERICA. He traveled across its width and breadth time and again, to raise funds for charitable causes, to visit old friends, to attend a rodeo or a polo match, or just for the sheer pleasure of seeing the natural wonders. "There ought to be a law," he said, "against anybody going to Europe until they had seen the things we have in this country."

And everywhere Will went he met the people, be they farmer, sheriff, storekeeper, or banker; he spoke to them, as friends do when they meet, about their daily lives, their business, their politics. Will knew more about the heartbeat, the aspirations, the fears, yes, and the pains of America, than probably anyone else of his time. Half-serious, as most of his jibes were, Will suggested that once, just once, the President of the United States come along with him on his travels to meet the real people of America.

Yes, Will loved America and its people, and that love was returned a millionfold. It was a happy love affair, joyous and deep. America loved Will as it had never loved any other private citizen before—nor ever would again. Americans would have gladly elected Will Rogers to any office he chose, except that he did not choose to enter politics. The only office he ever held—that of honorary mayor of Beverly Hills—was an office bestowed on him while he was absent. He first learned about it when he arrived back home and was met by a huge delegation. While "in office" Will paid out of his own pocket for a gymnasium for the local police department, and had a handball court built.

The California legislature soon after passed a bill that stated that in a town of the sixth class (Beverly Hills was in that class) the president of the board of trustees was constitutionally considered the mayor. Will Rogers was out of office. He took the loss in good spirit: "If I had known that Beverly Hills was a town of the sixth class, I would'a never taken the job."

America was bisected by one major highway. It led southward from Chicago to St. Louis; from there it turned more westerly through the Ozarks into Oklahoma and onward. It was U.S. Route 66. After Will's death this major two-lane highway was officially renamed the Will Rogers Highway. Along it the Okies from the Dust Bowl of the Southwest traveled all the way to California. Along this highway are also some memorabilia from the life of Will Rogers.

Take Chelsea, Oklahoma, a small town in the northeast corner of the state. Barely a few hundred yards off Route 66, atop a squat hill, is the town's cemetery. Buried here are Will's parents, side by side, the markers now faded by the constant breeze. Here, too, are some of Will's siblings: the two brothers he never knew; sister Zoe, who died as a baby; sister Maud, who had died in 1925. Here, too, is sister Sallie, who had raised Will after their mother had died when the boy was not quite ten years old. Just a few yards away is a newer grave. Will's niece Paula McSpadden Love is buried there. She helped raise Will's children, and for over thirty years she was the curator of the Will Rogers Memorial.

Less than twenty miles along Route 66 is Claremore, the county seat of Rogers County, named for Clem Vann Rogers, Will's father. Will always claimed this place as his hometown. Actually he never lived here, but as Will kidded, "only an Indian can pronounce Oologah." Here, high on the hill overlooking the town, stands the Will Rogers Memorial. Will had bought twenty acres, planning to build his retirement home here someday. Will never retired, and Betty gave the land to the state of Oklahoma, which built the Memorial on it. In the garden is the simple crypt where Will Rogers now lies buried. Here, too, lie Betty and their twenty-month-old baby, Fred Stone Rogers.

Route 66 continues through Tulsa and Oklahoma City, right past the grave of Wiley Post, on into Amarillo, Texas. Due westward now, the Will Rogers Highway continues, right past the Will Rogers Motel in Santa Rosa, New Mexico. Will stopped here one night; the motor court had a different name then. When he registered the owner recognized his famous guest. Will, in his usual manner, asked the man about the town, his business, his family. The man told about his sick child, feverishly tossing in the next room. Will asked to see the child. He had the greatest compassion for the worried father, having lost his own son, the youngest, during a diphtheria epidemic.

The man took Will next door. For the next two hours Will sat by the sick child's bed and told stories. The child, his pain and discomfort forgotten, listened attentively, so obviously enjoying the tales. Finally the child fell asleep. The next morning when Will was ready to leave he asked to see the child again. The crisis seemed to have passed during the night; the child's eyes were clear, and for the first time in many a day he was hungry.

The two men shook hands. The motel owner was reluctant to release Will's hand, and his words did not come easy. He had a request. Could he rename his motor court, using his famous guest's name? Will smiled: "I don't see how it's going to help any, but you can use my name." The motel has changed hands several times since then, and there is a bypass around Santa Rosa, but the Will Rogers Motel still stands, surrounded now by more modern accommodations.

And Route 66, the Will Rogers Highway, rolls on westward. Through Albuquerque, on into Arizona, on into California, until it reaches Los Angeles. Here Route 66 is better known as Sunset Boulevard. The Will Rogers Highway finally stops at the Pacific Ocean at the Will Rogers Beach, having just passed number 14253 Sunset Boulevard, the Will Rogers Ranch. Here Will and his family spent probably the happiest years of their lives.

If you visit there, you will find the books still on the shelves, the dishes set for a meal, the stuffed calf waiting for Will to toss his lariat. Everything here at the ranch is still exactly as it was that summer day in 1935 when Wiley Post set a small plane down on the polo field and first spoke to Will about coming along to see Alaska.

When some nation wants us to help 'em out, they use the same old gag: that America should exert MORAL LEADERSHIP, and we, like yaps, believe it, when as a matter of truth, no nation wants any other nation exerting "Moral Leadership" over 'em—even if they had one. We mean well, but wind up in wrong, as usual.

★

If America ever passes out as a great nation, we ought to put on our tombstone: America died from a delusion she had Moral Leadership.

Say, if we had any morals, we would use 'em ourselves.

★

No matter what we do, we are wrong. If we help a nation, we are wrong; if we don't help 'em, we are wrong. There just ain't any such animal as International Good Will. It just lasts till the money you lent 'em runs out.

★

I originated a remark that I think has been copied more than any little thing I've ever said—and I used it in the *Ziegfeld Follies* of 1922. I said America has a unique record: we never lost a war and we never won a conference in our lives. I still believe we could, without any degree of egotism, single-handed lick any nation in the world, but we can't even confer with Costa Rica and come home with our shirts on.

★

America means well, we mean better than any country in the world, but we just seem to come out wrong. We send men and money and everything. For a so-called smart nation I believe we can be the biggest yaps sometimes. And the funny thing is America never enters anything with any thought of gain. It's just as well that we don't.

★

What's the matter with us? No country ever had more, and no country ever had less. Ten men in our country could buy the whole world, and ten million can't buy enough to eat.

★

On account of us being a democracy, and run by the people, we are the only nation in the world that has to keep a government for four years, no matter what it does.

★

A bureau of something or other in Washington announced that America has reached the highest standard of living ever reached by any nation.

Course, we don't get meat as often as our forefathers, but we do have our peanut butter and radio.

★

On the Riviera in France, they found a bunch of people wearing no clothes and not particularly caring who they were married to, and they called it a cult.

Over here we call it society.

They say all nations are sore at us. Unfortunately for us they didn't get sore at us quick enough. If they had, we would have saved a lot of money. We are the ones that should be sore at them for not getting sore at us quicker.

Everything nowadays is a saying or a slogan. The prize one of all is: Two can live as cheap as one. That, next to "Law Enforcement" is the biggest bunk slogan ever invented. Why, two can't even live as cheap as two, much less one.

Even congress has slogans:

> Why sleep at home when you can sleep in congress?
> Be a politician, no training necessary!
> Join the senate and investigate something!
> Come to Washington and vote to raise your pay!

I have joined the great movement of Restoring Confidence. There is a lot of people who got Confidence, but they are careful who they have it in. We have plenty of Confidence in this country, but we are a little short of good men to place our Confidence in.

Where can you find a senator, or a congressman, or even a president who will not stand up from time to time and say: "My fellow Americans, America must lead the world. We must show these other poor boobs that our way is THE way." And so we set out helping the world—whether it wants it or not. Yes, folks, we are in the humanity business, and by golly, we are going to do it right!

It will take America two more wars to learn the words to our national anthem.

America is a great country, but you can't live in it for nothing.

We are the champion yap nation in the world for swallowing propaganda. You can take a sob story and a stick of candy and lead America right off into the Dead Sea.

We are always reading statistics and figures. Half of America do nothing but prepare statistics for the other half to read.

This is a peculiar country. A fool can make money—not only can, but does—but it takes real brains to give it away wisely.

Every invention during our lifetime has been just to save time. Two hundred years from now history will record: America, a nation that conceived many odd inventions for getting somewhere, but could think of nothing to do when they got there.

Brother, we are riding mighty high in this country. We are just sitting on top of the world. For every automobile we furnish an accident; for every radio we put on two murders; three robberies to every bathtub installed; building two golf courses to every church. Our courts are full, our jails are full, our politicians are full.

We are the first nation in the history of the world to go to the Poorhouse in an automobile.

With us it's: Nothing is too high! Get the Moon! We are just the guy that can run it, if we can reach it!

Whether we belong anywhere, or not, that don't matter. Get there— that's all.

There is nothing the American tourist won't carry off. The Grand Canyon is the only thing they haven't carried away yet, and that's only because it's a hole in the ground.

America invents everything, but the trouble is we get tired of it the minute the new is wore off.

The American people are a very generous people; they will forgive almost any weakness, with the possible exception of stupidity.

America has a great habit of always talking about protecting American interests in some foreign country. Protect them here at home! There is more American interests right here than anywhere.

All America has to do to get in bad all over the world is just to start out on what we think is a Good Samaritan mission.

Americans have one particular trait that they need never have any fear of some other nation copying, and that is we are the only people that will go where we know we are absolutely not wanted.

Last year Americans spent $700,000 to be insulted in Europe, and they could have got it done for half the money over here.

★

Imagine, with all our crime, and all our immorality in the papers, and our small attendance in our churches, and about as much contentment and repose as a fresh-caged hyena, we go to tell the whole world: we are the only one with the right idea!

★

When we start out trying to make everybody have "moral" elections, why, it just don't look like we are going to have enough Marines to go round.

★

There is one trait that I don't believe any other people in the world have developed to the extent that our folks have. It's almost impossible to show the American folks something that if you turn your head, they won't try to carry it home.

★

You know, I think we put too much emphasis and importance and advertising on our so-called high standard of living. I think that "high" is the only word in that phrase that is really correct. We sure are a-living HIGH.

★

If you can start arguing over something, and get enough publicity, and keep the argument going, you can divide our nation overnight as to whether spinach or broccoli is the most nutritious. We can sure get hot and bothered quicker over nothing and cool off faster than any nation in the world.

★

We are a good-natured bunch of saps in this country. When the president is wrong, we charge it to inexperience. When congress is wrong, we charge it to habit. When the senate is right, we declare a national holiday. When the market drops fifty points, we are supposed not to know that it's through manipulation. When a judge convicts a murderer, that's cruelty.

★

Of all the things that this country is suffering from, the greatest is an overproduction of organizations. When Judgement Day comes, half of America will be on their way to some convention, and the other half will be signing application blanks.

★

It will always seem funny to me that we think we are about the only ones that really know how to do everything right. I don't know how a lot of these other nations have existed as long as they have till we could get some of our people around and show 'em how really to be pure and good, like us.

If ever an industry is having a field day, it's the industry of paid leaders in every line who are explaining to their followers "what the government owes to them."

I haven't seen a copy of the Constitution in years—I guess they are out of print—but I don't remember anything in there about what it was to do. In fact, if I remember right, we owed more to the Constitution than it did to us.

There is still a lot of monkey in us. Throw anything you want into our cages, and we will give it serious consideration.

That's what makes us a great nation—we take the little things serious, and the big ones as a joke.

3 PRESIDENTS

WILL ROGERS MET most of America's presidents during his adult life, starting with Teddy Roosevelt. Will performed on the White House lawn when T.R. lived there, and the children watched in amazement all the tricks Will could do with a rope.

Woodrow Wilson really helped Will's career. Many times Wilson would attend the *Ziegfeld Follies*, and later the president would quote many of Will's quips. Since the audiences at the New Amsterdam Theatre were relatively small, these presidential references to "one of our foremost humorists" increased Will's importance.

Harding and Will never developed a relationship. For the *Ziegfeld Follies*, Will had written a sketch—in which he also appeared—lampooning an emergency session of the cabinet. A major crisis threatens the United States, but the president cannot be disturbed as he is involved in an important game of golf. This irreverence was naturally reported to Harding, and while there was no doubt about the truth, the president was not pleased by the humor. He would have appreciated less emphasis on his avid devotion to his pastime.

Later in the year when the *Follies* played Washington, D.C., the cast was alerted that the president would be going to the theatre that evening. Since the *Follies* were the most important show in town, it was naturally assumed that the president would honor it with his presence. Everyone in the cast was excited at the prospect. By curtain time the president had not arrived. The curtain was held until it was finally reported that the president had gone to another theatre, which played some unimportant, mediocre play. Will always thought that this was an obvious snub, and

48

he felt responsible for depriving the rest of the cast the honor of having performed before the president.

When Coolidge was in the White House, Will was a guest there on several occasions. He liked both Calvin and Grace Coolidge, but he joked more about Coolidge than he probably did about any other president.

Will had the highest regard for Hoover, the administrator of so many relief programs. And while many blamed Hoover for the Great Depression, Will came to his defense, albeit in his own way: "Don't you go and blame the Republicans for everything that's happened to us; they're not smart enough to have thought it up!"

Will liked Franklin D. Roosevelt very much. In their correspondence, Will, who couldn't care less about correct spelling, addressed him as "Franklyn." FDR allowed this to go on until he finally retaliated by addressing Rogers as "Wyll," offering that he would use the correct spelling whenever Will was ready to do likewise.

Both FDR and Will Rogers recognized each other's importance and the part each played during the early years of the country's worst depression. Will was invited to the White House, stayed overnight, and reported his findings to the president. One Sunday evening the president was scheduled for one of his "Fireside Chats." Will Rogers's program was on earlier in the evening, and Will had promised to talk on the problems the president might discuss. The president had a copy of Will's speech taken off the air and brought to him so that he could tailor his own talk accordingly. Said FDR after reading the transcript: "I could not have explained matters any clearer."

FDR and Will worked well as a team, though it was not always planned that way. FDR tried every possible way to help the country out of the depression, creating jobs for the unemployed, saving farms and houses from foreclosure, and it was Will Rogers who could easily either endorse and explain a program, or show up its folly.

Twice during national conventions Will Rogers' name was put in nomination. But Will wanted no part of it. "The country hasn't sunk so low that it wants a comedian intentionally in the presidency." He did however agree to run for the presidency—strictly for laughs—in the pages of *Life* magazine.

On election eve *Life* declared Will Rogers the "Unofficial President of the United States," elected by the vast silent majority. And Will, having now been elected, promptly kept his sole campaign promise: he immediately resigned.

I was up at the White House today. "Do you want me to tell you the latest political jokes, Mr. President?" I asked him.

"You don't have to, Will," he said; "I know 'em already. I appointed most of them."

The only way to keep a governor from becoming senator is to sidetrack him off on the presidency.

Isn't the presidency higher than senator?

Why, no! The senate can make a sucker out of any president, and generally does.

There come Coolidge and did nothing, and retired a hero—not only because he hadn't done anything, but because he had done it better than anybody.

I really can't see any advantage of having one of your party in as president. I would rather be able to criticize a man, than to have to apologize for him.

A man don't any more learn where the icebox is in the White House, than he has to go back to being a lawyer again.

Taxes are more important to every individual than the name of any man that will be in the White House.

The president is in favor of economy in all our various defenses. If we have another war, he will vote to have "a cheap war."

A president-elect's popularity is the shortest lived of any public man's. It only lasts till he picks his cabinet.

An emperor is bigger than a president; he is what a president would be if he dident have any congress or senate to see that he does nothing.

Mr. President, why do you feed all those senators for breakfast, anyhow? They will promise you anything while they are eating off you, and the minute they get out from there will vote against your measure. Get wise to 'em! They been kidding every president like that for years, and the ones in your own party is the worst.

It's a tough life, this being president and trying to please everybody— well, not exactly everybody, but enough to be reelected.

An awful lot of people are predicting the president's downfall—not only predicting, but praying. We are a funny people. We elect our presidents, be they Republicans or Democrats, then go home and start daring 'em to make good.

A foreigner coming here and reading the Congressional Record would say that the president of the United States serves solely for the purpose of giving a senator somebody to call a horse thief.

Our president delivered his message to congress. That is one of the things his contract calls for. It's one of the few stipulated duties of the president—to tell congress the condition of the country.

This message, as I say, is to congress. The rest of the people know the condition of the country, for they live in it, but congress has no idea what is going on in America, so the president has to tell 'em.

This whole thing of who is president is a lot of applesauce. We have lived under more than 30 presidents. They couldn't have all been great. In fact, if we told the truth about 'em, some of 'em was pretty punk. But we dragged along in spite of any of 'em.

A president just can't make much showing against congress. They lay awake nights, thinking up things to be against the president on.

★

Here we all are, we can't handle our own little affairs, and yet we start yapping about "what the president ought to have done."

★

No president can be himself. They are eating and sleeping in a show window. They are acting every minute.

★

Coolidge was the only president nobody ever knew when he was acting, and when he wasn't. He was like a ukelele. You know, you can't ever tell when somebody is playing one, or just monkeying with it.

★

Funny thing about the White House. It wears down the most hardy of our menfolk, but the women seem to thrive on it.

★

This country has been continually blessed with some fine charming women in the White House. Some of the men might have been able to stand a little overhauling, but there has never been a chirp of regret out of anyone about the female occupants.

★

The president goes on the air tonight. Even if he's good, there's plenty of 'em won't like it. He can speak on the Lord's Supper and he will get editorials against it.

★

America is just like an insane asylum; there is not a soul in it will admit they are crazy. The president, being the warden, us inmates know he's the one that's cuckoo.

★

Most of our presidents never went in much for plans. They only had one plan that said: "Boys, my head is turned; just get it while you can!"

★

In his message the president spoke of the high cost of living. That's all they ever do—just speak of it.

★

Distrust of the senate started with Washington, who wanted to have 'em courtmartialed; Jefferson proposed life imprisonment for 'em; Lincoln said: the Lord must have hated 'em for he made so few of 'em; Teddy Roosevelt whittled a big stick and beat on 'em; they drove Wilson to an early grave; and Coolidge never let 'em know what he wanted, so they never knew how to vote against him.

★

If the president will cuss the senate and the House out a couple of more times, he is liable to wake up a hero, for cussing congress is always popular.

★

If we can spare men like Teddy Roosevelt and Woodrow Wilson, there is no use in any other politician ever taking himself seriously.

It's not a disgrace not to be able to run a country nowadays, but it is a disgrace to keep on trying when you know you can't.

Men in America live, hope, and die trying to become president. If they can't make it, they accept the booby prize and go in the senate.

I'll bet you that even Cal Coolidge, who retired at his peak, wouldn't tell you that the worry didn't more than offset the glory.

This president business is a pretty thankless job. Washington, or Lincoln either, didn't get a statue until everybody was sure they was dead.

Say, this running a government is kinder like our movie business. You are only as good as your last picture. Things over which they have no control come along, and yet, if it happens and it's bad, why out they go.

They do love to be president. It's the toughest job in the world, but there is always 120 million applicants.

You know Lincoln's famous remark about "God must have loved the common people, because he made so many of them?" Well, you are not going to get people's votes nowadays by calling 'em common. Lincoln might have said it, but I bet it was not until after he was elected.

There wasn't any Republicans in Washington's day. No Republicans, no Boll Weevil, no income tax, no cover charge, no disarmament conferences, no luncheon clubs, no stoplights, no static, no head winds. My Lord, living in those days, who wouldn't be great?

Say, did you read what this writer just dug up in George Washington's diary? I was so ashamed I sat up all night reading it.

George Washington was a surveyor in his younger days. He was a good surveyor. He took the exact measure of the British and surveyed himself out about the most valuable piece of land in America at that time, Mount Vernon. George not only could tell the truth, but he could tell land values.

4 DEMOCRATS AND REPUBLICANS

DURING HIS LIFETIME Will Rogers lived under more Republican administrations than Democratic. Until his death in 1935 there were only two Democratic presidents in this century, Wilson and FDR. Since Will usually commented on the events of the day, naturally most of his quips were in response to Republican foibles. He sometimes, humorously, claimed to be a Democrat: "They are so funny, and I am supposed to be."

He was one of the few men who could address a Republican gathering one week and would be most welcome at a Democratic meeting the next week. His friends in Washington, D.C., were on both sides of the political aisle. His one standard for his comments was: "I usually give the party in power the more digs, because they do the country the most harm. Besides, they are drawing a salary to be knocked."

Actually Will chided both parties regularly for what he considered the narrow-mindedness of party politics. Wrote Will:

If political parties are supposed to have to vote together on everything, let each party only send one man from the entire United States. Party politics is the most narrow-minded occupation in the world. A guy raised in a straitjacket is a corkscrew compared to a thick-headed party politician. All you would have to do to make some men atheists is just to tell them the Lord belongs to the opposition political party. After that they could never see any good in Him.

To best demonstrate Will Rogers's impartiality between the two political parties, consider the legacy he left. Of his three children—Will, Jr., Mary, and Jim—one son is a registered Democrat, one son is a registered Republican, and Mary, who could break the tie, has never committed herself in public. Now nothing could be fairer than that.

I am not a member of any organized political party—I'm a Democrat.

★

The difference between a Republican and a Democrat is the Democrat is a cannibal—they have to live off each other—while the Republicans, why, they live off the Democrats.

★

The Democrats and the Republicans are equally corrupt—it's only in the amount where the Republicans excel.

★

The Republican and the Democratic parties both split. The Republicans have their splits right after election, and the Democrats have theirs just before an election.

★

It's getting so if a man wants to stand well socially, he can't afford to be seen with either the Democrats or the Republicans.

★

The Republicans have always been the party of big business, and the Democrats of small business. The Democrats have their eye on a dime, and the Republicans on a dollar. So you just take your pick.

★

Both parties have their good and bad times, only they have them at different times. They are each good when they are out, and each bad when they are in.

★

Democrats could live on little, because they never had anything else. But they sure don't live on little when they get into office.

Their greatest trait to recommend the Democrats is optimism and humor. You've got to be an optimist to be a Democrat, and you've got to be a humorist to stay one.

Democrats are the only race that can have an argument, even when they agree.

The Democrats are investigating the Republican slush fund. And if they find where it's coming from, they want theirs.

There ain't any finer folks living than a Republican that votes the Democratic ticket.

There is something about a Republican that you can only stand him just so long; and on the other hand, there is something about a Democrat that you can't stand him quite that long.

So many Republicans have promised things and then didn't make good that it's getting so a Republican promise isn't much more to be depended on than a Democratic one, and that has always been the lowest form of collateral in the world.

If I was running for office, I would be ashamed to let anybody know which one of those parties I belonged to.

The only way in the world to make either one of those old parties look even halfway decent is to keep them out of office.

The Democrats come nearer getting what they want when they have a Republican president than they do with one of their own.

Democrats never agree on anything, that's why they are Democrats. If they agreed with each other, they would be Republicans.

Republicans take care of the big money, for big money takes care of them.

This country runs in spite of the parties; in fact, parties are the biggest handicaps we have to contend with.

★

The Republican candidate says: "The majority of the country is prosperous." He means by that that the Republicans are prosperous, and he kinder insinuates that if a man don't know enough to be a Republican, then how can he expect to know enough to be prosperous?

★

Andrew Jackson was the first one to think up the idea to promise everybody that if they voted for you, you would give them an office, and the more times they voted for you, the bigger the office. That was the real start of the Democratic Party.

★

It was Andrew Jackson who said: "If he ain't of your party, give him nothing. Charity begins at the polls."

★

Senator Borah made an appeal to the country to donate a dollar or more to save the respect of the Republican party. I just mailed five dollars to make five Republicans respectable.

★

I received my five dollars back from Senator Borah that I sent him to clean up five Republicans. He wasn't able to raise the fund because people realized that it was a lost cause. You can't make the Republican party pure by more contributions, because contributions are what got it where it is today.

★

A Democrat at heart is just naturally an amiable fellow. He just wants to be known as a politician. Now a Republican don't. He just wants politics to be known as a sideline. He is sorter ashamed of it. He wants to work at it, but he wants people to believe he don't have to.

★

The trouble with the Democrats up to now has been that they have been giving the people "what they thought the people ought to have" instead of what the people wanted.

★

Republicans have a certain foresight and take over the reins of government about the time things are going good. And when they see pestilence and famine about to visit on the land, they will slip it back to the Democrats.

★

I don't know why it is, but Democrats just seem to have an uncanny premonition of sizing up a question, and guessing wrong on it. It almost makes you think sometimes it is done purposely. You can't make outsiders believe it's not done purposely, for they don't think people could make that many mistakes accidentally.

★

Republicans are overdoing this prosperity. They like to drive little cheap cars around and just love to play poor. I may start a candidate with the slogan: Come, Join the Democrats, and we will all be Poor, and Happy, and Moral again!

★

There is something about a Republican administration that it only functions one year in four. But they make sure that year is the presidential election year.

★

Every year it gets harder and harder to tell the difference between a Republican and a Democrat—course, outside of looks. Their platforms and policies become more and more alike. But I have found the sure way to tell one from the other this year. It's just the way they talk. The Republicans say, "Well, things could have been worse." And the Democrats say, "How?"

★

I see that the Democrats want to change the name of Hoover Dam. Lord, if they feel that way about it, I don't see why they don't just switch the two words.

★

Nowadays all a man goes into public office for is so he can try to find out something, then write a book about it when he comes out.

★

It's really remarkable how the politicians think of us. Their every thought is of us every fourth year.

★

The trouble with politics is that there is not enough jobs to go round. So next time that is to be one of the planks in the platform: A Job with every Vote! It's no harder to work for the government than it is to vote for it. In fact, most government jobs is not as hard.

★

A politician has to come in with some loot, and the more he drags in, the more solid he is at the next election. If it was in private life, and he put over some of the banditry that he does in official life, he would be caught and sent to jail, instead of back to congress.

★

There is no other line of business that any of them could get in where they would get one-tenth part of the publicity that they get in public office, and how they love it. Talk about actors basking in the limelight! Say, an old senator can make an actor look like he is hid under a barrel.

★

I don't think politicians get what's coming to them. They are lucky.

Politicians are doing the best they can according to the dictates of no conscience.

There is many scandals being whispered about, but in politics practically everything you hear is scandal, and besides, the funny thing is that the things they are whispering ain't half as bad as the things they have been saying right out loud.

They say the White House receptions are not as classy as the Republicans had, but what the Democrats lack in class nowadays, they make up in numbers.

Anyone can be a Republican when the stock market is up, but when stocks are selling for no more than they're worth, I tell you, being a Republican—it's a sacrifice.

I am asked to explain what the Democratic Party is trying to accomplish, what they are trying to get at. Well, they are trying to get at what few Republicans there are left.

A Republican friend showed up out here in California. He told me what their big mistake was in the last campaign. "Will," he said, "we went on the theory that Barnum was wrong, and that one wasn't born every minute. But now we see our mistake."

I am always kidding about something the Democrats did to the Republicans, then I got the Republicans on my back. Then I will sing the praises of some Republican uprising, and I will have all of the Democrats down on me. I tell you, there is just so much you can say in praise, or in reprimand, of either one of our political parties.

5 POLITICS

WILL WAS MOST INTERESTED IN POLITICS. He read every available newspaper, of whatever political persuasion. He said:

You can always tell the man that reads only one newspaper. You would be surprised how one bit of political news is so differently construed in different papers. Some public man is a horse thief in one paper, and then you pick up the other, and he is just about to be canonized and made a saint. Then the next paper will say: "Sure he is a horse thief in the daytime, but he repents at night!"

But Will's foundation in politics was not only based on newspapers. He read weekly magazines, monthly magazines, spoke with every elected or appointed official he could find. He asked a million questions and knew what he talked about, even though he hid behind his disarming opening: "All I know is just what I read in the papers . . ."

Based on his intimate knowledge, he summarized:

I can never take a politician seriously. They are always shouting that such-and-such a thing will ruin us and that this is the most eventful year in our country's life! No, Sir! This country is too big now. To stop this country now would be like spitting on a railroad track to stop a train. No element, no party, not even congress or the senate can hurt this country now; and a politician is just like a neck-tie salesman in a big department store. If he decides to give all the ties away, or decides to pocket all the receipts, it don't affect the store. It don't close. He closes, as soon as he is found out.

And if there was any doubt left where Will Rogers stood in his appraisal of politicians, he wrote: "I love a dog. He does nothing for political reasons."

A politican is not as narrow-minded as he forces himself to be.

★

A politician is just like a pickpocket; it's almost impossible to get one to reform.

★

The trouble with politicians is they see, but they don't see far. They wear reading glasses when they are looking into the future; they got their putter in their hand, when they ought to have their driver.

★

I am just like a politician—the less I know about anything, the more I can say.

★

Don't take politics serious, it's just another American racket.

★

Politics ain't worrying this country one-tenth as much as finding a parking space.

★

Politics has got so expensive that it takes lots of money to even get beat with nowadays.

★

What this country needs is more working men, and fewer politicians.

★

Many a public man wishes there was a law to burn old records.

★

Everything is changing. People are taking their comedians seriously, and the politicians as a joke, when it used to be vice versa.

★

American politics is the most obliging thing we have. One hundred million voters have six men in every state make up their minds for them every four years.

★

Politicians, after all, are not over a year behind public opinion.

★

In Europe public men do resign. But here it's a lost art. You have to impeach 'em.

★

Now about politicians—the least said about them, the best.

★

Every time we have an election we get in worse men and the country keeps right on going. Times have only proven one thing, and that is that you can't ruin this country, even with politics.

★

Every politician has some scheme in their district that they want to get done, and they are looking for an appropriation, so the vote trading will start. At the finish every state gets something they don't need; the politician gets reelected—thereby everybody getting something they don't need.

★

You know I believe that's what's kept us going so long is that our public men in high office are basically honest. It would be wonderful if we could say as much for our public men's ability.

★

Ain't it wonderful to have something come up in a country, where you can find out just how many political cowards there are?

★

I am a missionary. I am going to devote my life's work to rescue this country from the hands of the politician, and also rescue the politician to a life of Christianity.

★

There is nothing certain in politics, except salary and rake-off.

★

The party in power is always the worst, and every man looks good until he is elected.

★

My solution is to keep both political parties out of office one term and hire my good friend Henry Ford to run the whole thing and give him a commission on what he saves us.

★

If everybody didn't vote, then none of these politicians could get elected, and that would be the end of politics, and we would go out and hire us some good man to run the country—the same as we should now.

★

Politics sure is a gentleman's game. Everybody is of a high type—till the time comes when there is something worthwhile to be little over, and then they all revert to type.

You see the trouble with politics is—it breeds politics. So that makes it pretty hard to stamp out. The only way to do it is at the source. We got to get birth control among the politicians. We have to do that in order that they don't bring more politicians into the world.

People ain't any more interested in politics than they are in long underwear. Both sides have lied to 'em so often that we don't look on any candidate with admiration or with hate; we just pity 'em.

To get into politics in America, you need no qualifications. If you had a bad night the night before, and wake up feeling that there is nothing left in life for you, that you are no good to yourself, the world, or your friends, why, one day later finds your name on a ballot, running for something.

There is not a voter in America that twenty-four hours after any speech could remember two sentences in it. Politics amuse more people than they interest.

Anything important is never left to the vote of the people. We only get to vote on some man; we never get to vote on what he is to do. There is things about politics that is not just exactly 100 percent kosher.

The papers just came, having nothing but politics. It does seem that our country could be run much better by someone, if we could only think who.

There is very little dignity, very little sportsmanship, or very little anything in politics. It's only: Get the Job and Hold It!

In 1612 some wise guy decided that he would like to live off the other Virginians instead of off the forest, so they called him a politician. So politics started on these shores in 1612, and in the short space of over 300 years it has grown in leaps and bounds, where it is now America's leading racket.

A politician is nothing but a local bandit sent to Washington to raid headquarters.

America has the best politicians money can buy.

6 CONVENTIONS

IT SEEMED A COMPLETELY LOGICAL progression that the man who had for years commented on all aspects of the political spectrum should now be asked to report on national conventions. Thus, in 1920 Will Rogers was engaged by NEA (Newspaper Enterprise Association) to furnish "at least ten jokes a day," to be nationally syndicated. Will fully intended to cover the Republican Convention in Chicago and the Democratic one in San Francisco. He attended neither.

Under contract to Sam Goldwyn, Will was on location filming a silent motion picture called *Cupid, the Cowpuncher*. It was unthinkable to disrupt the shooting schedule to allow Will to leave.

Meanwhile at home, tragedy developed. The three boys, Will, Jr.; Jimmy; and little Fred Stone Rogers had complained of sore throats. On the advice of a physician the boys were put to bed and treated for tonsilitis. Betty debated about notifying Will, but decided not to bother him. Several days later when the sore throats were correctly diagnosed as diphtheria, Will was summoned. Driving through the night to reach his stricken sons, he arrived too late. In the early morning hours of June 17, Fred Stone Rogers died. He was not yet two years old.

It is most remarkable that Will, so distraught, could find the inner strength and concentration to send out the daily columns. The original manuscripts show his state of mind. The spelling, which ordinarily was inaccurate, is even more so; the typing, usually haphazard, is most erratic. Pages are inverted, typing begins at the bottom of a page rather than at the top; then that same sheet is inserted again in the typewriter, only this time upside down. It is quite obvious that while Will honored an obligation, his grief was paramount.

The Republican Convention of 1924, in Cleveland, was the first convention Will attended. Actually he claimed it was a waste of everybody's time, for President Coolidge could have been renominated by postcard.

The Democrats, on the other hand, staged a marathon fight that lasted through 103 ballots. Fortunately Will was appearing at the time in the *Ziegfeld Follies* again, and the convention was held at New York's Madison Square Garden. Thus he could cover the convention and then simply take a taxi to the New Amsterdam Theatre, in time for the show.

Flying to the Republican Convention of 1928, held in Kansas City, Missouri, Will took Western Air Express. As the plane landed in Las Vegas, Nevada, the right wheel broke and the plane flipped over, landing on its back. Will and a fellow passenger were stunned and slightly cut by flying glass. Undaunted, Will continued. Several hours later, because of severe winds, the regular mail plane abandoned the scheduled refueling stop at Rock Springs, Wyoming, and flew on to the emergency landing field at Cherokee, Wyoming. Let Will describe what happened next:

We got our gas and in taking off the wheel hit a big gopher hole and sprung a strut or brace that holds the undercarriage. We were going very slow at the time, and nothing happened, only that we couldent take off with that in that shape, so we phoned into Cheyenne and they sent out another plane and in a couple of hours, there it was.

Will reached the convention in ample time. It was not one of the more exciting conventions, and Will reported it faithfully—in his own style. What Will didn't report was an exchange with H. L. Mencken. "Look at the man," Mencken addressed a crowd of writers at an illegally stocked canteen, pointing at Will Rogers. "He alters foreign policies. He makes and unmakes candidates. He destroys public figures. By deriding Congress and undermining its prestige, he has virtually reduced us to a monarchy. Millions of American free men read his words daily, and those who are unable to read listen to him over the radio."

Will tried to defend himself. "Now Henry, you know that nobody with any sense ever took any of my gags serious."

"They are taken seriously by nobody except half-wits," Mencken continued, "in other words, by approximately 85 percent of the voting population!" It was quite a compliment for H. L. Mencken to admit that his friend Will Rogers was probably the most influential editorial writer of his day.

The Democrats gathered in Houston, Texas. Before leaving Kansas City, Will purchased a brown suit, especially for the convention in Texas. But arriving in Houston he found that a New Orleans company, strictly as an advertising stunt, presented presidential candidates with a washable seersucker suit. Since Will was the supposed candidate of the Bunkless party, he, too, was presented with a suit—and he promptly wore it. The extreme heat in Houston probably made the seersucker suit far more comfortable.

Will attended the 1932 Republican Convention in Chicago. Hoover, who had started his administration in a country apparently prosperous, was now being blamed for every aspect of the deep depression. When any man was down, Will Rogers never made him the butt of a joke, and Hoover was most certainly down. Whenever he could he would stress Hoover's past record of helping the sufferers both locally and abroad. But in his heart Will knew that Hoover's days in office were numbered.

That year the Democrats also met in Chicago. Here Will suddenly found himself with twenty-two votes nominating him for the presidency. Will simply laughed it off. Later, when he was asked to address the delegates, he told them exactly what they had to do: "No matter who is nominated, don't go home and act like Democrats. Don't say he is the weakest man you could have nominated. Don't say he can't win. You don't know what he can do or how weak he is until next November. I don't see how he could ever be weak enough not to win. If he lives until November, he's in!" The recording of this short address still exists, and the deafening roar at the end still shows the appreciation of the delegates. You can here them yelling "Go on! More!" It is one of the rare times in convention history that a speaker was urged to say more.

But Will Rogers, whose last convention this was to be, was never under the illusion that our national conventions were the ultimate example of democracy. His opinion of them, though he enjoyed them for what they were, was summed up in 1924. Said Will: "No one can possibly do anything to mar the dignity of a convention. The whole thing is applesauce."

Our National Conventions are nothing but glorified Mickey Mouse cartoons, and are solely for amusement purposes.

★

It takes a great country to stand a thing like a National Convention hitting it every four years.

★

I have been asked to cover the Republican Convention, to write something funny. All you have to do to write something funny about a Republican Convention, is just tell what happened.

★

Take any of those Party Platforms that they promise before election; why, they promise anything. The same fellows that make them out also make out these insurance policies. That is, what they say on one page, they can deny on the other.

★

An uninstructed delegate is one whom his district sent with a free rein to use his own judgment, but when he comes back he is supposed to give up 50 percent of whatever his vote brought.

★

An alternate is a man sent along to watch the delegate and see that he turns in the right amount. He, according to the rules, is to receive 10 percent of the gross.

★

An alternate is the lowest form of political life there is; he is the parachute in a plane that never leaves the ground.

★

A delegate-at-large is one who gets a room and bath at the hotel.

★

The chairman of a state delegation is a man that announces how many votes his state casts. The qualification for his job seems to call for a man that can't count. After he has announced the votes, they poll the delegates and he sees for himself just how near he guessed.

★

The poor fellow voting in the primary still takes it seriously and really thinks he has something to do with the nominations.

Spoke to a candidate today. He feels that if the nomination should ever accidentally get to a question of ability, he has a splendid chance.

★

One candidate has notified us that his acceptance speech will be very long. The other candidate says that his will be very short. I wonder why one of them don't announce that his will be very good?

★

I see that Mr. Coolidge is sending somebody to Kansas City to protect his interests. Say, if I had any interests to be protected in any political convention, I believe I would send the Marines.

★

The Democrats already have started arguing over who will be the Speaker at the next convention. What they better worry about is who is going to listen.

★

I asked Senator Penrose: "How come so many New York delegates are uninstructed?" And he remarked: "You can't instruct a New Yorker, he knows it all!"

★

Every seven years, some people have the itch; in a malaria country, every other day people have a chill; every forty years France and Germany fight; but every four years WE have politics and it hits our country like a pestilence.

★

The Democrats announced they are going to be so peaceful and hungry for harmony at their convention, that you won't hardly know they are Democrats. If they are like that, I certainly will ask for my money back. They have worked for years to bring their conventions up to a show, and now they want to spoil it.

★

Being with a loser may get you credit for being a game guy, but it don't bring you any federal pork chops.

★

You are a Favorite-Son candidate just as long as the winner is uncertain.

★

I still hope we can all find and settle on some man, and do away with both conventions. It would be such a good joke on the delegates.

★

It looks to me like any man that wants to be president in times like these, lacks something.

★

Tip to delegates who are coming to New York: leave your watches and jewelry at home; bring nothing but your alternates. It's a cinch you can't lose them.

★

Ohio claims they are due a president as they haven't had one since Taft. Look at the United States, they haven't had one since Lincoln.

★

The convention opened with a prayer, a very fervent prayer. If the Lord can see his way clear to bless the Republican Party, the way it's been carrying on, then the rest of us ought to get it without even asking for it.

★

As none of the politicians present knew how to pray, they called in a professional. Of course he had been told what to pray for.

★

The preachers are reading their prayers, which is new to me. Where I come from, if a man can't think of anything to pray about offhand, why, there is no need of praying.

★

The prayers are very long, but, of course, the parsons may know this audience and their needs better than me.

★

Prayers are getting longer each day. I don't know if that is through necessity, or not. Today's was the only strictly political oration I ever heard delivered in the guise of a prayer. The only reference to anything pertaining to the Bible, was the word Amen, at the finish.

★

Once during the prayer I was sure the speaker was referring to Our Savior, till they told me no, it was Herbert Hoover. In fact, he kinder give the engineer the edge over the carpenter.

★

Somebody prayed again today, but they are beginning to lose interest even in prayer, as none of their prayers up to now have been answered.

★

What a wonderful convention this would be if they just wouldn't start the balloting at all. The only thing that can spoil the convention, is for them to nominate someone.

★

The keynoter has the toughest job of any of them. If he points to accomplishments, he is sunk, and if he views with alarm, he is sunk, so we are liable to get two solid hours on the weather.

★

Of all the tips that's going round, why, everybody has a different one.

The bellboys where the delegates are staying are the only ones that haven't got a tip since the thing started.

The whole convention has degenerated into nothing but a dogfight for vice-president. Men who two days ago wouldent even speak to a vice-president, are now trying to be one.

There was a delegate with his little boy standing beside me on the floor of the convention, and I heard the little fellow ask his daddy: "Is that man praying for the convention?"

And his daddy told him: "No! He took one look at the convention, and he's praying for the country."

I am glad Chicago's children didn't come by on their way to school this morning and see how this wonderful system of choosing our country's leaders was conducted. They would never again have to ask: "What's the matter with the country."

Maybe in the old days, nominating speeches were just as idealess. But they were only listened to by delegates, and the man making the speech only had to appeal to intelligence as high as his own. But now, with radio, people are getting wise to the type of man that is supposed to save our country. So let's don't hold another convention till someone can think of a new speech.

The keynoter told things on Republicans that would have made anybody else but Republicans ashamed of themselves.

They are trying out the platform—the one they are going to speak from, not the one they are supposed to stand on after nomination.

As for drafting a platform, that's a lot of applesauce. Why, I bet you, there is not a Republican or Democratic officeholder today that can tell you one plank in the last election platform, without looking over the minutes.

Well, they just read the platform. It favors fixing everything the Republicans have ruined, and keeping everything that they haven't.

They read the platform. It's forty-five pages long. If they had come out in the open on every question, and told just where they stood, they could have saved themselves forty-two pages of paper. When you straddle an issue it takes a long time to explain it.

Talk about civilization! Why, if they ever took a sanity test at a political convention, 98 percent would be removed to an asylum.

From 10 o'clock in the morning until 6 at night, we heard nothing but "The Man I Am About to Name. . . ." You could never tell who they was going to nominate. They all kept the names until the last words. It was safer.

Talk about presidential timber. Why, man, they had a whole lumberyard of it here. There was so many being nominated that some of the men making the nomination speeches had never even met the men they were nominating. I know they never had, from the way they talked about them.

If we got one-tenth of what was promised to us in these acceptance speeches, there wouldn't be any inducement to want to go to heaven.

Personally I think the camera has done more harm for politics than any other one faction. Everybody would rather get their picture in the paper than their ideas.

There was ten cameras to every plank in the platform. There was more film wasted on the two conventions, than was used to make *King of Kings*.

I just want to go home and sleep for a month. I have looked at enough badges and heard enough speeches, that if I ever hear another man say "Back to Jeffersonian Principles!" or "The Grand Old Republican Party!" I will go to the gallows with a clear conscience.

Flew down here to Claremore, Oklahoma, to recuperate from one month of speeches. Heard a mule braying a while ago out at the farm, and for a minute I couldent tell who he was nominating.

★

It's a great game, this convention game. I don't suppose there is a show in the world with as much sameness in it as it has got. You know exactly what each speaker is going to say, before he says it; you know before you go who will be nominated; you know the platform will always be the same—promise everything, deliver nothing. You cuss yourself for sitting day in and day out and looking at such nonsense. But the next four years find you back there again.

7 CAMPAIGNS

APART FROM THE HARMLESS CAMPAIGN to run on the Bunkless party platform, Will Rogers allowed himself only once to be drawn into a political campaign. That was in October 1922 when he was asked by one of President Theodore Roosevelt's sons—Mrs. Rogers in her book thought that it was Theodore, Jr., while the *New York Times* reported that it was Kermit—to speak in support of his friend, Ogden Livingston Mills. Mills, a Republican congressman from New York's "silk-stocking" district, was running for reelection. At the appointed hour Will arrived at the meeting in New York's Town Hall. An alerted *New York Times* reporter covered the event, and this is what he heard:

I have spoken in all kinds of joints, from one of Mrs. Vanderbilt's parties on Fifth Avenue, to Sing Sing in Ossining, but this is my first crack at a political speech and I hope it flops. I don't want it to go over and then have to go into politics, because up to now I have always tried to live honest.

A great many think I was sent here by Mr. Mills' opponent, but this is not the case. I don't even know his opponent. But he must be a scoundrel. From what I have read of politics, every opponent is. He must also be a "tool of the interests"; I believe the least you can do is to say that in a political speech.

I don't know Mr. Mills, and that is why they have asked me to come here and speak, because I was perhaps better qualified to say something nice than some one who did know him. Now, as to Mr. Mills, I have read up on his family history. He comes from the old Mills family of New Jersey. There was Eleanor and Ogden. Eleanor, being rather wild, went

72

into the choir, while Ogden, being of more divine, spiritualistic nature, took to politics.

Events of the last few weeks have proved that Ogden's judgement was the better of the two. Statistics of the last congress show that not a single congressman was shot. The country has been wondering why. Probably it is the old theory that "they ain't worth the powder and lead!"

Now Mr. Mills is quite a novelty. He is one of the few men that didn't go into politics through necessity. He was wealthy when he started; not as wealthy as he is now, but he had some money. He went into politics to protect it, for they say there is honor among thieves.

Mr. Mills represents Fifth Avenue and Broadway. The dividing line of his district is Park Avenue, so he also represents the shady side of Park Avenue. And here are a few things which he has promised to do:

He represents the theatrical district and he has promised to keep all of us actors working; he is one hundred percent for the ticket speculator; he is for every industry in his district, no matter what they do; he is for a living wage for the bootlegger; he is the only congressman we can send to congress who can go into a Fifth Avenue home, without delivering something.

He is the only one you can accept a campaign cigar from and feel perfectly safe in smoking it.

And now I will tell you why I am here. I have no politics. I came here because a Roosevelt asked me to come here. A Roosevelt hint is the same to me as my wife's commands. I tell you how far I would go to do anything asked of me by a Roosevelt: I would even make a speech in favor of Harding!

As I said, I have no politics. When President Roosevelt, the Colonel, died, as far as I am concerned the Republican Party was buried right alongside of where the Democrats had been. You see, during the war I had said some complimentary things about the Colonel and his family, and some friend who heard it, wrote to Colonel Roosevelt, and repeated it to him. Colonel Roosevelt wrote me a nice letter from a trip he was on in Maine, and wrote the letter in longhand, in his own hand. He was about the busiest man in the United States at the time. I have said, along with my little knocks, nice things about men in public life, but he was the only man who ever took the time to write and thank me for it. He is the only big man who ever did a thing like that, so far as I know.

Now this gentleman Mills was a friend of his, and is a friend of his family. That is all I know about him. That is all I want to know about him. That is all you need to know about him.

The *New York Times* reported that Representative Ogden L.

Mills (R. New York) sat throughout the speech "with a stolid expression of countenance." Will Rogers summed it up correctly: "The poor fellow don't know it yet whether I am for him or against him!"

P.S. Representative Mills was reelected, and later—1932–1933—served as secretary of the treasury.

There has been an awful lot of people defeated in the primaries. Everybody was running that could get some cards printed. It was a great year for the printers.

★

So much money is being spent on the campaigns that I doubt if either man, as good as they are, are worth what it will cost to elect them.

★

Take your campaign contribution, and send it to the Red Cross, and let the election be decided on its merit.

★

If either candidate believes one-half of one percent of what any of his henchmen say, then neither one is smart enough to be president.

★

Did you ever see as much ground covered, and as many speeches made as those two vice-presidential candidates are making? It's out of all proportion to the position. One of them is going to get badly fooled—the one that is elected.

★

My idea of the height of conceit would be a political speaker that would go on the air when the World Series is on.

★

Most men that emerge from a campaign with any spoils were more lucky than competent. A good campaign manager can do more than an able candidate. "Trades," more than ability, make presidents.

★

We can get all lathering at the time over some political campaign promise, but if the thing just drags along long enough, we forget what it was that was originally promised. The short memory of the American voters is what keeps our politicians in office.

★

You see, if we didn't have two parties, we would settle on the best man in the country, and things would run fine. But, as it is now, we settle on the two most eager ones, and then fight over 'em.

It's fine for two candidates to want to run a campaign on a high plane, but politicians just ain't equipped to conduct anything on a high plane. They got their minds set on the tail end of Pennsylvania Avenue, and they will promise anything short of perpetual motion.

The trouble with our candidates is that after nomination they take things serious and lose the touch that put 'em where they are.

A few weeks ago the Republicans thought they could win with just anybody. Now they can't find anybody they think they can win with.

Herbert Hoover was the first elected presidential candidate I ever saw that kept his campaign promise. He had said he would follow Coolidge's policies, and he did! He went fishing too.

The American custom is when you can't beat a man at anything, why, the last straw is to debate him.

How often do politicians say: "I don't have to tell you what our great party stands for." Well, I don't care how smart an audience is, they couldent possibly know what their party stands for. The Supreme Court, with all its divided knowledge, can't tell you what either party stands for. About the only thing that you can safely say, is that both parties stand for reelection.

I see by this morning's paper where the Democratic candidate is going to make sixteen speeches, all different. Now offhand that looks like a pretty hard thing to do, but it's not. You can put sixteen different interpretations on the Democratic platform, and still not exhaust half the alibis.

If I was a politician, I would just pick out one good speech, and stay with it. But if a politician was that smart, he wouldn't be a politician.

There is really no difference in the two platforms. How could there be? They are both catering to the same voters.

Neither candidate may be his party's ideal of a president, but he is more their ideal of a president than any member of the opposition party that ever lived.

★

Half of each party is not really crazy about what their candidate stands for, but he stands the best chance of election, and that's the main thing to stand for.

★

All I know is just what I read in the papers, and I want to tell you, brother, when you read through one candidate's speech, including the denials, why, you have just about done a day's work.

★

There should be a moratorium called on candidate's speeches. They have both called each other everything in the world they can think of. From now on they are just talking themselves out of votes.

★

I honestly believe there is people excited over this election. They must think the president has something to do with running this country.

★

There is no law in Texas to apply to a Republican primary. You see Texas never thought they would come to a point where there would ever be any Republicans there. They also have no laws against the shooting out of season of reindeer or musk ox.

★

Let's have one issue where we can stand divided. What's the use of having elections if everybody wants the same thing?

★

Both sides are breaking their necks to find something to make an issue of. Mr. Coolidge has finally announced that his policy will be "Common Sense!" Common Sense is not an issue in politics, it's an affliction.

★

Mr. Davis, the Democrat, announced his policy will be "Honesty!" Neither is that an issue in politics, it's a miracle.

★

In the election that followed, eight million Americans showed they had "Common Sense" enough not to believe there was "Honesty" in politics.

★

I tell you the day has passed in America when a successful candidate can go about bragging on the fact that he was elected on $22.50 worth of five cent cigars! Besides, we don't want the type of man that's not big enough to hand out more than nickel cigars.

★

All you will hear from now until election will be: "We must get our government out of the hands of predatory wealth!" or "The good people of this great country are burdened to death with taxes!"

If you have a radio, the next few months is a good time to have it get out of fix. All you'd hear is candidates saying: "What I intend to do, is. . . ." What he intends to do is to try and get elected—that's all any of them intends to do.

Did you ever see the like of candidates everywhere? Every fellow over the age of 21 is running for something. You can always tell a poor business year by the number of candidates. When nobody else will give you employment, you feel like the country should.

You hear a lot of talk about the campaign this year being awful cheap, and maybe on the level, but I want to tell you that I would hate to offer one-hundred-and-fifty thousand dollars to either side. They would grab at a promissory note, or better, an anonymous check.

The Democrats are having a lot of fun exposing the Republican campaign corruption, but they would have a lot more fun if they knew where they could lay their hands on just a little of it themselves.

We are all excited now over this campaign, but six months from now we will look back and wonder why. Politics is just a custom and has nothing whatever to do with civilization.

One of the biggest bunks in these modern campaigns is these two candidates running from one part of the country to another to make a speech. I don't think I am betraying any national secret when I say that both of these boys are liable to get more votes if you can't see 'em.

It's too bad there is not some machine, or way, of registering just how many votes a candidate's speech gets, or loses.

Deals gradually come under the heading of "legitimate" campaign business. If you promise a man that if you are made senator, he will be made a judge, why, you have sold him something. You might promise voters a river to get a dam built on, and you have promised something, and you can't get the voters to distinguish the difference—if there is any.

Of all the bunk handed out during a campaign, the biggest is to flatter the intelligence of the voters. How are the voters going to be any smarter when the candidates themselves are no smarter.

The high office of president of the United States has degenerated into two ordinarily fine men being goaded on by their political leeches into saying things that if they were in their right minds, they wouldn't think of saying. So go fishing, then come back next Wednesday and we will let you know which one is the lesser of the two evils of you.

A clean campaign is one where each side cleans the other of every possible vestige of respectability.

★

The promising season ends next Tuesday, and at about 8 o'clock that same night, the alibi season opens, and lasts for the next four years.

8 ELECTIONS

WILL ROGERS WAS BORN NOVEMBER 4, 1879. That was a Tuesday, and being the first Tuesday in November, it was election day. It was not a presidential election year; just local offices were at stake. Will later kidded about it. Said he:

Women couldn't vote in those days, so my mother thought she would do something, so she stayed home and gave birth to me. That's why I have always had it in for politicians.

Rutherford B. Hayes was president at the time of my birth. I arrived amid a day of crooked ballots. The next year, 1880, why, Garfield was elected president on my first birthday. I didn't vote, but they voted my name every year up to 18.

I was never able to get elected to anything. But I am going to jump out some day and be indefinite enough about everything, so they will call me a politician; then I'll run on a platform of question marks and be elected unanimously, then reach into the Treasury and bring back my district a new bridge, a tunnel, or dam, and I will be a statesman. All I got to do is get muddled up enough.

For a man who was as astute as Will Rogers on all political matters, there are two points that are quite surprising. One was that he apparently never realized when American elections took place. For some reason he assumed that they always took place on his birthday. In his writings he would interchange "election day" with "November 4." He must have thought they were synonymous. Once, while on a trip to South America, he moved heaven and earth to hurry back to New York so that he would be present on election eve when the results came in. He managed to

79

arrive on November 4, only to learn that the election was still a couple of days off.

The other point is even more startling. Here was Will Rogers, whose waking days were filled with reading and talking about politics, who wrote more words on our elected officials than any other writer, and yet, Will never voted.

Perhaps he knew too much about it.

Well, this week takes care pretty much of the last of the primaries. This will throw thousands in every state back among the unemployed.

★

I certainly hope none of you readers are so simple-minded as to think you have anything to do with the nomination of the man you will eventually vote for.

★

In this country people don't vote for—they vote against. You know that.

★

Start having a presidential election nowadays and we'd have to postpone it. Neither side has got anybody big enough to run.

★

As you know, our presidential election is about to die out on account of lack of interest. Our two national parties have got to the point where there's no difference between 'em, anyhow. Whatever one will promise, the other will see him and raise him. So I propose a real big presidential lottery, and so give national elections the thing they lack now, which is dignity and prestige.

★

Ain't it funny, we can see our friends or neighbors go out, make bad investments, do fool things, but we never say a word. We let him risk his life and his money without any advice. But his vote? Why, we got to tell him about that, for he's kinder ignorant and narrow-minded, and don't see things our way.

★

Did you ever know a candidate that was not facing "a most critical time in the world's affairs" every time he spoke in public? I don't know what could be so "critical?" The world is going along as usual, having about the usual quota of wars, robberies, and murders.

Both sides are doing nothing but just looking at the next election. All you hear now is: "Do you think the president's going to be elected? And who will the other side run?"

We get pretty excited over politics, and pretty soon it's all over, and we settle down to cussing the guy we just elected. It just seems like we can't get a man that can take care of all of us after he gets in office.

There is one thing you can bet on this year. No voter is going to do anything that a politician thinks he will do. The way most people feel, they would like to vote against all of 'em, if it was possible.

It must be getting near election time. They have commenced taking up all the babies, and kissing them. Mothers, when you see a baby picked up by someone nowadays, it is either one of two men: a politician or a kidnapper.

With elections coming on, both sides are going to put their best side forward. They are just trying to figure out which side is their best.

In an election year, that's the year when congress really works—but it's for themselves, and you can't blame 'em. They have had a taste of being in congress, and they are seldom ever any good anymore for anything else.

Elections is just what we need. We don't know what we need 'em for, but it's for something, if only to get one-half of our folks sore at the other half.

No voter in the world ever voted for nothing; in some way he has been convinced that he is to get something for his vote. His vote is all that our Constitution gives him, and it goes to the highest bidder. He jumps the way his bread looks like it's buttered the thickest.

I have read about our two candidates relaxing. The time for a candidate to relax is after election. In fact, everything they do after they are in office looks like it was done when relaxing.

Elections mean nothing in our lives. All we do is just dig up their salary, and they all get the same, Republicans or Democrats—so you see, there is no way we can win.

If I was running for office, I would rather have two friends in the counting room, than a Republican slush fund behind me.

More candidates have been defeated after the polls closed, than were ever defeated during election day.

The Democrats not only have a good candidate, but they got money, which it's better to have than a good candidate.

When there is money in an election, it's always in doubt.

One of the evils of democracy is you have to put up with the man you elected, whether you want him, or not.

A flock of Democrats will replace a mess of Republicans, but it won't mean a thing; they will go in like all the rest of 'em, go in on promises and come out on alibis.

Elections are really a good deal like marriages, there's no accounting for anyone's taste. Every time you see a bridegroom, we wonder why she picked him, and it's the same with public officials.

Napoleon said one time an army traveled on its stomach. I don't know what soldiers do, but I know what voters do in regard to their stomach. They go to the polls, and if it's full, they keep the guy that's already in. But if the old stomach is empty, they vote to chuck him out.

Who cares who is elected nowadays? They are not in office three days till we realize our mistake and wish the other one had got in.

★

Our system has been that when a man is defeated at election, he is appointed to a bigger job than the one he was defeated for.

★

No elective candidate is ever as bad, or as good, as we expect him to be.

★

Honest, did you ever read as much bunk and applesauce piled into one campaign? There wasent any more truth in over half of what any so-called orator said; if it wasn't a "deliberate lie" why, it was an "exaggerated falsehood."

★

If your side lost, don't take it too much to heart. Remember there is always this difference between the United States and a dictatorship: a dictator runs the country, but here, the country runs the president.

★

A "Lame Duck" is a congressman who had his official position shot from under him by the excellent judgment of the voters back home.

★

Some congressmen are "Lame Ducks" because their constituents could think faster than they was.

★

A lot of people are confused as to just what is meant by a "Lame-Duck" congress. It's like where some fellow worked for you, and their work wasn't satisfactory, and you let 'em out. But after you fired 'em, you let 'em stay long enough so they could burn your house down.

9 INVESTIGATIONS

THE TEAPOT DOME SCANDAL and subsequent investigations, the Seabury investigation into New York City politics, Wall Street, J. P. Morgan, were only a few of the headline-making hearings. The newspaper reports of the testimony presented made juicy reading. It also produced some unintentional humor, which made the entire investigation seem inane. Take, for example, the earnest witness who swore he heard a little black bag mentioned, and that someone said 80,000. A later witness laughed when asked about the 80,000 and swore that what was said was 80 cows *and* . . . and he insisted that the previous witness must have misunderstood.

It is little wonder therefore that Will Rogers had much material for his columns. But his most cogent suggestion appeared in a weekly article:

Well, all I know is just what I read in the papers. All we have been able to read here lately is about somebody testifying before somebody else's committee, and I have been reading the testimony.

Now I have an idea I want to lay before you. Everybody is offering suggestions at how to improve education. We are learning them all kinds of courses. We have courses in Business Administration, Salesmanship, Public Speaking, Etiquette, Banking, Dairying, Fertilizing. Everything that a person can think of, we have a course in it that you can take at some college. Now what I propose is a course in "Public Testifying."

Most of our public men spend over half their time testifying on the stand. Now what has brought forth this idea of mine is the testimony that has been delivered on the stand. Did you ever in your life see men get as flustrated and tangled up as these fellows do on the stand? It looks like the smarter the man, the bigger sucker he is when he is being questioned. The minute a witness has had any education, or thinks he knows something, why, the less convincing he is on the stand. I think of all the bunch on the witness stand that lawyers are the worst. You never read a lawyer's testimony in any case in your life and could tell heads or tails. They think they are so smart that they have to hide something, and they are generally more scared than any other class of witness there is. The smart fellow has so many different angles that he is trying to use a little of all of them and winds up by making everybody believe that he dident tell half he knew, and dident know half he told.

So I am going to start a school of "Public Testimony." Instead of being layed out like a school, it will be layed out like a court. Instead of teachers, we will have 'em made up as sheriffs and bailiffs and jurymen and judges. The minute a man is elected to office, like senator or congressman, why, we will have him come and spend a few weeks in the school, and then, when he goes on to his public office, he will be all set for the first investigation. We will teach 'em not to be nervous, not to let the other fellow get 'em rattled, and have 'em all trained to tell where they got every dollar they used in their campaign, and how much they paid for each vote. In other words, it will persuade our big men to turn honest after elections, and trust to the mercy of the jury.

It's really patriotic reasons that make me want to do this. For I am afraid that foreign nations will read some of our papers and find the testimony of some of our men who are in the Cabinet and high in public office, and they will judge them by that testimony. They will think they are no smarter than their testimony.

My school for Public Testimony that I wrote you about is gathering recruits every day. Men that had no idea they would be called on a month ago, are now enlisting for short courses.

★

Ex-presidents are awful scarce, but you can't hardly shake a bush without a congressman running out, afraid that you are looking for him for an investigation.

★

What does the Senate do with all the knowledge they demand from other people? They never seem to use it.

★

The very day that all this testimony came out, in the same papers, there was a picture showing a Negro with one of those truth machines fastened on his wrist. They are supposed to tell when you are lying. That very day, in Washington, there were guys testifying with nothing on their wrists, but silk shirts. God bless America for a sense of humor.

★

If they had ever taken one of those truth machines to that investigation in Washington, there would have been more Americans sailing for Europe than went during the war.

★

I have a scheme that I think would add to the efficiency of these investigations. That is, have certain days for certain things. Say, for instance Mondays. Everybody that wants to confess, come and confess on Mondays. Tuesdays is for accusations. If you want to accuse anybody, come Tuesday and accuse from 9 A.M. to 6 P.M. Then that leaves Wednesdays, Thursdays, Fridays for denials. You see, it takes longer to deny than anything else.

★

I tell you folks, if American men are as dumb as some of them have appeared on the witness stand this year, civilization is tottering.

★

The only trouble about suggesting that somebody ought to be investigated is that they are liable to suggest that YOU ought to be investigated. And from the record of all our previous investigations, it just looks like nobody can emerge with their noses entirely clean.

★

I don't care who you are, you just can't reach middle life without having done and said a whole lot of foolish things. If I saw an investigating committee headed my way, I would just plead guilty, and throw myself on the mercy of the court.

★

Imagine a congress that squanders billions, trying to find out where some candidate spent a few thousands.

★

You can't believe a thing in an official statement. The minute anything happens connected with official life, why, it's just like a cold night back home—everybody is trying to cover up.

★

America never has been represented at any investigation ever held. It's always only the two sides who are interested in the outcome of it.

★

The queerest investigation has sprung up in Washington. Mr. Wheeler, one of the presiding questioners at one of the various investigations, was himself indicted in his home state, and he turned around and caused an investigation to be made, and a committee formed, to investigate where they got the grounds to indict him.

Now the people who had him indicted will appoint a committee to investigate where he found out that he had been indicted.

Those boys in Washington have had a lot of fun investigating. You see, a senator is never as happy as when he is asking somebody a question, without the party being able to ask him one back.

At this investigation, did you read where one fellow said he was nicked for 75 thousand berries for the campaign fund? And here the president was elected by the biggest majority of any president. What would these boys spend on an election if it happened to be close?

Some think these investigations will not do much good. But any time one half learns how the other half lives, why it does us all good.

These hearings in Washington uncover a lot of things these old boys have done that are within the law, but it's so near the edge that you couldn't slip a safety razor blade between their acts and prosecution.

I do joke about our prominent men, but at heart I believe in 'em. I do think there is times when traces of dumbness crop up in official life, but not out of crookedness.

There is many an investigation going on in Washington. I never saw such an eager senate. You see, there is something about a Democrat that makes 'em awful inquisitive, especially if it's on a Republican, and there is an awful lot to find out about most Republicans.

It seems the senate committee has been trying to find out where this bird got his clutches on all this stack of dough. Any time a man has got more than a senator, they are suspicious of him, and rightly so, for they know how they got what they have.

The more a man has got, the more he hates to be investigated, for things that might pass as honest in a court of law, don't sound so good when some bird blats them out at an investigation.

★

The American people would trade 10 investigations for one conviction.

If congress would only hang somebody, no matter if they were guilty or not, just for an example, why, we could forgive them for all their investigations.

You know, these senators may be doing all this investigating just to get out of the senate during the day.

Our investigations have always contributed more to amusement than they have to knowledge.

Investigations run along for weeks, and hundreds come to get their names in the papers. I can't help but believe that all these Washington hearings must be sponsored by the hotels and railroads. There can't possibly be any other reason for holding them.

The attorney general can report nothing but investigations during the past weeks. What's wrong with Justice?

   I won't commit myself; if I did, I would be overruled by the Supreme Court.

You know, there is two places where what a person says should not be held against 'em in a court of law. One is at a dinner, and the other on the witness stand of a Washington investigation. Both affairs are purely social, and should be covered only by the society editor.

I know a man that went to Washington to testify, and there was twenty-nine cabinet and ex-cabinet members in line ahead of him; so he had to just write his confession, and mail it in.

I suppose by the time this reaches an eager public that he will have resigned, as I see where he says he "won't quit under fire!"

   That is the usual remarks before leaving.

In Washington these days there are politicians acting honest now that never acted that way in their lives.

10 CRIME

DESPITE THE FACT THAT TODAY'S BLARING HEADLINES seem to indicate that America is deep in the grip of a crime wave, little has really changed since the days of Murder Incorporated and the gang wars of the twenties and thirties.

From the neighborhood bootlegger to Al Capone, from Dillinger to Bruno Hauptmann, their exploits made the front pages. With speakeasies an accepted way of drinking, with police a willing—and paid—accomplice, regard for law and order was at an extreme low. It was difficult to espouse law enforcement when lawlessness was everywhere.

Chicago, the headquarters of several gangster organizations, was the hub of criminal activities. Rarely a day went by without a machine-gun execution, followed discreetly by an ultralavish gangster-style funeral.

Of all the crimes, kidnapping was the one Will abhorred most. Though a peaceful man, and slow to anger, he publicly recommended a mandatory death penalty for anyone found guilty of kidnapping. The most famous case during that period was, of course, the Lindbergh kidnapping. Just two days before the child was taken, Will had visited the Morrow home at Englewood, New Jersey, where Charles and Anne Lindbergh were staying. Will had played with the small boy, probably remembering his own lost boy. When time came to leave, the little boy had climbed into Will's car, wanting to leave with him. Will was the last newspaperman to see the child.

Months later, after the trial and conviction of Bruno Hauptmann, Charles and Anne Lindbergh wanted to escape the constant barrages by the press and radio. There was only one place where they could have unencroached privacy—Will Rogers' ranch. While the world looked for them, the Lindberghs mourned the loss of their firstborn. Will saw to it that they were not disturbed.

Will Rogers was given the opportunity to visit Al Capone in jail. He interviewed him for the longest time and made notes. But he never submitted the story. "There was absolutely no way I could write it and not make a hero out of him. What's the matter with an age when our biggest gangster is our greatest national interest."

We don't give our criminals much punishment, but we sure give 'em plenty of publicity.

★

Some new plan has got to be worked out in our prison system. Of course this may be a radical suggestion, but couldn't they fix some way where the guards carried the guns, instead of the prisoners?

★

Papers have been commenting on the novel way the state of Nevada executed a man for committing murder. The novelty of that was that a prisoner was executed in any way for just committing murder.

★

I see a lot of men are advocating letting everybody carry guns, with the idea that they will be able to protect themselves. In other words, just make civil war out of this crime wave.

★

If you think that being armed protects you, why, how about the amount of policemen that are shot down in New York? They are all armed.

★

Of course, the best way out of this crime wave would be to punish the criminals, but, of course, that is out of the question! That's barbarous, and takes us back, as the hysterics say, to the days before civilization.

★

Supply and demand regulate robberies the same as they do anything else. The supply of people who have money to be robbed of will never exceed the demand to rob them. In other words, as soon as there is a man that has a dollar, there is a robber to take it.

★

Robbery statistics were published today. They can show you the statistics but no robbers. We go to great lengths to keep track of what a robber did, but do nothing to find out where he went.

Here is a usual AP dispatch: Four prisoners, three serving life terms, escaped from prison today!

Nowadays the sentence reads: "You are sentenced to prison as long as it's made comfortable for you and you desire to remain. In checking out kindly let the warden know, so he will know how many will be there for supper."

Our big problem is this discontent in our prisons. Hardly a day passes that prisoners don't show some little outward sign of uneasiness, such as shooting a few guards, burning some buildings, or giving some hint publicly that they want to participate in this area of prosperity through which we are struggling to make both ends meet. Personally I would like to see 'em all turned out, as I have always felt we had the wrong bunch in there.

There must not be such a thing in this country as an "amateur crook." Every person that is caught in some terrible crime, you find where he has been paroled, pardoned, and pampered by every jail or insane asylum in the country. Some of these criminals' records sound like a tour of a one-night theatrical troop.

It must be awful monotonous, belonging to one of these state parole boards. There is days and days when they just have to sit around, waiting for new criminals to be caught, so they can parole them.

Is our court procedure broken down, lame, or limping? Something sure is cuckoo. It looks like after a person's guilt in this country is established, why, then the battle as to whether he should be punished is the real test of the court. It seems if he is lucky enough to get convicted, or confesses, why, he has a great chance of going free.

If there is one thing that it would be laughable for this country to try and show the rest of the world how to do, it would be to run a court. Of all the cockeyed things we got in this country at the present time, it's some of our judges and courts and justices. Why, we got more crooks out on bail than we got people for 'em to rob!

Oh, we are living in progress! All of our boasted inventions, like the auto, and the automatic; and our increased drug output, lost confidence in our justice, graft—top to bottom, all these have made it possible to commit anything you can think of, and in about 80 percent of the cases, get away with it. If anybody is caught nowadays, why, it will be accidental.

★

The toughest part of robbing nowadays, is to find somebody that has something.

★

If there is one thing that has increased crime, it's been the automatic pistol. It's made no practice necessary to be an outlaw. Give any young egotist two shots of dope and an automatic and he will hold up the government mint—and he'll get his money quicker than you can get it with a bona-fide check.

★

Robbing is one profession that certainly has advanced in this country. And the remarkable thing is that there is no school to learn you to rob. No other line, outside of drinking, can show the progress that robbing has had. We spend billions of dollars on education, and we're no smarter today than 30 years ago. And we spend nothing to foster robbing, and here it is, one of the most skilled industries we have.

★

Robberies! Where they used to take your horse, and if they were caught, they got hung for it; now they take your car, and if they are caught, it's a miracle, and they will perhaps have the inconvenience of having to go to court and explain.

★

Headline in the paper says: "Crooks from Other Cities Are Coming to Los Angeles!" I guess the landlords there are going to have competition.

★

American murder procedure is about as follows: foul enough to commit a crime, dumb enough to get caught, smart enough to prove you was crazy when you committed it, and fortunate enough not to hang for it.

★

We are always saying let the law take its course, but what we really mean is: let the law take our course!

★

There is a thousand policemen to see you don't park your car too long, where there is not one to see that your house is not robbed or your child is not kidnapped.

★

Every man on the street can have an automatic pistol in every pocket, yet he will never be searched. But you let your taillight be out, and you're in for life.

14,000 people were fined last year for parking more than six inches from the curb; five were convicted for selling liquor, and three of those got retrials. Two murderers were convicted, and then released as insane.

We don't seem to be able to check crime, so why not legalize it and put a heavy tax on it? Make the tax for robbery so high that a bandit could not afford to rob anyone unless they knew they had a lot of dough. We have taxed other industries out of business; it might work here.

You know, every man convicted for murder in court is not guilty, and on the other hand, volumes of propaganda and lengths of petitions have nothing to do with guilt or innocence.

Pardoning sure has been one industry that hasn't been hit by recession.

I met the head of the antinarcotic work in this country. Say, let him tell you what is happening to the youth of this country through drugs! Talk about crime waves, why, it's nothing but heroin. They got to rob to supply the dope. And talk about profit in things! Opium, from the time a certain amount leaves its original owner, until it is split and passes through thousands of hands, why, a grain of it sells for 9 thousand times as much as it originally cost!

★

In Memphis today, over 25 policemen went to a hospital and volunteered to give blood transfusions to a kid that was near death. I know that I am out of order in speaking of the good things that cops do, but I am one of the old-fashioned people who believe if some one pounces on me, I could holler for a policeman, and he would come and help me out.

11 RECESSION

WILL ROGERS LIVED THROUGH A NUMBER OF RECESSIONS, but the most devastating was the Great Depression of the thirties. Starting with the stock market crash of 1929, conditions worsened, and by the time of Will's death in 1935, there was still no sign of recovery. For the last five years of his life Will tried to help wherever he could, and however he could. Whether he was asked to contribute funds or to assist at a benefit, he was eager to help out. In fact, if he heard of a benefit anywhere in the country to which he had not been asked, he would wire immediately and offer his services.

Will realized that he was in a unique position to instill hope and confidence in the masses who had nothing, who were hungry, who went without, and to whom the future promised no improvements. By this time his columns, both daily and weekly, reached 40 million readers—approximately one-third of America's total population. It has not been determined how many millions listened to his radio program, but it was a fact that American families found Will Rogers's comments on a Sunday evening far more inspirational than many a sermon.

With such an enormous following, Will was keenly aware of his responsibility, yet he could not simply "preach optimism"; there had to be a ham sandwich at the end somewhere. He knew that none of the plans, and there were hundreds, could solve all problems overnight. "Plans," he warned, "can get you into things, but we just will have to work ourselves out of this."

Will felt that the key to the depression was unemployment. With great compassion he wrote:

For millions of folks it is a very hard time. There is nothing that they personally can do to help their position. Their living has always been made by working, by holding an honorable job, but there is no job to hold. Inflation, deflation, on the gold, off the gold—the whole mess are just little side issues compared to reemployment of those out of work.

Ideas? Schemes? Everybody has some scheme or plan to save the country. I gather that from the pamphlets that people send me. Somebody is sure doing good that is in the printing line. Every guy that's got a scheme, racket, idea, hallucination, gets it put in a pamphlet form, and while the letter *R* comes pretty late in the alphabet, they must have me mixed up with the letter *A*. I seem to be the first to receive these Depression Solvers.

Will had a suggestion to all those who favored him with their plans: "Don't send me your suggestions! You just go ahead and solve the depression, THEN you can wire me collect that you have done it."

Last year we said: "Things can't go on like this!" And they didn't—they got worse.

★

There is not a man in the country that can't make a living for himself and family. But, he can't make a living for them AND his government, too, not the way this government is living. What the government has got to do is live as cheap as the people.

★

One of the most honest divorce reasons I ever heard was given the other day by some fellow: "She suits me fine, your Honor, but I can't afford her."

★

Why don't somebody print the truth about our present economic condition? We spent years of wild buying on credit, everything under the sun, whether we needed it or not, and now we are having to pay for it, and we are howling like a pet coon. This would be a great world to dance in, if we didn't have to pay the fiddler.

★

There is quite a few problems that is agitating the country that I'm not really 100 percent decided on myself. I would never make a good economist. You know, an economist is a man that can tell you anything

about . . . well, he will tell you what can happen under any given
condition, and his guess is liable to be as good as anybody else's, too.

★

I can't figure whether we made any progress in the last hundred years, or
not. There was no unemployment in those days. If a man wasn't
working, he sat in front of the grocery store and whittled. Also, if a man
was idle in one part of the country, you didn't hear about it in the other
parts of the country.

★

This thing called statistics was the worst thing that was invented; it's the
curse of the world. We wouldn't know how bad the others were doing if
we didn't have statistics.

★

Every day brings new schemes in the papers for relief. I guess we will
just have to save ourselves accidentally. That's the way we stumbled on
prosperity.

★

I don't know any more about relieving depression than a prominent man
does. But it looks like the financial giants of the world have bungled as
much as the diplomats and politicians.

   This would be a great time for some man to come along that knew
something.

★

The way I figure this thing will end is that the depression won't be
solved. It will just remain with us, and as a new generation grows up,
why, they won't be used to anything else, and they won't mind it.

★

The depression won't end till we grow a generation that knows how to
live on what they got.

★

I am going to Washington as a delegation of one from the American
Comedians' Association to get us some aid. No industry has been hit
worse than us professional humorists. There is just too much unconscious amateur talent among our elected officials.

★

We have eleven million unemployed, counting the four million that do
nothing but keep statistics on things that we would be better off if we
dident know.

★

The reason there wasn't much unemployment in the last ten years
preceding the depression was that every man that was out of a job went to
work for the government—federal, state, or city.

Every morning some court declares this law, or that conviction, illegal. In other words, the way the courts are going now, they may declare this whole recession and everything connected with it, illegal, and that it all has to be done over again.

I never realized that elections were so near till we see by the papers this morning that each political party has some plan of relieving the unemployed. Both parties have discovered that while these folks are not working, there is nothing in the Constitution to prevent them from voting.

This recession has taught us one important fact, that we haven't got as many "big men" as we thought we had. We used to think every head of a big organization was a "big man," and he was, as long as everything was running in spite of him. Big men are just like livestock now; they are selling at just what they are worth, no more.

The trouble with us today is we are in such bad shape that it takes us all day to tell about. We keep yapping for the good old days. Well, we might just as well wake up, for those cuckoo times are not coming back any more.

Well, the old year is leaving us flat, but in reality it's been our most beneficial year. It took some of the conceit out of us.

The president in his message said that "during the last 12 months we have suffered with other nations from economic depression."

Yes, and we have suffered alone, too.

I don't think the Republicans, or even Russia, is responsible for this depression. I think the Lord just looked us over and decided to set us back where we belonged.

Everybody kinder tries to explain the cause of this depression, that's where they all fall down. They offer every manner of different excuse. Why don't some of 'em just say, Boys, I don't know where this thing come from.

There is no reason to know where all this depression comes from. If a snake bites you, you ain't going to stop and study out where he come from and why he was there at the time, you want to start figuring on what to do with yourself right then.

Well, I'll tell you, the country is doing fine, if we can just keep some prominent man from getting up and crab it by saying: "We have reached the bottom."

12 INFLATION

BORN ON THE LAND, Will knew two basic investments: livestock and land. Whenever Will was able to do so, he bought land. He always felt that real estate—and California, of course, was the place for it—was the most secure investment. Only once did he try stocks, when he followed Eddie Cantor's advice. But that was short lived, and Will was grateful when the crash came. "I guess I will just have to give thanks that we had invested in land, instead of Wall Street, even if we can't sell the land and have to pay taxes on it, we can at least walk out on it. Still, I got some you can't, unless you have Divine power."

The land he referred to was beach property in Santa Monica, California. Will had bought a quarter-mile stretch on advice of a broker. Within days William Randolph Hearst wanted to buy that particular stretch to build a very private beach house for Marion Davies. Will was amazed at the amount of the profit on such a short-term investment. Emboldened by the success, he bought a one-mile stretch. When Will died, the family still had the property. The city of Los Angeles eventually passed a resolution exchanging the ocean frontage for a lot of equal value in downtown Los Angeles. The city council felt that the beach property should not be held in private hands, but should be made public. Today that is the Will Rogers Beach, a state park. The downtown property proved a most equitable exchange and a perfect hedge against inflation.

Whether Will invested in land because he realized the dangers of depressions and inflation, or whether it was just the innate shrewdness of a country boy, can best be judged by what he said:

99

I have been accused of being worried over this inflation. I wasn't worried. I was just confused. There is quite a difference. When you are worried, you know what you are worried about, but when you are confused, you don't know enough about a thing to be worried. You see, medical science has developed two ways of actually tracing insanity. One is if the patient cuts out paper dolls, and the other is if the patient says: "I will tell you what this economic business really means."

The papers every day tell in big headlines what gold sells for. They just as well tell us what radium sells for—who has any of either?

★

We read headlines where gold is going up and it's almost driving us nuts, because we ain't got any to sell. A female movie star out here in Hollywood, for whom things haven't been breaking too good lately, is just getting along great—she's turning in an old gold wedding ring every day, and she told me she's set for several weeks yet.

★

I see a committee that was investigating the high cost of living, turned in their report: "We find the cost of living very high and we recommend more funds to carry on the investigation."

★

You ought to have been in the cattle business the last few years. Let me say right here, boy, they are coming back. You steak eaters better get yourself a bankroll, or change your diet.

★

Say, did you read about this society woman on Long Island suing her ex-husband again? She claims she can't properly raise their child on $50,000 a year.

Someone's been feeding that young one meat!

★

We couldn't spell a billion dollars, much less realize it, count it, or anything. But now, as a nation, we learn awful fast, till it won't be long now and we'll be working on the word trillion—that follows billion. You'll read: "Congress has been asked to appropriate 2 trillion dollars to relieve the descendants of a race of people called 'Wall Streeters.'" This is a worthy cause and no doubt this small appropriation will be made, after all, they are the wards of the government.

★

With old inflation riding the headlines, I have read till I am bleary-eyed, and I can't get head from tails of the whole thing. We are living in an age of explanations, and plenty of 'em, too, but no two things that's been done to us have been explained twice the same way, by even the same man.

★

We got inflation and a lot of us dumb ones are trying to figure out just what it is. All you can learn about it is: money will have to be cheaper! Cheaper than what? Even if a dollar is worth only 10 cents, how are you going to get your clutches on it any easier than now?

Unless they give it away, I can't see where it's going to be any big help to anybody.

★

Inflation? When congress becomes ten percent efficient, why, that is inflation!

★

To inflate, or not to inflate, that is the question. Whether it's nobler in the minds to suffer the slings and arrows of Southern politicians, or to take up inflation against a sea of economists, and by opposing, end them.

To expand, to inflate; to inflate, perchance to dream, aye, there's the rub. For in that sleep of inflation, what dreams may come puzzle the will, and make us doubtful whether to bear those ills we have, or fly to others we know not of.

★

This inflation was brought on by the actions of many peoples of the whole world, and its weight will be lifted by the actions of many peoples of the whole world, and not by a Republican or a Democrat.

★

Inflation? I don't know what it's all about. I don't know any more about this than an economist does, and God knows, he don't know anything!

★

Got a wire from an old boy in Parsons, Kansas, and he wanted me to enter in a hog-calling contest. You know, I used to be an awful good hog caller when hogs were cheaper, but the way hogs have gone up in price, it's changed the whole system of calling 'em. I hollered all morning just for three slices of bacon and it didn't come, so there ain't much use of me howling my head off trying to get a whole hog to come.

★

Of course our government is costing us more than it's worth, but do you know of any other, cheaper government that's running around? If you do, they sell you a ticket there anytime.

Fifteen hundred Americans who have been living in Paris for years have decided to come home on account of the price of our money.

Now there is a bunch of folks who will be an awful big help to us!

★

Papers all excited today over the dollar being worth sixty cents. Well, it's been sixty cents for months. It's a good argument for us dumb ones to stay out of, so may the loudest man win.

13 GOVERNMENT

IT IS QUITE OBVIOUS when one reads Will Rogers' writings that he always chided government for practicing far more politics than concern for the welfare of the people. More than once he warns the government: "When it comes to a showdown, Washington must never forget who rules—the people."

America realized that here was the only voice, Will's, which seemed to represent the people. Washington, after years in power, had not only grown well entrenched, but arrogant. A senator, or a congressman, were men of great political power, who could award contracts or jobs, who could swing millions of dollars of the taxpayers' money to a district, or a company. Even though these men in Washington were held in awe by the people and a partisan press, Will just kidded them, while throwing velvet-tipped harpoons. They were most definitely velvet-tipped, but they were harpoons, nevertheless. Yet there was one remarkable quality to these harpoons. They left no permanent scars, even though they never missed the most sensitive spots.

When Will chided Washington that the Air Defense Program turned out more air than defense, a congressional investigation ensued. After viewing the feeble efforts to contain a flooding Mississippi River, Will wrote: "I have more confidence in high ground than any government commission." He was invited to appear before a congressional committee to testify as to what he thought should be done to help those who had been driven from their land. Suggested Will: "Hire a boat builder!"

The power in Will's hand rivaled that of the government; he was the single most prominent spokesman for the average American, who would have liked to say what Will said for him. Such power in a lesser man could have been most dangerous, but never once did Will misuse it. Nor did he ever overstep his bounds. He just watched the government and reported his point of view.

At one time, while in the Capitol, and walking through Statuary Hall, one of the lawmakers observed that some day Will's statue would stand in there. Will doubted it, but he thought about it. Finally he said: "Well, if they ever do, I want to stand where I can keep an eye on our Hired Help."

Jo Davidson, the world-famous sculptor, created a startling likeness of Will. There are only two copies in existence. One stands at the Will Rogers Memorial in Claremore, Oklahoma. The other is in Statuary Hall in Washington, D.C. In a typical Will Rogers stance, hands thrust deeply into trouser pockets, the head inclined and slightly to the side, Will seems to be peeking around the corner at both Houses of Congress. "I still feel," he seems to be saying, "that congress isn't doing the best they can. They are only doing the best they know how."

We are a nation that runs in spite, and not on account of our government.

★

Lord, the money we do spend on government, and it's not a bit better than the government that we got for one-third the money twenty years ago.

★

Our government is the only people that just love to spend money without being compelled to, at all. But the government is the only people that don't have to worry where it is coming from.

★

We say the government is nutty, and throwing away money. But any time any is thrown our way, we have never dodged it. Well, if the government is throwing the money away, the only thing I see for the ones that they are throwing it to, have 'em refuse to take it. But you haven't heard that, have you? So don't be so critical of the present plans as long as you are living on the loot from them.

★

Just been reading of a fund the government has, called the Conscience Fund. If you feel that you have cheated the government, you send them the money. Say, how about the government having a Conscience Fund? They have skinned us many a time!

★

You see, what will have to come eventually in government affairs, will be to consider ability, instead of numbers. The law won't just say: "Elect so many men each time!" No! It will say: "Find some man that knows just as much as a hundred others put together. Well, take him, and get rid of the hundred!"

★

Our Secretary of State Kellogg's peace treaty—a lot of people don't seem so enthusiastic about it. I also have a scheme for stopping war. It's this: no nation is allowed to enter a war till they have paid for the last one.

★

It's a tough baby, that secretary of state thing. You come in there labeled a statesman, and limp out headed for the ash can of political hopes.

★

They are always wanting the government to spend the taxpayers' money to build something. Every congressman wants to get an appropriation to dam up his client's little stream with federal funds. If the politicians have their way, there won't be a foot of water in this country that's not standing above a dam.

★

If you got a river near your house, and the government hasn't *damded* it up yet, why, it's only because you haven't sent them a blueprint of where it is, and haven't asked them to put one in for you.

★

We are going on the assumption that nothing in public life (or out of it, for that matter) is any good. Now what we have set out to do is to find the worst. It's no trouble to pick out the bad, but I tell you, when you sit down to pick out the worst, you have set some task for yourself.

★

Say, can't you just see a cabinet meeting?

The secretary of war reports: "Sir, wars—none; peace—none; average: 50 percent."

The postmaster general reports: "Sir, so many letters sent, so many letters received, so many letters lost."

The secretary of agriculture reports: "Sir, farms in the U.S.—eleven million; farms mortgaged—eleven million; farms carrying second mortgages—10,998,634. The department reports progress."

The secretary of labor reports: "Sir, number of people laboring—ten million; people living off people laboring—ninety-eight million, including twenty-three million government employees."

★

Daylight savings time. Well, it's an hour earlier here today. It seems kind of funny, with the government spending everything to sort of save a little daylight nowadays.

★

Alexander Hamilton started the U.S. Treasury with nothing—and that was the closest our country has ever been to being even.

★

America is the only consecutively losing big business in the world that keeps on losing, and still keeps going.

★

There's dozens of great humanitarian things that could be done if the tax money was properly applied. It's the waste in government that gets everybody's goat.

★

The way we do things, always have done things, and always will do things there just has to be so much graft. We just have to get used to charging so much off to graft, just like you have to charge off so much for insurance, taxes, and depreciation. It's part of our national existence.

★

The Treasury department has saved some money, but it showed that it cost fifty million more to save it than it did the same department last year, showing that even the cost of saving money has gone up.

★

England has a great custom in government. They can bring before the House of Commons, in open session, any cabinet member or the Premier, and ask him what he has done and what he has in mind for the future, and he has to tell 'em.

We don't do it over here. It would be embarrassing to our officials to have to admit what little they had done, and extremely humiliating to explain what they had in mind for the future, when they had nothing in mind after their appointment.

★

Speaking of members of the cabinet, if they are not impeached, we never hear of them again. They only have one obligation here. They have to sign the payroll in person.

★

I doubt if Barnum's Circus has housed as many different kinds of species as have been in our government employ during its existence. Yet as bad as they are, they can't spoil it, and as good as they are, they can't help it. We are just flowing to the sea. Corruption can't retard us, and reformers can't assist us; we are just flowing along, in spite of everything.

★

When a man is working for the government in an elected office, he never knows how long it will last. He can only give half his time to his job. He has to give the other half to trying to find out where he is going when this is over. So I believe, if we guaranteed them something permanent, they would do better.

At least we always have the satisfaction to know that they couldn't do worse.

★

If there is one thing that we want to inculcate into the minds of the youth of this country, it is that honesty and fair dealing with our own government is the foundation of this nation. Our history honors many names whose morals would not stand the acid test, but our history honors no man who betrayed, or attempted to betray, a government trust.

14 DIPLOMACY

IN APRIL 1926 WILL ROGERS had lunch with George H. Lorimer, editor of the *Saturday Evening Post*. Will suggested a series of articles, giving his personal observations on conditions in Europe. The *Post* had recently featured a series "Letters of a Self-Made Merchant to His Son," so Will suggested that his articles be called "Letters of a Self-Made Diplomat to His President" by Will Rogers, Ambassador Without Portfolio. The two men came to an understanding, and on May 1 Will left for Europe aboard the *Leviathan*.

As an introduction to his "diplomatic mission" Will had to explain his qualifications, which had made his selection for "this delicate task" a most natural choice. Here is what "diplomat" Will Rogers wrote:

A few words might not be amiss as to why I was chosen. I will try to explain the whole thing in a few words, in a way that will entirely eliminate my own personal achievements. I only relate them to show what I had done before being chosen by our President to embark on this mission to carry out my policies in his name.

From my earliest birth I was always doing things and letting other people take the credit. I started the Spanish-American war in '98. But I never said anything. I just sit back and let the *Maine* get the credit. I was the one who told Roosevelt to call his regiment the Rough Riders, even if there wasent a horse nearer Cuba than Lexington, Kentucky.

I managed William Jennings Bryan's nomination in '96. But on account of his losing the election, I have always claimed that I advised him strongly against running. I wanted him to be the only man that ever was

108

nominated and then wouldent run. I advised Teddy Roosevelt to go ahead and run for Vice-President, that something would turn up. We split over Taft, I wanted him to reduce and Roosevelt dident.

The Democratic Conventions of the early Twentieth Century was held much against my advice. I said they not only should not convene in New York City in 1924, but that they shoudent convene at all, to save all their money and buy all the votes they could in 1928.

I don't care how unostentatious you do things, the news of them will gradually leak out. So, of course, the President heard of me and my underground methods of doing things and that's how we got together. Now comes the most remarkable thing about our relation, and that is we have had no personal contact or agreement about taking up this work for him. In other words, our understanding has been so perfect between each other that we haven't even had to talk it over. There is a kind of mental telepathy between us. I just felt that he needed a foreign Diplomat that could really go in and dip, and he didn't even have to ask me to do it; that same intimate understanding that had told me he needed someone, had told him that I was the one he needed. And that's all there has ever been between us.

Of course we have foreign Ambassadors over there, but they are more of a social than a diplomatic aid to us.

Naturally, in the course of human events I will have to communicate with my Master. We only had one understanding before I left and that was that everything between us must be carried on in an absolutely confidential manner, and not get out to the general public. So it was decided to carry it on by postcard. Just another example of typical American Diplomacy.

These articles proved so popular that the first seven installments were published in book form as *Letters of a Self-Made Diplomat to His President*, while the other three were published in a book as *There's Not a Bathing Suit in Russia & Other Bare Facts*. Later Will wrote a set of five more articles for the *Saturday Evening Post* entitled "More Letters from a Self-Made Diplomat," and another series of five articles entitled "Letters of a Self-Made Diplomat to Senator Borah."

There is one thing no nation can accuse us of, and that is secret diplomacy. Our foreign dealings are an open book, generally a check-book.

★

Diplomacy was invented by a man named Webster, to use up all the words in his dictionary that dident mean anything.

★

A diplomat has a hundred ways of saying nothing, but no way of saying something.

★

A diplomat is a man that tells you what he don't believe himself, and the man he is telling it to don't believe it any more than he does.

★

Diplomats are just as essential to starting a war as soldiers are for finishing it. You take diplomacy out of war, and the thing would fall flat in a week.

★

Nowadays we have diplomats work on wars for years before arranging them. That's so that when it's over, nobody will know what they were fighting for. We lost thousands and spent billions, and you could hand a sheet of paper to one million different people, and tell 'em to write down what the last war was for, and the only answer that will be alike, will be "d—— if I know!"

★

Diplomats are nothing but high-class lawyers—and some ain't even high class.

★

Diplomats write notes because they wouldent have the nerve to tell the same thing to each other's face.

★

It's great to be friendly with a foreign nation, but it's terribly expensive. If the worst comes to the worst, and we do have to be friendly with any of 'em, why, let's pick out little ones that haven't got the nerve to ask for much.

★

It's a funny thing that you can't deal with nations like you can with businessmen. That's on account of having what they call, diplomats. A diplomat is a fellow to keep you from settling on a thing so everybody can understand it.

★

Paper says: "The new ambassador arrives in London in a fog."
    That's the way all of 'em have arrived, and most of them have remained in one.

★

Since I got started on all this foreign mess (which I don't know any more about than you do), I come to think that nobody knows anything about any country, not even his own. The smartest statesmen are the worst fooled when anything comes up right quick. I think a country is harder to understand than a woman.

★

Diplomacy is a great thing if it wasn't so transparent.

★

That's called "diplomacy," doing just what you said you wouldn't.

15 ARMED FORCES

WILL'S FIRST CONTACT WITH ANY ARMY was during the Boer War in South Africa. He had left home to visit the Argentine, which proved most disappointing. Then Will was offered a job on a cattle boat going to Durban, South Africa. After the cattle had been driven to their destination, 150 miles into the interior, Will looked for another job. He finally landed one with the British Army, breaking horses. Within days the war was over. Will's wanderings continued. Finally in Johannesburg he saw a sign advertising *Texas Jack's Wild West Show*. The hours and weeks and months Will had spent perfecting his roping tricks were now to pay off, and his show-business career was about to begin.

When America entered World War I, Will had three children and was over-age. He did the next best thing. He pledged $100 a week for the duration of the war to the Red Cross, a pledge he fully discharged. He played in every army camp in the New York City area, as he was then appearing in the *Ziegfeld Follies*. When the war was over, Will, unlike so many others, never forgot the veterans. He continued to play benefits, visited veterans hospitals, and donated liberally to the Red Cross.

Hal Roach told the story of Will's performance at the Arrowhead Springs Veterans Hospital in California. Roach had agreed to put on a special Christmas show at the hospital, and he had asked Will to perform. On the appointed day Will left Los Angeles to drive to the hospital. As was his practice he probably drove too fast, and he was stopped by a policeman in Azusa. He was taken before a judge who recognized Will, but still fined him $100. Will was annoyed; he had been delayed and he disliked being late for any appointment, especially a benefit. When he finally arrived at the veterans hospital, he delivered one of his funniest monologues ever, entirely about the trip to Arrowhead Springs and the mishaps along the way.

On another occasion Will had been asked to perform a benefit at a veterans hospital. This was a special group of seriously wounded and amputees. Will entertained them for over an hour, then disappeared. When he was finally located by the commanding officer, Will was in the men's room, crying over the tragedy of the men he had just seen. Will never forgot the debt owed those who fought for their country.

When Will returned from a trip to Europe just before America entered World War I, reporters met the ship, as was the practice at that time. Spotting Will, they surrounded him—he was always good for a story. Had he not been concerned about the great danger of German submarines, they wanted to know. He shook his head. "No," he said, "not only wasn't I worried, but I worked out a plan to git rid of those submarines!"

"How?" the reporters wanted to know.

"Simple," said Will, "all you have to do is heat the North Atlantic to the boiling point, and then when the water bubbles, the submarines will just rise out of the water and you can shoot 'em down." The reporters smiled, but they were not satisfied. "Just how do you propose to heat the North Atlantic?" they wanted to know.

"Don't bother me with details," Will laughed as he walked down the gangplank, "I'm a policy maker!"

Ain't it funny how many hundreds of thousands of soldiers we can recruit with nerve, but we just can't find one politician in a million with backbone.

These big wars over commerce are pretty bad. They kill more people, but one over religion is really the most bitter.

★

A country is known by its strength, and a man by his checkbook.

★

If we were told tomorrow that the future and safety of our country depended on football and athletics, why, everybody, the whole country, would be out practicing. But when any sane person absolutely knows that the success of the next war is in the air, why, they just drag along and think somebody is kidding 'em.

★

If you want to know when a war might be coming, you just watch the U.S. and see when it starts cutting down on its defenses. It's the surest barometer in the world.

★

We are the only nation in the world that waits till we get into a war, before we start getting ready for it.

★

Was talking to a lady congressman and she said to me: "Why do all those men say that all that armament will bring peace?"

I told her: "Well, even if it don't bring peace, it will come in mighty handy in case of a war."

★

I told our secretary that I wished we had the biggest navy in the world, the biggest army, and by all means the biggest air force, but have it understood with the taxpayers that they are only to be used to defend the home grounds.

Be ready for it, and then just stay at home!

If you think preparedness don't give you prestige, look at Japan. We are afraid to look at them cross-eyed now for fear we will hurt their honor. Before they got a navy, neither them, nor us, knew they had any honor.

★

It ain't your honor that is respected among nations, it's your strength. These nations would have just as much honor without any navy, but the navy helps to remind you of it.

★

Holland, Belgium, Switzerland, and half a dozen other countries got just as much honor as England or France, but you don't see them with a permanent seat on the League of Nations.

★

We better start doing something about our defense. This old "Economy" is a good slogan. It's a great horse to ride, but look out you don't ride it in the wrong direction!

★

I tell you, war is a business with some of these other nations. Their soldiers are trained between wars—not after one starts.

You see, we have been lucky that way, all of our wars have waited on us till we could get ready. But one day we may have one where the enemy won't wait!

You think that's kidding? Well, you are just another senator if you do.

★

I was just thinking about these budget hearings. There were these generals that congress won't listen to in regard to preparedness in peacetime, yet they will stake their entire future on them in war.

★

We start sinking our navy to save taxes. To reduce your navy in these times is exactly like a man who is not doing so well financially, cancelling all his life insurance, figuring it's a dead loss because he hasn't died yet.

★

When we nearly lose the next war, as we probably will, we can lay it onto one thing—the jealousy of the army and navy toward aviation. They have belittled it since it started and will keep on doing it till they have something dropped on them from one, and even then they will say it wasn't a success.

★

If America don't look out, they will be caught in the next war with nothing but a couple of golf clubs.

★

In the next war, you don't want to look out, you want to look UP. When you look up and you see a cloud during the next "War to end Wars," don't you be starting to admire its silver lining till you find out how many enemy planes are hiding behind it.

★

Why don't we either go on and build a great defense, or not have one hardly at all? For running second don't get you anywhere in anybody's war.

★

Why shouldent we have the biggest army and the biggest navy and the biggest air force in the world, we are the greatest nation.

★

People are not going to quit fighting, any more than individuals are going to quit fighting. A nation is nothing but a boy grown up and he hasent any too good an education in growing up.

★

The one thing these old boys with a big navy are scared of, and that's submarines. They are always claiming they are inhuman, and not a civilized mode of warfare.

It would be rather interesting to see published the names of the weapons that are considered a pleasure to be shot by.

★

They are bringing soldiers back from Europe. Would have brought them back sooner, but we didn't have anybody in Washington who knew where they were. We had to leave 'em over there so they could get the mail that was sent to them during the war. Had to leave them over there, anyway; two of them hadn't married yet.

★

Ever since I can remember telling jokes, I have used kidding stuff about us going into somebody's country, and it's always been tremendously popular stuff, for not a soul wanted us to be sending marines out over the world. You know, like a big city would send policemen to places where they heard there was trouble.

★

It had just become almost impossible for a country to have a nice home-talent little revolution among themselves, without us butting in. Everywhere an American went to invest some money in the hope of making 100 percent, why, here would be a gunboat to see he had all the comforts to which he had been accustomed.

★

Did you know that we sent marines into Vera Cruz, Mexico, one time? Oh, we was in Nicaragua, Haiti, San Domingo, China, Mexico. Anywhere in the world we could find a place where we had no business, why, there is where we were. It was just during our adolescent period in our life as a nation, when we thought it was up to us to regulate the affairs of everybody.

★

If we could just let other people alone and do their own fighting. When you get into trouble 5,000 miles from home, we've got to have been looking for it.

★

If we are out, upholding downtrodden nations, it will take a bookkeeper to keep track of our wars.

★

Lord knows how many men we lost. Finally we got out. It's wonderful now to go to sleep at night and know that we haven't got scouts out, looking for wars or private revolutions for us to get mixed up in. Just think of being a spectator once again!

★

Did you ever notice how much more peaceful it is all around when our Marines are at home, instead of prowling around? Why, if we keep 'em at

With actor David Landau in scene from film *Judge Priest*.

Frames from Will Rogers' travelogues on Ireland (1926).

With band leader Ben Bernie, Christmas benefit, 1934.

With Tom Mix (December 16, 1932).

Will and Babe Ruth visiting Children's Hospital in Boston (April 25, 1929).

Will, never a pilot, poses at the controls of an experimental plane.

With houseguest Prince Ferdinand, the son of the German crown prince.

On Bootlegger, one of Will's favorite polo ponies.

Favorite pastime, roping and tying calves (1935).

Resting and reading between takes on set of *Too Busy to Work* (September 22, 1932).

Will and Betty returning from Europe aboard the *Ile de France* (September 25, 1934).

Before departure for Point Barrow, Alaska. On right, the famous Alaskan flier Joe Crosson (August 15, 1935).

Will in his office on wheels, typing out his daily column.

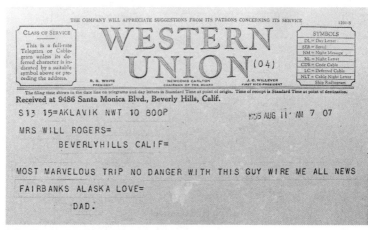

WESTERN UNION (04)

CLASS OF SERVICE

This is a full-rate Telegram or Cablegram unless its deferred character is indicated by a suitable symbol above or preceding the address.

R. B. WHITE
PRESIDENT

NEWCOMB CARLTON
CHAIRMAN OF THE BOARD

J. C. WILLEVER
FIRST VICE-PRESIDENT

SYMBOLS

DL = Day Letter
SER = Serial
NM = Night Message
NL = Night Letter
CDE = Code Cable
LC = Deferred Cable
NLT = Cable Night Letter
Ship Radiogram

The filing time shown in the date line on telegrams and day letters is Standard Time at point of origin. Time of receipt is Standard Time at point of destination.

Received at 9486 Santa Monica Blvd., Beverly Hills, Calif.

S13 15=AKLAVIK NWT 10 800P   1935 AUG 11 AM 7 07

MRS WILL ROGERS=

     BEVERLYHILLS CALIF=

MOST MARVELOUS TRIP NO DANGER WITH THIS GUY WIRE ME ALL NEWS

FAIRBANKS ALASKA LOVE=

    DAD.

Last telegram to Betty (August 11, 1935).

Barely fifteen miles from Point Barrow—their destination—Will Rogers and Wiley Post died in this lagoon.

Close-up of the smashed engine. While there are several theories for the cause of the crash, no definitive explanation has ever been offered. [Photo courtesy Smithsonian Institution, Washington, D.C.]

August 22, 1935. Prior to a simple service for Will Rogers at the Wee Kirk o' the Heather, his flower-covered casket lay in state in Forest Lawn Memorial Park. Honor guard of United States fliers stood at attention as more than fifty thousand people filed past. Many had waited in line all night.

Rogers crypt on grounds of Will Rogers Memorial, Claremore, Oklahoma. In 1944 Will's remains were brought here from California. A month later when Betty died, her body and that of their infant son Fred Stone Rogers were buried by his side.

Early photo of Will Rogers Memorial, Claremore, Oklahoma.

"The White House on the Verdigris," Will Rogers' birthplace in its new, safe location.

One of two stars embedded in the sidewalk on Hollywood Boulevard, Hollywood, California. This one, at number 6401, with the symbol of the motion-picture camera, recognizes Will as a film star; the other star, at 6608, displaying a microphone, pays tribute to Will as a broadcaster.

Jo Davidson, the world-famous sculptor, created this statue at the Will Rogers Memorial, Claremore, Oklahoma. An identical copy stands in Statuary Hall, the United States Capitol, Washington, D.C.; at Will's suggestion it is positioned "so that I can keep an eye on our hired help." [Photograph courtesy NBC, Project XX]

home a while, why, we are liable to get out of the habit of wanting to send 'em away off, every time we heard of some little nation about to pull off a local amateur revolution.

★

Most of our Marines are back in America. It's the first time in years. From what I hear, some of the boys like it here—they think this is a great country and a lot of them are going to take out citizenship papers.

★

I will never joke about old soldiers who try to get to reunions to talk over the war again. To talk of old times with old friends is the greatest thing in the world.

★

Us letting the veterans entirely alone, and not caring, now that we don't need him—or think we don't—is like lots of people we have, who allow their old parents, or grandparents, to be sent to a sanatorium because they were getting to be too much trouble and too much in the way for them to take care of at home.

I am not so sure myself of "No More Wars," and there is a bare possibility that we might want to use these boys again. The best insurance in the world against another war is to take care of the ones that fought the last one.

★

There were bands playing, soldiers marching, orators orating, telling you it's your duty to buy Liberty Bonds . . . and now, years later, no bands, no marching, no orators, just a patriotic girl, or a broken piece of human frame, trying to sell a poppy for a few cents, made by even a more unfortunate brother in one of our veterans' hospitals. There is only one sure way of stopping war, that is to see that every "statesman" has the same chance to reflect after it is over that these boys making the poppies have had.

★

I tell you, any experiment that is being made in the air is not a waste of time or money. Our defense, offense, and all, have got to come from the air.

16 BUDGET

WILL ROGERS FIRMLY BELIEVED in fiscal responsibility in government and business. As for himself, if he believed in it, he certainly managed to hide the fact. For Will money was meant to do things, to bring joy to people, not to be saved, hidden away, or doled out in carefully preplanned droplets. This is not meant to give the impression that he was irresponsible with money. Far from it. He always knew his obligations and met them, but to friend and stranger alike he was an easy touch. Anyone could approach him with a hard luck story, and Will would do anything he could to help out. Many is the story where Will would give away the last dollar in his pocket to some unfortunate, only to find himself in the position of having to borrow carfare home.

He never kept any business records, and yet he knew almost to the dollar how much money he had in the bank and what obligation it would cover. When he was in the *Ziegfeld Follies* he would usually carry as many as ten uncashed weekly paychecks in his pocket. Then he would deposit them all at once and almost break Flo Ziegfeld's precariously financed company.

In the twenties Will made films for Hal Roach Studios. His salary was $2,500 per week, but many times he would neglect to pick up his paycheck at the office. Sometimes weeks would go by before he would come around to collect his pay—probably because some major payment was due, or the bank balance was low. By that time the total amount of those checks represented a substantial sum. "Don't you have a bookkeeper?" Hal Roach asked Will.

"No," Will replied, "I just put a check in the bank and then draw on it till it's gone."

Betty discovered Will's way with money early in their marriage. Having been raised in a home that practiced the old-established virtue of thrift, she decided that the new family needed a budget and a savings plan. She persuaded Will that while they toured the vaudeville circuit they should put aside one dollar each day. They bought a large awkward strongbox with handles and a slot and religiously deposited a dollar every day. Touring the eastern theatres it was usually a greenback that was tucked away at the end of each day, but out west most dollars were silver, and the box grew heavier and more awkward. It was in Butte, Montana, that the box, and 125 days' savings, was stolen. Betty was heartsick, but Will tried to console her and made light of the episode. But the experience hardly served to impress Will with the advantages of a strict budget or savings plan.

Many years later, on the ranch in Santa Monica, Betty was still trying to get Will to stick to some kind of budget. There were guests for Saturday night dinner, including the well-known actor Harry Carey and his wife Olive. Will and Harry had ridden through the canyon earlier in the day, and Will had a new project in mind.

"Blake," he began. Will always used Betty's maiden name when the topic was serious. "Blake, we will need a dam up in the canyon to keep that whole mountainside from sliding down on us."

How much would it cost, Betty wanted to know. Will thought about it for a moment and then offered that it would probably cost about $25,000. That's when Betty put her foot down. "We can't do it this year," she said firmly. "It is not in our budget!"

Will looked at her mischievously, then left the room. When he returned some minutes later, he was grinning like a kid.

"Blake," he said, "Monday morning you order a crew to get started on that dam. I'm leaving tomorrow. I just booked me a little lecture tour for $25,000. So now the dam *is* on this year's budget."

You have a budget like you have a limit in a poker game. You're not supposed to go beyond it till at least an hour after the game has started.

They sent the Budget to congress. It took the head men of every department 6 months to think up that many figures. We won't run over the budget limit, till maybe as late as August. When we do, it'll make another department in Washington.

★

Funny thing showed up in the papers. Something we hadn't heard of in so long that it seemed like reviving an article from King Tut's tomb. It was the Budget! They are even talking about balancing him. Course they won't be able to do that—you take a rope walker that's laid off for years, and they never come back—but it's good to hear the old boy's name mentioned again. Budget is the name, spelled B-U-D-G-E-T, pronounced bud-jet.

★

All you read about Washington is how they are going to spend those billions of dollars. There hasent been even one suggestion as to where it was to come from. It must be marvelous to belong to some legislative body, and just pick money out of the air.

★

There is a lot of schemes in congress to spend these five billion dollars. Now there is something you got to have a plan for—you can't spend five billion dollars in the old-fashioned way. I bet you could put a strong man in the Treasury warehouse full of hundred dollar bills and give him a scoop shovel, and he couldn't shovel out that much money in the rest of his life.

★

I don't know where any of all this money is coming from that we are spending now, any more than a congressman does. But if Americans are going to stop, and start worrying about whether they can afford a thing or not, you are going to ruin the whole characteristic of our people.

There wouldent have been a dozen automobiles sold last year if that was the case.

★

They sent the Budget to congress. There's things on there that you had no idea existed. Do you know it cost 345 million just to make these figures to tell us how much we was in the hole. That's like hiring a man to tell you you are broke.

★

Get this item of our national expense: interest on debt is 731 million dollars! They keep juggling with millions and we owe billions. Let's sell off enough of this country to somebody and pay off all national debts, then the taxes wouldent be nearly so much.

The Democrats will agree to peddle Texas, and I am certain the Republicans will let Massachusetts go.

Look at the president. He started in with the idea of a balanced budget, and said that was what he would hold out for. But look at the thing now. Poor president, he tried but couldn't do it by persuasion and he can't do it by law. So he may just have to give it up and say: "Boys, I have tried, but I guess it's back to the old ways of an unbalanced budget."

The president has been going out to his camp every weekend and it hasent been all for pleasure. One weekend he took our secretary of war, and he told him: "The treasury has gone and let the politicians overdraw our bank balance. Now we got to make it up in some way. How about lopping part of your army off? Take some oats from your mules, or something. Go back to your office and see who would be least needed in our next war, and give 'em two weeks notice. We got to be prepared, but see if we can't be prepared a little cheaper. We got to get this thing balanced up before the next election; after that, you can have all the help you want. But we got to stop Alexander Hamilton from laughing in his grave.

★

The budget is a mythical beanbag. Congress votes mythical beans into it, and then tries to reach in and pull real beans out.

17 EUROPE

WILL'S FIRST TRIP TO EUROPE came about strictly by a set of unusual circumstances. During his haphazard school days there had been several pictures in the class atlas that left lasting impressions. One was of wolves jumping at the throats of terrified horses as they raced, pulling a sleigh across the Russian steppes. Another was of gauchos herding cattle on the plains of the Argentine. Willie, the schoolboy in the Indian Territory, promised himself that he would most certainly try to steer clear of the former and go and see the latter.

In 1902 Will had enough of being a rancher for a while; he wanted to go somewhere. He sold his herd of cattle, persuaded his friend Dick Parris to come along as his guest, and struck out for the Argentine. Since the Argentine was generally south of Oologah, it seemed to make perfect sense to head for New Orleans to catch a ship.

The two young men were disappointed to learn that no ships left New Orleans for Buenos Aires and that they would have to make arrangements to depart from New York. Thus on about March 18, 1902, Will and Dick took the steamship *Comus* enroute to New York.

In New York City they learned that no ship was expected to leave for the Argentine for some months and that the wisest thing they could do would be to go to London. There, they were told, ships left for South America almost every week.

Will and Dick behaved like tourists and took part in the required sightseeing in New York City, and about March 28 they sailed aboard the U.S.S. *Philadelphia* for England.

In London, Will dragged Dick to all the important sights. They visited Westminster Abbey where "a curious sort of sensation" crept over Will, even though he had not "personally known any of the men buried there." They went through the Tower of London, walked around Piccadilly Circus, which Will thought to be "a good location if they ever want to put on a show." They sat in the visitors' gallery in the House of Commons. They spied King Edward as he passed by, during preparations for the forthcoming coronation. But as Will wrote home: "I doubt that the King recognized me." The Grenadier Guards, resplendent in their bright red uniforms and high busbies, drew this comment: "Can you imagine a flock of these located in front of the White House with Teddy Roosevelt there? But different nations have different ideas of humor."

On April 10, 1902, Will and Dick left London for South America aboard the *Danube*. Will's first trip to Europe had finished. This one had been strictly for pleasure; the next one would be in pursuit of a career.

On that next visit Will was booked into the Wintergarten in Berlin for the month of April 1906. He left New York in plenty of time to spend a few days in Paris before going on to Berlin. He was very successful in the German capital, except for one incident, which taught Will the archaic practice of lese majesty. During a performance in Berlin, Will saw a uniformed fireman stationed in the wings. Thinking that it might be a good gag to rope him, Will threw his next loop over the fireman, pinning his arms to his sides, and dragged him on stage. Instead of the laughter he expected there were gasps. The manager rushed on stage, apologized, saying that the American's rope had slipped. The incident prompted Will to write home: "In Germany they have cultivated everything they got, but humor."

An engagement in London's Palace Theatre followed. Will must have remembered that only four years earlier he and Dick Parris had been just visitors, while now he was the featured performer at the top vaudeville theatre.

Will visited England and the continent several more times, but he was always glad to put his feet back on American soil.

You know, of course, or perhaps you have had it hinted to you, that we stand in Europe about like a horse thief.

Now I want to report to you that this is not so. It is, what you'd call, erroneous. We don't stand like a horse thief abroad. Whoever told you we did, is flattering us.

★

Been reading editorials on: What would Europe do if we were in difficulty and needed help?

So this is in reply to those inquiries: Europe would hold a celebration.

★

Some Americans in Europe are traveling incognito. They are not bragging on where they come from and nobody knows they are Americans.

★

All Americans are wired for sound, and before they go abroad they ought to detach the wiring.

★

I had been over to Europe two or three times, years ago, but I thought, well, I will go and see if the boys have scared up anything new. They hadn't anything new but the prices.

★

I told you how bad it's getting with the tourists over there. Some of them are getting almost what they deserve.

★

Everybody in Europe talks about how we are hated. Well, I would just casually, in order to keep up the conversation and not change the subject, nonchalantly remark: "Will you enumerate to me the nations that you people can call bosom friends?"

Well, they had never thought of that.

★

All of Europe wants to be our partners. That's one good thing about European nations. They can't hate you so badly they wouldn't use you.

★

I would like to stay in Europe long enough to find some country that don't blame America for everything in the world that's happened to 'em in the last fifteen years: depression, disease, fog, famine, and frostbite.

Now the birthrate is falling off, so I am going to get out of here before we get blamed.

Passports, that's one thing you want to carry in your hand in Europe. They just seem to get a pleasure out of having you dig for it.

Flying over Holland in an airship is the only real way to see it, cause if you are down on the level—and if you are in Holland you will be standing on the level—Holland's highest point is eight feet six and a third inches above sea level. That is called the mountainous region of Holland. That's where they do their skiing and winter sports.

Lithuania? Why, I never even heard of it. President Wilson is the one that laid all these countries out. Any time a committee would come to him with ten names signed to an application, he would give 'em a country.

This Monte Carlo is a queer layout. It's the only country in the world that has practically no rural population. You either live in the city, or you don't live in Monte Carlo. If you are out of town, you're in France or Italy; or if you get too far out in the country, you're in Spain or Switzerland.

Well, to make a fair bankroll short, it don't take me long to learn the game of roulette pretty quick. When I bet without a system, they looked at me like I was crazy. I don't know why, because I was losing just as good as they were.

I see where six members of the Greek cabinet were executed today for negligence. I hope that will be a lesson to our cabinet.

Well, if you get your schooling from an Irish history book, you shoot anybody. The theory is—and they are just about right—that everybody that ain't been shot, should be shot.

They expressed sympathy for Ireland, but from the looks of the casualty lists lately, I think, England needs it more.

★

Well, today is the seventeenth of Ireland. Of all the nationalities that have helped to root the Indians out, the Irish are the only ones that have made enough of an impression on everybody till we celebrate their holiday.

★

I like Ireland perhaps better than any other foreign country. They got humor, and while they think they take life serious, they don't. They will

joke with you, sing with you, drink with you, and, if you want, fight
with you—or against you, whichever you want—and I think, if they like
you well enough, they would die with you.

★

France and England think just as much of each other as two rival bands of
gangsters; a Frenchman and an Italian love each other just about like
Minneapolis and St. Paul; Spain and France have the same regard for
each other as Fort Worth and Dallas; Russia hates everybody so bad, it
would take her a week to pick out the one she hates most.

★

A bunch of American tourists were hissed and stoned yesterday in
France, but not until they had finished buying.

★

Most of the secretaries of state I ever heard of, gained fame by sending
diplomatic notes to some nation. So why can't the present secretary of
state send one too? Why don't he send a note demanding the protection of
our American tourists in France? They have been skinned alive there for
years.

★

I see where they captured an American spy in France. He must have
been working on his own, for we already know all we want to know
about 'em.

★

Nice, France, is pronounced neece, not nice. They have no word for nice
in French.

★

France says that this year's harvest of tourists has not reached the
expected yield. The number has been beyond expectation, but the
shakedown per person has been very low. Where tourists used to carry a
letter of credit when leaving America, they are now carrying lunch
boxes.

★

Before the war, Germany led the world in lots of things. She lost all of
them; now here she is back where she was. It's a great argument against
war. It just shows you can lick a nation, but when you let 'em up they can
still beat you at the same things they could before, which takes away the
only reason left for having war.

★

I visited every nation that was supposedly the winner in the last war; then
I visited Germany, which is humorously referred to as the loser. I tell
you, if the next war is anything like the last one, I wouldent give you a
nickel to be the winner.

They live there in Rome amongst what used to be called Culture, but that don't mean a thing. Men in Washington live where Washington and Jefferson and Hamilton lived, but as far as the good it does them, they might just as well have the Capitol down at Claremore, Oklahoma.

They got a lot of things they call Forums in Rome. They are where the senators used to meet and debate—on disarmament, I suppose. I dident know before I got there, and they told me all this, that Rome had senators. Now we know why it declined.

Sight-seeing is no pleasure. Over there they go in great for ruins. Now a ruin don't just exactly spellbind me. I don't care how long it has been in process of ruination. I kept trying to get them to show me something that hadn't started to ruin yet.

Rome wasn't built in a day—it's not a Miami Beach by any means.

Rome has more churches and less preaching in them than any city in the world. Everybody wants to see where Saint Peter is buried, but nobody wants to try and live like him.

Rome is the oldest uncivilized town in the world. New York is just as uncivilized, but it's not as old.

There is quite an argument in Rome over the exact spot of Caesar's death. Some say that Caesar was not slain in the Senate; they seem to think that he had gone over to a senatorial investigation meeting at some committee room, and that is where Brutus gigged him. The moral of the whole thing seems to be to stay away from investigations.

They used to have a wall around Rome. It got so the wall wouldent keep the people from getting out. You can't keep people in a place with a wall. That wall system is a failure, and always was.

I have just arrived back from Europe, in company with 5,000 other half-wits. We are the only people in the world that will go where we are absolutely not wanted.

18 ENGLAND

THE YEAR IS 1926, THE MONTH IS MAY. Will Rogers and his fourteen-year-old son, Will, Jr., arrive in Southampton aboard the *Leviathan*. It is twenty-four years since Will first visited England, and much has changed.

Will has been the star in the *Ziegfeld Follies*, Broadway's most colorful and elaborate musical extravaganza. He has starred in thirteen major motion pictures and a dozen Hal Roach comedies; he has produced three films of his own, and he now writes a weekly column that is nationally syndicated and read by more Americans and Canadians than any other newspaper column. Will Rogers is famous now.

England, too, has changed, especially now, for she is in the midst of a general strike. While Will was escorting his son from Parliament to the Tower, and from London Bridge to Trafalgar Square, they had a firsthand view of how a British general strike compared to an American. "Colleges like Oxford and Cambridge turned out and they did police duty or ran engines on the railroads or drove buses. I think even the Lords took up some useful occupation. And here, to me, was the greatest thing of all: Not a striker ever did a thing to interfere with any of them, even if they were trying to do the strikers' old jobs."

Will found out that "the House of Commons and the Americans there were the only unruly ones." On the other hand:

The hard thing in this British strike from an American standpoint, is to look at an Englishman and judge from the way he is working, whether he is on strike, or not. There is not an American that wouldn't say England is on strike. But they wouldent be at all; it would only be teatime. That is why this strike looks so small. There is only five million out on this one, but at teatime there is 51,683,423 on strike. You see, that is why it is so hard to excite people that are used to that much leisure every day, anyway, whether there is a strike, or not.

But despite the strike, Will and his son had a very hectic stay. Will called on Lady Astor, one of the famous Langhorne sisters of Virginia; had dinner with Sir James Barrie, the spiritual father of Peter Pan and the Little Minister. Their introduction—though each knew who the other was—went supposedly like this:

"Barrie said: Are you a writer?"
"So I said: Yes, Sir, are you?"
"He said: No."
"I said: Well, I am, if you ain't, because we are certainly opposite."
"He said: What did you write?"
"I said: Tobacco ads."
"Well, come to find out that Mrs. Astor had of course tipped him off to me and the rascal was kidding me all this time. But anyway, we broke even, for neither one of us had read anything the other had written."

Will visited the Prince of Wales at York House and came away with the prophetic summation: "Just between you and me, Calvin, he don't care any more about being King, than you would going back to being Vice-President again."

After a short trip to the continent, where he had personal interviews with Benito Mussolini, the dictator of Italy, and Primo de Rivera, the dictator of Spain, Will returned to England to pick up a Russian visa, and flew to Moscow.

England is having their troubles. Their Labor government is having tough sledding, almost as bad as our efficiency government.

★

England has a Labor government, but nobody has ever accused ours of doing a tap of work. When a man goes in for politics over here, he has no time to labor, and any man that labors, has no time to fool with politics. Over there, politics is an obligation, over here it's a business.

★

I went to Hyde Park, London, where, if you have anything against the government or King, why you jump up on a box and get it out of your system. They sink the navy, impeach the Crown, and cancel the debt, and when they finish, they are just as happy as if it had been done. It's real democracy. Over home, you have to be elected to the senate before you can do it.

★

Now here is one thing about England's government where they are more democratic than ours. When a guy don't suit them, there is no waiting to oust him. The minute the majority are at outs with the reigning Premier, why, they can call for a new election and he is out, maybe before he even has time to learn where the icebox is at 10 Downing Street.

★

Just like to show you what our English cousins are doing in the way of toting the mail; headline reads: "The British Post Office showed a Profit at the End of the Fiscal Year of seventy million dollars! Last year 57 million post office profits was applied to reduction of taxes."

We lost 150 million a year, so who's looney now? And they also run the telephone and telegraph, so when you say that a government can't run a business, you mean OUR government can't run it!

★

England had an earthquake yesterday. There is a cricket match going on here that has been for three months—one game! The earthquake didn't even wake up the spectators.

★

That cricket game that I told you about, well, I have been thrown out of the grounds twice for applauding. They contend I was a boisterous element.

★

"Sir" is about the lowest form of title there is. It's the Ford of titles.

★

England has the best statesmen, and the rottenest coffee of any country in the world. I just hate to see morning come, because I have to get up and drink this coffee.

★

Poor coffee and no bathtubs have drove more Americans out of England than unfamiliarity with their language has.

★

England has been the daddy of the diplomat, the one with the smooth manners. Still going after what he wants, but always a gentleman. You know, that's one thing about an Englishman, he can insult you, but he can do it so slick and polite, that he will have you guessing until away after he leaves you just whether he was friend or foe.

19 RUSSIA

WILL MADE TWO TRIPS TO RUSSIA, the first in 1926, the second in 1934. In the mid-twenties much myth and misinformation was disseminated about Russia, primarily by self-styled experts. Will wanted to see for himself:

Now everybody had said to me in going in: don't take anything with you; they examine everything. They look at every card. Don't take a thing or don't write a thing while you are in there; everybody is a spy and everybody is listening to what you have to say.

Well, they throwed such a scare into me that I stripped myself down till I dident have a single piece of paper about me but my passport. I tore up two handfuls of cards that people had given me of people in Russia to look up for them. I dident know exactly how some of these folks might stand, and if they caught me with these names, I might be suspected of being a spy, or something. Outside of my passport, if I had been run over in Russia, nobody in the world could have told where I was from, or who I was.

I took only one suit and four extra shirts, as I was told if I took in too much, I would be suspected of capitalistic tendencies. I debated with myself a long time in the hotel in Berlin the night I left whether two extra pair of socks instead of one would constitute capitalistic affluence. I wouldent risk it. I even dident get a shave for a few days, figuring I might pass as a native.

Naturally Will decided to fly into Moscow; the picture of the yelping wolves was still quite vivid in his mind. From Koenigsberg, he was the only passenger aboard a Russian airline using a German-made plane. Will had second thoughts about his

131

trip. Here he was, alone with two Russians, the pilot and a mechanic, and there was no way to communicate. He spoke no Russian and they spoke no English. Why was he here?

Why was a bonehead like me breezing into Russia, or off into anywhere? What was the matter with the Verdigris bottoms down in old Rogers County, Oklahoma? Why, there I used to be scared to climb up as high as the barn loft, unless there was a load of hay being pitched in. I could understand a man flying out of Russia, but not in there.

We went into Moscow right on the dot, not a minute late. I went into a little customs office. They took my passport, but instead of like lots of countries, where they take it away and hold a clinic over it, why, this old boy give it a peek and shoved it back to me. I opened up the grip, he got one peek, dident even feel in there. Talk about not bringing in anything, why, I could have had a grand piano in there and he would never have seen it. And as for looking what you had in your pocket or had on your person, why I could have had two years' collection of the Congressional Record.

Now as a consequence of getting rid of all those cards and addresses, I dident have a soul in the world to go to. And as for the next popular illusion: "Oh, they will take care of you; they will just take you and show you just what they want you to see; you won't be allowed to see anything." Well, I tell you, I was so lonesome and it was humiliating on me. I wanted to hire my own detective and have him watch me, just to keep up the popular tradition.

Will's observations, though now over fifty years old, still show his incredible understanding and insight.

The second trip to Russia, in 1934, was with Betty and the two boys. On their trip to Asia, the four Rogers family members traveled from east to west along the Trans-Siberian Railroad to Moscow. While not taken in by propaganda, Will saw much that gave him cause to be concerned.

I am the only person that ever wrote on Russia that admits he don't know a thing about it. On the other hand, I know just as much about Russia as anybody that ever wrote about it.

If you want to start an insane asylum that would be 100 percent cuckoo, just admit applicants that thought they knew something about Russia.

Communism to me is one-third practice and two-thirds explanation.

One thing though, that a Communist can do, is explain. You can ask him any question in the world, and if you give him long enough, he will explain their angle, and it will sound plausible.

You know, these Russian rascals, along with all their cuckoo stuff, have got some mighty good ideas. If just part of 'em work, they are going to be mighty hard to get along with.

The Russians figured out everything in their communistic system, except how to get enough to eat.

You see, the Communism that they started out with in Russia, you know, the idea that the fellow that was managing the bank was to get no more than the man that swept it out, that talked well to a crowd, but they got no more of that than we have.

Everybody gets what he can get, and where he can get it; and it takes about two to watch one, and then four to watch those two.

What they need in their government is more of a sense of humor, and less of a sense of revenge.

Communism is like Prohibition; it's a good idea, but it won't work.

In 1926 I went into Russia, that was before they had their five-year plan. They was just messing along a good deal like we are now, without any plan.

I see where somebody has started a movement to "unrecognize" Russia. I imagine their recognizing us hasen't turned out so hot for them, either.

Russia's made great strides since I visited the place eight years ago, and most of it has been by eliminating Communism.

I'll be glad to answer any question about Russia. Anything I don't know about the country I can make up. For Russia is a country that no matter what you say about it, it's true. Even if it's a lie, it's true.

★

Communists have some good ideas, of course, but they got a lot more that sound better than they work.

★

If Socialists worked as much as they talked, they would have the most prosperous style of government in the world.

★

Have the people got anything to say about the government in Russia? I have an answer to that. Yes, they have—but they must say it to themselves, and under their breaths.

★

The question arises: How is Russia getting along? Well, to be downright honest with you, it's getting along better than we want it to. Think that over.

★

Siberia is still working, and it's just as cold on you to be sent there under the Soviets, as it was under the Czar.

★

The only way you can tell a member of the party from an ordinary Russian, is that the Soviet man will be in a car.

★

The one thing that impressed me most is that every person in Russia works—women digging subways, women carrying bricks, climbing up ladders with bricks. If women over here keep telling American women that they should have equality with men like they do in Russia, well the difference as I could see was that the women had a pick and shovel—and the men didn't.

★

Their big export is caviar; that's a kind of gooey mess of fish eggs that I suppose is without a doubt the poorest fodder in the world. I was surprised, I dident think a fish in Russia would lay anything but hard-boiled eggs.

★

The Russians are sure giving us a run around. In fact the Russian oil people have got our oil people right where the Russian wheat people have got our Farm Board. Why does it always look like nobody knows what the Russians are doing?

★

Funny thing about these Russians. They are sure tough to find out anything really directly from. I know now how they can go to all these conferences and bring home the bacon, while we are gabbing our heads off about "humanity" and "we want to disarm down to the last man," and all that hooey for home consumption. Why, they just sit there and take it all in, haven't said a word, but when it is added up, they go home with the goods.

★

It sure looks like Russia and China are arranging the details for a war. The thing that makes me believe that some day China and Russia will fight, is that nobody knows what they would be fighting about. Anyhow, according to the Communists all are equal—so I guess they will all be generals.

★

Russia spent so much money on propaganda in other countries. Tell me, what should they care about Communism in Chicago or London? Fix up Moscow and show the world what can be done under Communism, and they will get all the converts they need, and never spend a dime on propaganda.

★

I have been reading about this American Communist meeting. You just try to pay the fares of any of them, and offer to send 'em to Russia, and you would have to call out the Marines. The old Communist teaches his doctrines, but he wants to do it where he is enjoying the blessings of Capitalistic surroundings. He preaches against the pie, but he sure eats it.

★

There is as much class distinction in Russia today as there is in Charleston, South Carolina. Why, I went to the races there, and the grandstand had all the men of the party, and over in center field, stood the mob in the sun! Well, there was Bourgeoisie and Proletariat distinction for you.

★

I can't understand by what reckoning the Soviets think that everybody connected with running the government should be a nonbeliever. Just what quality does that add to government?

If the Bolsheviks say that religion was holding the people back from progress, why, let it hold 'em back. Progress ain't selling that high; if it is, it ain't worth it!

20 DISARMAMENT

WILL ROGERS WAS A MAN OF PEACE. Time and again he wrote of the terrible aftermath of any war. But he was also a realist. Having traveled more than most of his contemporaries, including America's elected officials, he looked at disarmament with little optimism. His writings clearly indicate that he suspected the motives of most participants to these disarmament conferences, including America's. He had seen preparations for war, on land and in the air, and he warned his readers. While politicians predicted "Prosperity Around the Corner," Will scoffed that "war is closer around the corner than prosperity." Yet all the time he hoped that mankind would prove him wrong. Will did not live to see the outbreak of World War II in 1939.

Despite his misgivings Will covered the various disarmament conferences, whether they took place in Washington, D.C., or elsewhere. Soon after the first of the year in 1930, a disarmament conference was to convene in London. Wrote Will:

When I was a little boy out in the old Indian Territory, I remember seeing a sheriff disarm some men one time, and it always fascinated me, but I had never seen it since. So when I got to New York last Friday, and they told me that they were going to disarm whole nations over in London next week, why, I grabbed the fastest thing there is, the *Bremen*.

But it had not been quite that simple.

Indeed, when Will learned that the conference was to open the following week and that the American delegation had already sailed, he thought he could not possibly attend. But he was told that the German ship *Bremen* was to leave at midnight and, being a far faster ship, would arrive in London ahead of the American delegation. Will did not have a passport, and he had not come to New York prepared for an overseas trip. He contacted his boss at Fox Films, Winfield Sheehan, who in turn pulled some strings in Washington, and Will was issued a temporary passport. Then Will scurried down Seventh Avenue where some stores stayed open late.

When the hour approached for the *Bremen* to depart, Will could be seen climbing up the gangplank, wearing an almost new blue-serge suit, while under his arm he carried several paper bags containing the rest of his luggage: changes of underwear, a half-dozen shirts, socks, handkerchiefs, and toilet articles, all bought at the last minute.

Reported Will from London:

The American delegation just arrived. They brought eighteen type-writers—not the machines, but the ones that run them. That's four and a half blondes to the delegate, and I can write in longhand everything that will be done here in the next month.

On February 9, 1930, Will Rogers summed up the conference:

Nobody is going to disarm in the least. You know these men that are gathered are not the idealists that think: 'Oh, we can't have war; it's too terrible, we must not have war!' That would be wonderful, but these men know history too well, they know each other too well, and they know that war is not only a possibility, but a probability.

There were other disarmament conferences, and agreements to sink parts of navies, and limits were set—yet within nine years the world was at war.

Other nations are anxious to confer when we are building ahead of them, but when they are ahead, why should they confer?

★

Wars don't diminish our preparedness. It's peace that's devastating, that's when we are attacked by disarmament conferences.

★

This disarmament thing is only a tax-saving conference and not a humanitarian one. They want to eliminate the battleships, and not a word is said about restricting the things that you are going to be killed with in the next war.

★

We are in the midst of a disarmament conference to disarm ourselves of the things we figure won't be used in the next war, which will leave more money to develop the things that will be used. You can't say civilization don't advance, however, for in every war they kill you in a new way.

★

Take these disarmament conferences now, why, it's like holding a traffic conference and just discuss the limiting of horses and buggies. I wonder if we ever get so civilized that one will be held to limit submarines, airplanes, and chemicals.

★

No nation can tell another nation what they need to defend themselves. That's a personal affair. If I sleep with a gun under my pillow, I don't want somebody from across the street to advise me that I don't need it.

★

These so-called treaties are really a funny thing. You ask: "Does it prevent war?"
　"No!"
　"Does it ensure peace?"
　"No!"
　"Is it for anything?"
　"No!"
　"Is it against anything?"
　"No!"
　I think the whole thing is just to find out if we can write.

★

Lots of people feel discouraged over the ending of this disarmament conference without doing anything. But I don't! I think it was the most successful conference we ever attended. It's the only one where we lost nothing, promised to give up nothing. It's the first one in our history where we come out as strong as we went in.

Sometimes you wonder whether the boys we elect to govern us are with us or against us. Take these disarmament conferences. It looks like the other side won't join us in disarmament, but that don't seem to worry us. If they don't want to disarm with us, we will shame 'em into it—if we have to sink our last life preserver to do it. We will show 'em we are right! We will do it alone!

The way to make 'em disarm is to start building and quit begging 'em to disarm.

I been reading a lot about this disarmament conference that's been going on for quite a while. So far it seems to be a Disagreement Conference.

The last conference was a success because we did all the sinking, and the next conference will be the same success, under the same conditions. It's a mistake to say that disarmament is not possible. It is possible as long as we provide all the sinking.

Well, I am glad we found that out as quick as we did.

This might be just the ideal time for disarmament; it's not done for humanitarian reasons; it's only done for economic reasons. The whole thing seems too good to be true, but the whole world is changing, so maybe they are going to turn human.

The disarmament conference has us blaming the other side for knowing enough to keep their country protected. That's like blaming a heavy-weight champion for knowing how to box. When we have had as many wars as they have, our statesmen may know as much as theirs, but I doubt it.

Our secretary of state spoke last night in Plattsburg on disarmament. It is a good idea for Plattsburg, and even Chicago and New York, but our delegation can starve to death trying to get the other side interested in equal disarmament.

Disarm? Let's get the best defensive force in the world. Second money in defense is sorter like running second at a presidential election. If America has the best defense in the world, then just sit back and take care of our own business, you can bet nobody is going to come over here and pounce on us.

The Chinese don't go to disarmament conferences. Course there's millions and millions of 'em, but what has humanity got to do with a conference? It is funny, what a respect and national honor a few guns will get you, ain't it? China and India with almost half the population of the entire world, have not only never been asked to confer, but they have not even been notified. Yet you give India England's navy, and China ours, and they would not only be invited to the conference, but they would be the conference.

★

Here's one thing you got to keep in mind on all this disarmament thing. It takes years to get even plans scrapped. What I am getting at, by the time all these marvelous plans are about to be in effect, none of these men might be in power, and who knows what the next man's ideas are?

But they are conscientious men, and let us hope that they are followed by men of the same type. You can't get nothing without trying, and if no effort is made toward peace, why, we can't expect any.

21 ASIA

UNLIKE MOST WRITERS OF HIS TIME, Will Rogers traveled extensively. His columns bear the datelines of many places around the world. It was partly restlessness that drove him to peek over the horizon, to be doing something every waking minute, and partly it was an unquenchable thirst for firsthand knowledge of the things he intended to write about.

Despite the fact that Will Rogers was a very poor sailor, and dreaded the thought of a long ocean voyage, he visited Asia twice. Late in 1931, when Far East politics seemed to reach the boiling point, Will was aboard the S.S. *Empress of Russia*, headed for Japan. He almost had second thoughts, but: "I have already learned to pronounce two towns and one general's name, so I am not going to turn back." Everything seemed to be going well until November 25. "When you reach the 180th meridian sailing west, you lose a whole day. Don't ask me why. If you come back this way, you get it back. If you don't, you just lose it. The way days are now, it don't look like it's worth coming back for. We go to bed tomorrow night, Thursday, and wake up Saturday—maybe." Two days later, November 27, Will wrote: "I told you we was going to lose a day for no other reason than to make somebody's calendar come out even. Well, we lost a day. We gained a typhoon. We lost a lifeboat and I lost my whole internal possessions. An Oklahoma prairie product has no business on the ocean when it's washing away lifeboats." By December 1, Will wrote: "This ocean is just as innocent looking today, just like it hadn't done a thing." The following day he was up and about, and suggested that "there ought to be a law against making an ocean this wide."

After touring Japan, Will flew to Korea. From there he flew to Dairen and on to Mukden in Manchuria. Most of the Sino-Japanese war news came from there. On to Harbin in North Manchuria, where Will took a boat to Peiping (now Peking). Here he was presented to China's emperor, who gave Will a mink-trimmed kimono to take back to Betty. On Christmas Day—one of the few Will ever spent apart from his family—he was in Shanghai. By plane he continued to Hong Kong, Singapore, Malaya, across India, Pakistan, and the Middle East, to Europe. His reports from that trip have remained uncanny analyses, showing Will Rogers' talent as a reporter and his understanding of Far East politics, accurate even today in the glaring light of perfect hindvision.

Will's second visit took place in 1934. This time Betty and the boys, Will, Jr., and Jimmy, joined him. Daughter Mary could not be persuaded to give up her summer stock theatre commitment. On July 22 they sailed aboard the S.S. *Malolo* for Hawaii. President Franklin D. Roosevelt was there on vacation, and Will spent many hours with him. It was Will's first trip to Hawaii, and after visiting the naval installations, he wrote: "You don't have to be warlike to get a real kick out of our greatest army post, Schofield Barracks, and the Navy at Pearl Harbor. . . . If war was declared with some Pacific nation (everybody knew it could only mean Japan) we would lose the Philippines before lunch, but if we lost these, it would be our own fault."

After an enjoyable stay, the family boarded the S.S. *Empress of Canada* to continue their trip to Japan, Korea, Siberia, and on the Trans-Siberian Railroad to Moscow. Leaving Hawaii, Will wired his daily column in which he quoted President Roosevelt's parting advice: "Will, don't jump on Japan. Just keep them from jumping on us."

The date was August 12, 1934. The attack on Pearl Harbor was still seven years away.

In China, you get into power through an army. You may ask: "How do you get votes with an army?" Votes? What votes? There is no voting in China; voting just ain't done in up-to-date Chinese circles. There has been nothing voted by the people of China since Genghis Khan called for a vote of confidence in twelve hundred something. He not only called for a vote, but brother, he got it!

The Chinese are the most fortunate nation in the world, for they know that nothing, absolutely nothing, that happens to 'em can possibly be any worse than something that's already happened to 'em.

In the old days in China, the rulers promised 'em nothing, and made good. But nowadays, they get promises. So you see yourself just how much better off they are. No comparison to the old days.

Sounds like our 100 percent American campaign pledges, don't it? Their promises are fulfilled, too, just like ours.

When American diplomacy gets through messing around in China, I can tell them what caused this original dislike of us over there. It was our missionaries who had been trying to introduce Chop Suey into China. Now China didn't mind them eating it, but when they tried to call it a Chinese dish, that's what made 'em sore at us.

You know the Chinese are the most patient race of people in the world; they have waited four thousand years for something good to happen to 'em, and as it hasent, they are all set for another four thousand.

They had emperors in China. Of course it's been hundreds of years since their emperor had done any real empering. But emperors could behead people. Now a president can't do that, as much as he would like to; but say, if our president could do a little beheading . . . eh, what?

Always dodge the expert, you know, the one who lived in China, and knows China. The last man that knew China was Confucius, and he died feeling that he was becoming a little confused about 'em.

China, even if they never shot a gun for the rest of their lives, is the most powerful country in the world. You could move the whole of Japan's seventy million into the very heart of China, and in seventy years there wouldent be seventy Japanese left.

Ain't it funny, the Chinese don't get wise to themselves and really learn how to live right? But they just don't think that a car and a radio is essential to their happiness. So it will just about be their luck to go on living like that another five thousand years, while we have everything down so perfect that we can live a whole lifetime in a couple of years.

★

I came to Peking here and I been looking at walls and old palaces till I am groggy. The Forbidden City—that's the way to attract attention to anything: call it "Forbidden," and you couldn't keep an American out of there with a meat ax.

Well, this wasn't "forbidden" any more than Palm Beach, but by calling it "forbidden" they grabbed off the yokels, me included.

★

You know, those chopsticks are really not so difficult; with just a little practice, you can get so you can do quite a bit of gastronomical damage with 'em. They are great if you are on a diet, or have a tendency to eat too fast.

I got so that finally, I could catch flies with mine.

★

The Chinese are the only ones that have mastered mass production and mass distribution, too. They have arranged wars, famines, droughts, floods, and disease, so that it takes care of the surplus. Hundreds of millions have lived on the same farms for four thousand years. They can't overproduce anything—if they do, they eat it. If they don't produce it, they don't eat it; so you can't beat that for balance of production versus consumption.

★

We always think of the Japanese as the egotists, but the Chinese got him licked on it. The Chinese has books to show that he has been educated for thousands of years. I don't mean he is distant, like a strange Englishman. No, the Chinese are the most friendly folks and you can't help but like 'em. But back in that nut of theirs,.they feel that all this modern junk you are lording over them will pass in time, and they will be in command.

And the rascals might be right, at that.

★

As far as our trade is concerned, you can't force 'em to buy your goods. Japan has found out that any door is open to those that have the best product at the cheapest money. A manufacturer can sit in his office and if his car is cheaper and better than any other car, dealers will come clear there to buy 'em.

★

The Japanese are mighty polite and nice, and they want you to see and like their country. They got everything we got, and if they haven't, you show it to 'em and they will make it.

★

The Japanese are manufacturing so many different things and doing pretty good and away underselling anyone else. Well, that's going into economics and when you go into them, you have entered the forest without an ax, or light, or compass. The only thing you can go by, is results, and the Japanese are getting 'em.

★

Plenty of excitement in these countries. Japan's cabinet resigned.

It's funny, we can't ever have any luck like that.

★

In parts of India, they have a law that if a man is married and is unfaithful to his wife, her family can take him out and publicly shoot him. There is no trial or anything. It is just their religious and state custom. Well, anyway, if that was the custom over in America, I would take every cent I make and put it into an ammunition factory.

22 NEW YORK CITY

FOR A YOUNG MAN who had grown up on the limitless prairie of the Indian Territory and to whom the horizon was a challenge, not a border, the confining canyons of New York City seemed somewhat less than awe inspiring. The year was 1902, and by this time Will Rogers had visited other large cities such as St. Louis, San Francisco, Buffalo, and Kansas City. When he first visited St. Louis he was indeed impressed: "Every guy thinks that the first time he sees anything, that is the first time it ever existed. I will never forget the first time I went to St. Louis. I thought for sure I was the first one to find it."

Will came again to New York City in 1905. This time he was a member of *Colonel Zach Mulhall's Wild West Show*, which came to Madison Square Garden as part of the annual Horse Fair. It was really what today would be called a rodeo, featuring trick riding, roping, and bulldogging. One evening, a Texas Longhorn steer became terrified by the noise and the lights and tried to escape the arena. The animal jumped a barrier and raced up a stairway leading past ringside boxes to the mezzanine. Spectators and musicians scattered in terror. Will, who had not been part of this act, pursued the frightened animal into the stands. This is what the *New York Herald* of April 28, 1905, reported: "Will Rogers, a Cherokee Indian, and three other cowboys had joined in the chase, and Rogers got a rope over the steer's horns as it turned to run down into the arena. Rogers clung to the rope, but was dragged over seats and down the stairs." A man on foot can hardly impede a runaway steer. As it was, Will at least slowed the animal down, while Tom Mix, another member of the group and not yet world famous, missed the steer, but caught an usher instead.

When Colonel Mulhall was ready to return to the Indian Territory, Will decided to stay behind and break into vaudeville. Will never again moved back to the land of his youth. He visited there as often as his busy schedule permitted, but he never lived there again. New York had become his new temporary home.

For years Will lived in and around New York City. During the vaudeville days he and Betty would live in some of the theatrical hotels around Times Square. While most of the records are lost, some stationery Betty used to write home still shows the old names. There is the King Edward Hotel at 145 West Forty-seventh Street (330 rooms, 250 baths, singles $1.50, singles with bath $2.00, suites $4.00). The hotel was torn down some time ago, and on its site now stands a modern parking garage.

Will and Betty lived on West 113th Street, just off the Columbia University campus. This is where Will Rogers, Jr., was born. The family also lived in Forest Hills, and in Amityville, Long Island. This was where James B. Rogers, Will's second son, was born.

After traveling the vaudeville circuits, Will and Betty would always return to New York City. And it was here, in New York City, where Will's career took two sharp turns.

The first was an engagement on the New Amsterdam Theatre roof, Ziegfeld's famous *Midnight Frolic*. Here Will began to rely more on his topical humor, playing down the roping act. And these verbal comments on current events spawned a lecture career, radio talks, and indeed, the weekly and daily columns.

The other new venture begun here was the first motion picture Will made for Sam Goldwyn. It opened up an entirely new direction, a motion-picture career, in which Will Rogers became the top box-office attraction.

It must be admitted that the motion picture *Laughing Bill Hyde* was actually filmed in New Jersey, but it was in Fort Lee, which is on the western edge of the Hudson River, and in full view of Manhattan. So it can justifiably be claimed as part of the "greater New York City area."

Never a day passes in New York without some innocent bystander being shot. You just stand around this town long enough, and be innocent, and somebody is going to shoot you.

★

One day there was four innocent people shot. That's the best shooting ever done in this town. Hard to find four innocent people in New York.

★

I see where New York is going to make their nightclubs close at 3 in the morning, and the people are kicking about it. Well, I say they ought to close 'em. Anybody that can't get drunk by 3 A.M. ain't trying.

★

I see where a New York City alderman was robbed. I thought it was an unwritten law that crooks did not bother each other.

★

New York's mayor called a committee of one hundred to stop small graft. He said that it was growing to such proportions that it was interfering with large graft, and that couldn't be allowed in New York.

★

The mayor of New York called in a hundred prominent citizens to discuss graft with him. A man naturally wouldn't call in 100 poor men to discuss graft, as they would have no technical knowledge of the subject.

Anyhow, these 100 met and adjourned, without adopting any resolution to either halt or increase it. It seemed everyone was satisfied as it is.

★

We're having a primary in New York City, to see who will be the Democratic candidate for mayor. I don't see why they don't have the governor for mayor? He could hold both jobs. He could run this town in the evenings. And come to think of it, that is when New York City needs running. Everybody is asleep here all day.

★

The past week was kinder eventful here in the old townsite of New York. They had a primary election, and the mayor was defeated. He says he will retire to private life, and that he retires a poor man, which, I guess, constitutes a record for a New York Tammany mayor after 8 years of opportunity.

★

You know, the more they knock New York, the bigger it gets. They don't have any tax money, so the city is just like a modern human being—it has to exist on borrowed money.

★

Say, did you read about the Ku Klux Klan coming to New York? Well, you ain't going to get me to say anything about it. I don't want any white-robed gentlemen leading me forth in the middle of the night, and massaging me with any tar, and sprinkling feathers on me for a chaser. I ain't got much education, but I do have a powerful lot of common sense.

★

New York is just like us individuals, they are finding it tough to dig up the money it spent last year, that it didn't have.

★

New York is getting like Paris. Its supposed devilment is its biggest ad. The rest of the country drop in here and think that if they don't stay up till four A.M. that New Yorkers will think they are yokels, when, as a matter of fact, New Yorkers have been in bed so long, they don't know what the other half is doing. New York lives off the out-of-towner trying to make New York think he is quite a fellow.

★

We had quite a panic here the other day in New York, in the subway. Several people were trampled on and crushed. The cause of the trouble was that someone hollered out: "Here is a vacant seat!"

★

New York is in the midst of what they call a jubilee. It's celebrating something and nobody can find out just what. Personally I think it was to celebrate the starting of the hat-check privilege.

★

New York is so situated that anything you want, you can get in the very block you live in. If you want to be robbed, there is one living in your block; if you want to be murdered, you don't have to leave your apartment house; if you want pastrami or gefillter fish, there is a delicatessen every other door; if it's female excitement you crave, your neighbor's wife will accommodate you.

★

New York, that city from which no weary traveler returns without drawing again on the hometown bank.

★

New York, that city of skyscrapers, where they have endeavored to make the height of their buildings keep pace with their prices. That city of booze, boobs, and bankrolls, where the Babbitts from Butte and Buffalo can pay the speculators $8.80 for a $2.20 show, view the electric signs until 12 o'clock, and then write home of his Bacchanalian revels.

23 LABOR

LOOKING BACK ON THE ROARING TWENTIES and the Terrible Thirties, the general impression is that everything was perfect in the twenties and that precisely on Black Tuesday, October 29, 1929, the stock market plummeted, beginning the worst depression in America's history. Unfortunately, that was not exactly how things were.

While the twenties are depicted as a decade of almost uncontrolled revelry—with dancing and drinking, despite Prohibition; with money being made on almost any kind of speculation; with morals loose—there was much hardship, too. Unemployment figures were staggering, both early and again late in the twenties, long before the stock-market crash. Governmental statistics, as they always do, indicated that one million unemployed was about the norm to be expected with a labor force of 47 million. In 1928 the number of unemployed (1,982,000) was almost twice that figure. By 1933 the number of unemployed had risen to 12.8 million.

As far as Will Rogers was concerned there were two major problems facing the working man. One was the scarcity of jobs, the other was the seeming drive to call a strike whenever contract negotiations did not immediately produce the desired benefits.

Will stated time and again that he felt the most important duty the government had to perform was to provide a job for anyone who was willing to work. As early as 1928 he advocated public-works programs, rather than having some agency simply hand out welfare payments, without the recipient performing some labor. He felt that the self-respect of any individual demanded the

150

contribution of something in return for the assistance furnished. Even if such labor was only three hours a day, he thought that America would gladly offer a living wage if those three hours produced something of tangible benefit to all. Of course, the numerous "alphabet" agencies were still five years off.

As for the seemingly endless number of strikes, Will suggested arbitration. It was Will Rogers's concept that all workers had a perfect right to organize, to form unions for their collective betterment. But it was his conviction that strikes were the very last recourse, not one of the first. Especially during the depression, when millions were out of work, when men fought each other for the opportunity to just stand in line for a job opening, Will suggested that all disputes should be submitted to binding arbitration. Will was of the opinion that strikes are too costly, not only to employers and employees but to their families, to the ultimate consumers, and to the country. Besides, when it's finally settled, little is really won and labor and management have "lost face." Said he: "I see where another strike is ended. Nobody won anything, but they always word the agreement in such a way that it looks like both sides gained something. China has a word, it's called 'face,' you know, saving face: How-can-I-do-nothing-and-still-make-it-look-like-I-did-something!"

Samuel Gompers spent his life trying to keep Labor from working too hard and he has succeeded beyond his own dream.

★

Labor leaders don't do any laboring after they are able to lead.

★

Unions are a fine thing, for they are in every line of business. Bankers have their association for mutual benefit, governors have theirs, all big industries are banded together in some way. But a strike should be the very last means, for it is like war, it always falls on those who had nothing to do with calling it.

★

It's a tough time for any group to start making demands. The farmer deserves a profit, but the guy that's not eating deserves a meal more. The stockholder deserves his dividend, but the unemployed deserves his job more.

★

Don't it look like in a case of a labor dispute, it would be best for a man to keep on working, but the workers send two men, the owners send two men, and the government two men, and they confer? Even if they were months settling this, and Labor won, their benefits would go back to the time when the first protest was made.

That way nobody would be hurt much, and the Labor leaders and management could cuss each other in a room, the same as they do now in the newspapers, yet nobody would have to be idle, listening to 'em.

★

Machines are a great thing, but if one replaces a hundred men, it don't buy anything, it don't eat anything, while a hundred men would spend their pay back for food, shelter, and hundreds of various commodities for themselves and their families. So you can have all the theories and plans you want, but folks got to have work.

★

I asked Mussolini about his no-strike plan. He told me that he had formed Labor, Capital and government into a trust, and everything has to be submitted to this body. He said: "A strike is just like two men shooting at each other out there on a public square that is crowded with people. Everybody gets hit more than the two men shooting at each other."

★

Don't it look like there ought to be some civilized way of finding out what the employee and employer owed to each other?

★

There is only one form of employment in our country that I can think of, that has no bright spots, and that is coal mining. There is generally an overproduction and they are out of work; if not that, it's a strike. Then when they do go to work, the mine blows up. Then, if none of these three things happen, why, they still have the worst job in the world.

★

By the way, who owns the coal mines, anyway? There is always trouble in the coal mines, and nobody knows who the owners are. Nobody should be allowed to employ Labor that can't deal with them personally. The miners can't be wrong all the time.

★

If I was a coal-mine owner, and couldn't understand my help any better than they do, I would resign and announce to the world that as an Industrial leader I was a bust, and that I would devote my life to seeing that the world burned cow chips.

★

I see where the coal strike was settled in the usual way—with the public paying more for coal.

★

Did you see what the senate voted for yesterday? A week's work is to consist of thirty-six hours!

I doubt very much if the people working now will agree to an increase in time of work, like that. We stick to the old American principle of only working when the boss is looking.

24 CONFERENCES

THE POST-WORLD WAR I ERA was glutted with conferences. There were peace conferences, economic conferences, prearms limitation conferences, arms limitation conferences, Pan-American conferences, naval disarmament conferences, etc. And quite naturally, each of these conferences had a superabundance of committees. Will Rogers just could not let it pass unreported:

At the Pan-American Conference they have done nothing but form committees, and then those committees would form subcommittees, and the subcommittees would form advisory committees, and they have just committeed their self to death.

In years to come, the question will be asked by some fond child of its father, who was a delegate to this conference: "What did you do father at the big conference?"

"Why, I was the fellow who thought of all the different names for all the different committees. If it hadent been for me, they wouldent have known what to call their committees, and if they hadent had names for the committees, the conference would have been a failure—for forming committees was the sole accomplishment of the conference."

At this same Pan-American Conference (1928), Will also suggested some other improvement which international conferences could well adopt, though it is most doubtful that they ever will:

We stood while twenty-one nations played their national anthems. The conference is already a standing and musical success.

I have one suggestion to offer for international goodwill, that is, have an international national anthem that goes for everybody when it is played. It's for all. Make it short and it will please every nation. Some of these anthems today were longer than their countries records. I propose Irving Berlin as its composer.

When you have stood in the tropical sun for twenty-one national airs, you are about ready to vote for your nation to annex the other twenty.

Yours, groggy from martial music,

Will Rogers.

Congress ought to pass a law to prohibit us conferring with anybody on anything—till we learn how.

I have often said that it is cheaper for America to go to war than it is for us to confer with anybody. It's funny, we can talk our heads off until it comes to a time when it means something, and then we are as dumb as an oyster.

I am going to attend the peace conference. I noticed all the wars of the last few years had more fighting at the conferences than they have at the original, so I don't try and make the original any more.

It's kinder like Hollywood weddings. I get a bundle of invitations every day to attend the wedding, but I would rather wait a few weeks and take in the divorce.

We have a delegation at Geneva on narcotics. We want to limit the output. We don't manufacture it and the other nations do, so you already know where that conference will end.

We get nothing at a conference, only the trip.

A conference is just a place where countries meet and find out each other's shortcomings, and form new dislikes for the next conference.

That's where these other nations got us. They can play a half-dozen conferences at once, while with us, if we can find a man to send to one, why, we are lucky, and we always feel uneasy till he gets home.

I'll bet there was never a war between two nations that had never conferred first.

A conference is held for one reason only, to give everybody a chance to get sore at everybody else.

Mr. President, will you please do me and America a favor? If you see some guy that looks like he is going to attend a conference, just casually dent his bean! If you see a committee starting off for anywhere, deport them to Atlanta, and let them join something there. If we have any Foreign Relations Committee, discharge them, and take the money we save by it and spend it on Better Babies Week.

★

We get all excited over each of these conferences, and we think it is the last word, and that it will settle everything. Then two weeks after it's over, we can't for the life of us remember what happened. We are all plodding along, just as though we were in our right mind.

★

Do you remember some of the statements before the London conference started? The world was to stop revolving, the air was to lose its oxygen if the conference failed. Well, the thing has flopped and we are getting along better than ever. It just shows that nothing is important a month later. All these statesmen really thought they were going to make history. Well, history makes itself, and the statesmen just drag along.

25 WOMEN

MAN IS THE PRODUCT of his innate drive and his environment. Will grew up in a time when women were considered frail creatures, to be cherished, protected, and generally put on a pedestal. Not too many women raised in the comfortable East would willingly venture into the still-rough West. In the West women lived a paradoxical existence. Though they were appreciated, it did not keep them from having to work at least as hard as their men. The hours were long, conditions hard, comforts few. In case of illness, or childbearing, the nearest neighbors or medical help were usually hours away. Women learned to be co-worker, wife, mother, nurse, and quite often even surgeon. It was the West—Wyoming—which first gave women the right to vote (1869), recognizing full well that there was indeed an equal partnership.

The women in Will Rogers's life were few. His mother, whom he adored, died when he was ten years old. Even though his father remarried, Will was sent to stay with his married sister Sallie, sixteen years his senior. Though Will was the youngest of eight children, only three sisters lived to adulthood. When his sister May died in 1909, Will made a point of coming back to Chelsea, Oklahoma, as often as he could. He would divide his time equally between the two remaining sisters, staying half the time with Sallie, and half the time with Maud, across town.

His love and respect for both was profound. When Maud died in 1925, he grieved for her and wrote a touching tribute.

Will married in 1908 and years later bragged that one of his accomplishments was the fact that he still had the same wife he

157

started out with. In show business, and especially in Hollywood, that was rare indeed. The "wicked stage" teemed with temptation. Appearing in the *Ziegfeld Follies*, surrounded by hand-picked beauties, Will never succumbed. In fact, there is no indication that he ever even tapped one of the lovelies on the shoulder. He was a private man and he loved his wife.

Years later, in Hollywood, while filming *They Had To See Paris*, a scene called for Will to kiss his screen wife, the famous actress Irene Rich. But Will tried to postpone the scene as long as he could. Finally the director, Frank Borzage, took Miss Rich aside and told her that she would have to take the initiative, and kiss Will. As the cameras rolled and Will unsuspectingly went through his lines, Irene Rich suddenly grabbed him and kissed him squarely on the mouth.

Will was so stunned, he just stood there, muttering in embarrassment: "I feel like I been unfaithful to my wife!"

Will's regard for women was not based on the fact that they were women, but on what they did and what they knew. Among the people in Washington he respected most was Alice Roosevelt Longworth, daughter of Teddy Roosevelt, and wife of Nicholas Longworth, Republican Speaker of the House of Representatives. Will felt, and always said, that Mrs. Longworth was the most politically astute person in Washington, and that he would rather talk to her for ten minutes than to anyone else for an hour.

Grace Coolidge was another woman Will greatly admired. He had been to the White House several times, had met Calvin Coolidge and his wife on a number of occasions; and while he liked the President, still he thought more highly of Mrs. Coolidge. Said Will: "Mrs. Coolidge had more magnetism than any woman I've ever known. She could run things—Calvin couldn't, but she could."

What's this generation coming to? I bet the time ain't far off when a woman won't know any more than a man!

★

Money and women are the most sought after and the least known about of any two things we have.

If you let women have their way, you will generally get even with them in the end.

If women must insist on having men's privileges, they have to take men's chances.

The League of Women Voters are here in convention, demanding these planks in the next platform: Democratic women want birth control for Republicans, and Republican women want equal corruption for both sexes.

There are two types of men in the world that I feel sincerely sorry for. One is the fellow that is always saying: "I know the Mississippi River"; and the other one is the fellow that thinks he knows women.

Another American woman just swam the English Channel. Her husband was carried from the boat, suffering from cold and exposure.

Yours, for a revised edition of the dictionary explaining which is the weaker sex.

You know, women always could endure more than men. Not only physically, but mentally—did you ever get a peek at some of the husbands? But they can stand more pain, in fact, there is just lots of things where they are superior to the so-called male.

You can't pass a park without seeing a statue of some old codger on a horse. It must be his bravery, you can tell it's not his horsemanship. Anyhow, women are twice as brave as men, yet they never seem to have reached the statue stage, but one is due.

Although the gamest women can keep back tears in sorrow, they can't keep them back in happiness.

The Nineteenth Amendment, I think that's the one that made women humans, by Act of Congress.

Everybody is always asking: "Has women voting made any real change in our political system?" It has! It has doubled the number of candidates.

Women havent been able to harrow much of a role as far as cleaning up our national pastime is concerned. I think they take it too serious. I believe they would get further if they kinder ridiculed the men.

They can do that in everything else, so why can't they do it in politics?

I wouldn't be a bit surprised that it won't be no time till a woman will wind up in the senate. 'Course, up to now there has been no need for anything resembling a woman in the senate, especially an old woman, for there is more old women in there already than there is in an old ladies' home. But they been in there on a pension and they are awful nice old fellows and they don't do any particular harm.

'Course, they don't do any great good, either.

Women promised us that if they had the vote, they would clean up politics. About all they have added to the whole voting and political thing is just more votes and more bookkeeping. But it ain't the women's fault. Politics is bigger than any race and it's bigger than any sex.

Women are not the weak, frail, little flowers that they are advertised. There has never been anything invented yet, including war, that a man would enter into, that a woman wouldent, too.

You know what has hit us? The return of the longer dresses. You see, according to law, fashions must change every year, and in order to change dress styles, you have to either go up or down—crossways don't count. Well, skirts had just gone so high, there wasent anything to 'em.

Now watch marriages pick up, concealment will beat exposure anytime.

The whole country had gone "legs!" Every imaginable shape, size, and contour was on free exhibition. You see, short dresses was made for certain figures, but fashion decrees that everybody be fashionable, so that meant there was folks trying to keep up with fashions that while they might be financially able, were physically unfit.

So now, with longer skirts that will all be remedied. Every girl gets an even break—till she hits the beach.

Imagine the idea that "a woman couldn't live happily at home and have an active mind!" The only nuts I have ever met among the female gender has been these female bugs that think the world owes them a career, and the brightest and most active brains have belonged to our everyday women, who you never hear saying very much; but if you talked with them, you would soon see they had pretty sound ideas on about everything.

Women voters, do you think they are a-buying "Glorious Tradition" at the polls? No, sir. They want to know what kind of break they are going to get in Commerce and Industry. If they are going to make the living for the family, they want to know what kind of inducement the government is going to make to them for doing it. They are no smarter than their mothers were, but they think they are. So what we got to do, is to make 'em think we think they are.

26 TAXES

WILL WAS IN FAVOR OF TAXATION. There were, however, certain inequities he objected to. "You can't legitimately kick on income taxes, for it's on what you have made. But look at land, farms, homes, stores, vacant lots. You pay year after year on them, whether you make any money or not. Every land or property owner in America would be tickled to death to pay 45 percent of his profits, if he didn't have to pay anything if he didn't make it."

Another unfairness to the average wage earner, Will felt, was the tax-exempt bond—only rich men could afford them, while poor ones couldn't and had to pay full taxes.

In 1924 Will also espoused a plan which is now again being considered, a national sales tax: "Why don't they put a big sales tax on everything of a luxury nature? Every time you see a big 10- or 12-thousand-dollar limousine going down the street, you would know the fellow in there had already paid the government a big percentage of tax on it to help run the country. Let the working man know the rich have paid before they get their luxuries. No slick lawyer or income tax expert can get you out of a sales tax. It's so much a dollar on every luxury you buy."

Another tax project Will poked fun at was inheritance tax: "The secretary of the Treasury come out with a plan for a tremendous big inheritance tax. That is, men who died and on an estate of say, ten million dollars, the government would take about 90 percent, and then give the offspring ten. Then on an estate of 100 million, the government just takes all of that, and notifies the heir: 'Your father died a pauper here today.'"

In the twenties the government published a list of the largest income tax payments. Chided Will: "Don't feel discouraged if a lot of well-known men were not as wealthy as you thought. They are just as rich as you thought. This was only a test of their honesty, and gives you practically no idea of their wealth at all."

Income tax has made more liars out of the American people, than golf has.

★

The crime of taxation is not in the taking of it, it's in the way it's spent.

★

I see a good deal of talk from Washington about lowering taxes. I hope they do get 'em lowered down enough so people can afford to pay 'em.

★

They will have to lower income taxes, but of course, people are getting smarter nowadays; they are letting lawyers, instead of their consciences be their guides.

★

If you make any money, the government shoves you in the creek once a year with it in your pockets, and all that don't get wet, you can keep.

★

There is a tremendous movement on to get lower taxes on earned incomes. Then will come the real problem: Who among us on salary are really earning our income?

★

You should get a new kind of tax every year or two, so they don't know how to beat it. When this one first come out, the first year, every man was down for two or three times the amount that he pays today. We had no tax experts, and no lawyers that made a specialty of showing you what you could take off. You simply had a wife and so many children, that was about all as far as you knew what to charge off.

★

Every time congress starts to tax some particular industry, it rushes down with its main men, and they scare congress out of it. As it is now, we are taxing everybody without a lobby.

★

A fellow can always get over losing money in a game of chance, but he seems so constituted that he can never get over money thrown away to a government in taxes.

★

Alexander Hamilton was the man that originated the "Put and Take" system into our national Treasury. Us taxpayers put it in, and the politicians take it out.

★

In the early days, they used to pay their whole year's taxes with a few sacks of tobacco they raised on their farm. Now, the same farm, you put another mortgage on every time a tax comes due.

But, mind you, in those days there was only 26 senators and about 50 congressmen to support. It's a good thing we haven't got any more states to add on, for we would go broke.

★

This is income-tax-paying day. No two can agree what is deductible. When your form's made out, you don't know whether you are a crook, or a martyr.

★

Taxes is all there is to politics. You take taxes out of politics, and you don't have any politics, or taxes, either. You see, you have officeholders to pass bills about taxes, and what is the money from those taxes for? Why, it's to pay those same officeholders that passed those tax bills in the first place!

★

If I was running for president, I certainly wouldn't pull that old tax-saving gag. I would just announce: "Folks, I don't believe I will be able to save you anything. The only thing I would advise you to do, is not to have anything they can tax away from you!"

★

The lower-tax issue has been dragged out and dusted off. When a party can't think of anything else, they always fall back on lower taxes. It has a magic sound to a voter, just like fairyland is spoken of and dreamed of by all children. But no child has ever seen it, neither has any voter lived to see the day when his taxes were really lowered.

★

They are talking about some kind of big overhaul on this tax thing. Different conditions make different taxes. There should be a distinction between earned and unearned income. For instance, a man that earns every dollar by his work or efforts, then another earns the same by having enough money invested to bring him in that much. One has his principal to fall back on, and the other has nothing to fall back on when his earning capacity has diminished.

★

It ain't taxes that's hurting the country, it's interest.

★

Baseball is a skilled game. It's America's game—it, and high taxes.

27 WALL STREET

THE FOLLOWING IS PART OF WILL'S ACCOUNT of his one and only venture into the stock market. It was written before the famous "crash" of October 29, 1929, even though it did not appear in print until November 10:

Now that stock market is a puzzle to me. I never did mess with it, except one time in New York last year, when everybody was just raking in money with a shovel—or so they all told me. I was hearing that Eddie Cantor, the actor, was piling up a fortune that Rockefeller couldent vault over. Now I had known and been a friend of Eddie's for many years, so I hold out some dough on Mrs. Rogers—out of my weekly stipend, and go over to the New Amsterdam Theatre one night and call on Eddie.

When I was admitted, I felt like a racketeer that had finally gained admission to J. P. Morgan's sanctum. Eddie thought I had come to persuade him to play a benefit for some improvident fellow actor (as I had often done with him in the past). But then I quietly whispered to him that I wanted him to make me a few dollars without me telling jokes for them, or what went for jokes. I told him about the amount that I had been able by judicious scheming to nick from Mrs. Rogers. I told him that I wanted to get in on this skinning of Wall Street. Everybody was doing it and I wanted to be at the killing. I dident have anything particular against Wall Street, but knowing the geographical and physical attributes of the street, I knew that it was crooked. You can stand at the head of it and you can only see to the bend. It just won't let you see all of it at once, as short as it is.

Well, Eddie had just that day made fifty thousand, according to closing odds. I says, show me the fifty. He then explained to me that he hadent

165

the money, that that's what he could have made, if he had sold. But he hadent sold, as tomorrow he should make at least another fifty, or even if he only made 49, why, it would help pay for burnt cork, which he uses for his makeup.

Eddie dident much want to take my money, knowing how hard I had worked for it, both from the theatre manager, and Mrs. Rogers. But I went on telling him I was 49 years old, and had never in my life made a single dollar without having to chew gum to get it. So he says, "Well, I will buy you some of my bank stock. It's selling mighty high and with this little dab you got here, you won't get much of it, but it's bound to go up, for banks make money whether the market goes up or down. Even if it stands still, they are getting their interest while it's making up its mind what to do. I will get you some of this stock. You don't need to pay me for it, just let it go. Put it away and forget it. Then some day, when you want, you can send me a check for it."

Well, just think of that. Here I was going to break Wall Street on credit! Well, I shook hands, and went back to my own dressing room at my theatre, and I never was as funny in my life as I was that night. I had Wall Street by the tail, and a downhill run.

I stayed up the next night till the papers came out, to see what OUR bank had closed at, and after reading it, I stayed up the rest of the night, wondering if Eddie could possibly be wrong. Well one little drop brought on another, till one day I received a letter from Eddie's broker, saying that my check would come in mighty handy, and for me to please remit undernamed amount.

Well, in the mean time I had used up most of the money celebrating the fact that I had bought the stock. Each night I began to get unfunnier and unfunnier. The strain of "being in the market" was telling on me. Eddie could laugh at a loss, and still remain comical. But when there was minus signs before my lone stock, I just was not unctuous. I dident want to tell Eddie, but finally I sent for his personal Aide-de-Camp, and told him that on the morrow, when the market opened, among those desiring to dispose, I would be among those present. I got out with a very modest loss.

The next day that stock went up big. But the whole thing is no place for a weak-hearted comedian, and from now when Eddie wants to help me, he can just give me some of his old jokes.

It might be interesting to note here that on the day the news of Will Rogers's death became known, Fox Film Corporation—whose biggest star Will was—dropped ⅞ of a point.

I tell you this country is bigger than Wall Street, and if you don't believe it, I'll show you the map.

★

There's a proverb on Wall Street: What goes up—must have been sent up by somebody.

★

Don't gamble; take all your savings and buy some good stock, and hold it till it goes up, then sell it.

If it don't go up, don't buy it.

★

The senate's been investigating Wall Street for ten days, and all they found is that the street is located in the sharp end of New York City; that not only the traders, but the street itself, is short, and that neither end don't lead anywhere.

★

The senate passed a bill to regulate Wall Street. The government is going to put traffic lights on it; it's always been a hit-and-run street.

★

All the big financiers and stock-market writers are saying: good values are worth as much as they ever were! But that's the trouble, nobody knows what they ever were worth.

★

The New York Stock Exchange is having their own investigation. They are investigating 14 different stocks that have been acting so funny, that Wall Street itself didn't know what they were doing. In other words, you can fool the public, but you mustn't fool the members of the lodge.

★

Here yesterday was a good illustration how these market boosters can pull a bad one. Yesterday, farm machinery went up on the stock market. Now there is not a farmer in the United States that can pay his taxes, or his groceries. How is he going to buy any farm machinery? If he wanted to, he couldn't. So that raise don't look so hot—that's like Christmas trees going up at New Year's.

★

They ought to do with Wall Street like they do with farmers—say: "How much gambling did you do last year?"

"Your Honor, I bet a hundred thousand dollars!"

"Well, this year we want you to cut down to 75 thousand, and we will pay you thirty thousand for not betting the other twenty-five."

We ought to legalize horse racing in every state. Sure people will bet, but at least they get to see the horses run and you certainly can't see General Motors and General Electric and General Utility run when you bet on them.

Stocks, why anything that looked like a stock, would sell. People would wire in: "Buy me some stocks!" The broker would answer: "What kind?" The buyers would wire back: "Any kind, the Republicans are in, ain't they all supposed to go up?"

Imagine people whose whole idea of our country is gained from what it does every day in a stock market!

Headline on the financial page says: "This week's clearing rise to five billion." We had been led to believe there was no such thing as billions, only in a government deficit.

Read this: three hundred thousand dollars for a seat on the Stock Exchange! You pay that for a seat where nobody sits down. They stand and yell and sell something they haven't got, and buy something they will never get.

That's not a seat; that's a license to hold a sucker up when he buys, and blackjack him when he sells; to commit petty larceny when he buys, and grand larceny when he sells.

They are talking about putting another tax on the New York Stock Exchange. So they say they are going to New Jersey. Well, there is no industry that could move easier. All they have to do is change their telephone number, pick up the blackboard, and tell the loafers where to meet tomorrow.

This stock-market thing was a great game, but, after all, everybody just can't live on gambling. Somebody has to do some work.

28 AGRICULTURE

YOUNG WILLIE GREW UP surrounded by the activities and hard work demanded by country life. His father's ranch controlled 60,000 acres of open grazing range along the Verdigris River. After Willie was given his first pony for his fifth birthday, he explored every single acre. From his own father, and from his friends and neighbors, he learned early the vagaries of life on the land, of the utter dependence on weather and market conditions. Later, Will ran away from one of the many schools he had been sent to and worked as a cowboy in Texas. He took part in many a dusty, tiring drive to bring cattle to railheads for shipment to markets.

When Will inherited the old home ranch, he tried farming. By then much of the open range had been fenced, and farmers and ranchers had settled the area. Since Will was busy with his show-business career, he asked his nephew Herb McSpadden to manage the farm. Through the difficult times of the twenties and the hard depression years of the thirties, the Rogers farm—like most of the farms of the drought-stricken Southwest—struggled to survive. Will had to use his show-business earnings to sustain the farm. He knew the plight of the farmers and ranchers firsthand, and he spoke for them. Despite his success, he never forgot his beginning, and he never missed a chance to come home and walk the land of his youth.

"I am just an old country boy," he said once during the depression, "yes, and I been lucky enough to be eatin' regular; and the reason that I have been is because I've stayed an old country boy."

The farm is mostly gone now. A few acres of the original Rogers ranch are still owned by the family. Some acres were sold after Will's death; some were deeded to the state for a park. The most fertile acres, the low-lying parts along the Verdigris River, are now covered by Lake Oologah. Man-made for flood control, the lake is part of an inland waterway, linking Oklahoma with the Gulf of Mexico.

The two-story house where Will was born was moved to higher ground to save it from the rising lake. Today, the house stands in a small state park, looking out on white sails, fishermen, swimmers, and motorboats towing water skiers over the submerged prairie, where once there were huge herds of cattle and a waving sea of bluestem grass.

Every farmer in Oklahoma has a picture of the new Farm Board hung on their wall, right in between the two mortgages.

★

Just read the Farm Bill. It's just a political version of Einstein's last theory. If a farmer could understand it, why, he certainly would know more than to farm—he would be a professor at Harvard.

★

The president appointed a committee that is to bring milk and honey to the famished agrarian. It looks like an awful simple problem they have to solve. All they have to do is to get the farmer more money for his wheat, corn, and cotton, without raising the price to the man that buys it.

★

The Farm Board Committee will meet and then appoint a subcommittee, and the subcommittee will appoint an investigating committee, and just before the next election, the investigating committee will turn in a report: "After due examination, we find the farmer really in need of succor, and we advise making one out of him at the coming election."

★

Farm relief, tax relief, flood relief—none of these have been settled, but they say they are getting them in shape for consideration at the next session of congress, with the hope that those needing relief will perhaps have conveniently died in the meantime.

★

Did you know that the Farm-Relief plank was exactly the same in the last two conventions? They hadn't even gone to the trouble to reword their promise! It just looks like they said: "Well, what did we promise him last election? Oh, we promised him relief. We'll do as well for him this time, and promise it to him again. As long as we don't give it to him, we can keep on promising it."

★

What has the poor farmer done against the Almighty that he should deserve all this? If it's not the heat, it's the deep snow; if it's not drought, it's a flood; if it's not boll weevil, it's the tariff; if it's not relief he needs, why it's rain. There is only one pest he is free from—that's income tax.

★

Everybody wants land irrigated by a government dam. For as everyone knows, new land with plenty of water will raise quite a bit. But so will old land, if it's fertilized. So why should the whole of American taxpayers pay for water for newly irrigated land any more than they should pay for fertilizer for old land?

★

I hope they don't irrigate more land, so they can raise more things that they can't sell and will have to plow up more rows, and kill more pigs to keep 'em from becoming hogs. What our secretary of agriculture is trying to do is to teach the farmer acreage control, and the hog birth control, and one is just as hard to make understand, as the other.

★

I have to put a stamp on all my letters, not like those boys in congress. I can't help increase the post-office deficit, like they can. We can't get the farmers any subsidy, but those boys in congress managed to get themselves quite a few little rake-offs.

★

I can tell you in a few words what the farmer needs. He needs a punch in the jaw, if he believes that either one of the parties cares a *dam* about him after election. That's all the farmer needs—and that's all he'll get.

★

Well, why don't the big farming states of the middle- and northwest vote for the Democrats? Because they are Republicans! Why? Because they were against slavery? When was they against slavery? In 1861! Well, ain't slavery over? Yes, it's over for everybody but the farmer!

★

The good people of Dakota offered to give the president a farm, if he would live on it. I wouldn't advise you to give those people too much credit for generosity. There is not a farmer in any state in the West that wouldn't be glad to give him his farm, if he will just paint it, fix up the fences, and keep up the series of mortgages that are on it. And if you think the president ain't smart—you just watch him not take it.

★

If your crop is a failure these days, and you don't raise anything, why, you are fortunate. Because it costs you more to raise anything than you can sell it for; so the less you raise, the less you lose, and if you don't raise anything, why, you are ahead.

★

The farmer wears out one automobile a year just running back and forth to town, to stall off interest on his mortgages. It's not lack of relief, or surplus, it's interest that's driving the farmer to the poorhouse.

★

Men bet thousands of dollars every day on racehorses, yet they don't interfere with the horse raiser in Texas. They get their gambling just the same, but they don't manipulate the price of horses all over the country. But a guy can sit in Chicago, produce nothing, and yet put a price on a farmer's whole year's labor.

The Russian peasant knows there is no use raising anything if you can't sell it for what you want. And you know yourself, Mr. President, those peasants in our middle west are either hollering for higher prices for their grain, or cheaper prices for what they need. So you see, Mr. President, Russia's problem is about like your problem, except that your peasants can vote, and the Russians can't. But we are hardly in a position to blame the Communists for not finding a solution, when we pay 600 congressmen billions of dollars, and they can't find one either.

Do any of you radiator folks know what a combine is? Well, here is all it does—just one machine, and in one trip over the ground. On the front of it is an arrangement that makes a deal to take over the ground from the bank that is holding the present mortgage. Then, just a few feet behind that, are the plows that plow the ground, and right in the furrow is the seeder, then another plow that plows the furrow back where it was in the first place. Then comes the fertilizer, and then the sickle that cuts the grain. Then into the threshing machine and out into sacks. Then, near the back end is a stock-market board, where a bunch of men that don't own the farm, the wheat, or the combine, buy it back and forth from each other, and then announce to the farmer that on account of supply and demand, the wheat is only worth two bits.

That's what you call a combine.

29 EDUCATION

IT IS GENERALLY ASSUMED that Will Rogers was an uneducated—or at best, little educated—cowboy, who just happened to think of quotable things. No such thing; nothing could be further from the truth. Will had just about as good an education as the Indian Territory of the 1880s and 1890s could offer. He went to the best schools, including two years to the Kemper Military School in Boonville, Missouri.

Of course, it must be also stated that Will was not the most cooperative student, that he did not like formal schooling, and that he apparently had a system all his own:

My father sent me to about every school in that part of the country. In some of them I would last for three or four months. I got just as far as McGuffey's *Fourth Reader*, when the teacher wouldent seem to be running the school right, and rather than having the school stop, I would generally leave. Then I would start in another school, tell them that I had just finished the *Third Reader* and was ready for the *Fourth*. Well, I knew all this Fourth Grade by heart, so the teacher would remark, "I never see you studying, yet you seem to know your lessons." I had that education thing figured down to a fine point. Three years in McGuffey's *Fourth Reader*, and I knew more about it than McGuffey did.

But I don't want any enterprising youth to get the idea that I had the right dope on it. I have regretted all my life that I did not at least take a chance on the Fifth Grade.

This may have been as Will reported, but he did attend schools until he was nineteen years old, and his report cards show that he was quite a good student. But that was only the formal education

173

of his life. Will was possessed by a lifelong thirst for knowledge—any knowledge. It was not just political information, or farming and ranching; no, anything he came across he wanted to know. The story is told that Will was being shown through a new government building in Washington, D.C., when the officials conducting the tour, and who were indeed very honored to have him there, suddenly noticed Will was missing. When he was finally located, he was on his hands and knees, being shown how mosaic floors were laid.

Will Rogers may not have had a college degree, but through his traveling, his reading, his contact with people, he was among the best-informed men of his time. And as for those college degrees, he could have had those too. For he was approached numerous times to accept honorary degrees. But Will would have none of it.

I received a nice letter from a college president. He wanted to give me a degree and he said they had given them to the Cabinet, the Supreme Court, and leading industrialists. I have had this same play come up a time or two, and I think those guys are kidding. If they are not, they ought to be.

Degrees have lost prestige enough as it is, without handing 'em around promiscuously. Let a guy get in there and battle for four years if he wants one, but don't give him one just because he happens to hold a good job in Washington, or manufactures more monkey wrenches than anybody else, or because he might be fool enough to make people laugh.

Keep 'em just for those kids that have worked hard for 'em. Keep 'em believing in 'em. They are stepping out in the world with nothing but that sheet of paper. We offer him nothing, so let's at least not belittle his badge.

Everybody is ignorant, only on different subjects.

There is nothing as stupid as an educated man if you get him off the subject he was educated in.

★

America is becoming so educated that ignorance will be a novelty. I will belong to a select few.

★

All I know is just what I read in the papers, and that's an alibi for my ignorance.

★

I have a lot of big ideas, they just don't seem to work out. There must be a bit of college professor in me somewhere.

★

Today I got my official document from the Red Cross headquarters of being made a life member. Well, sir, I am crazy about it for two reasons; one, of course, is that it is one of the greatest organizations in the United States (including the world). I think it is greater than the Republican Party.

The other reason is it looks like a diploma. You know I never had any kind of diploma—I never finished from anything. I always did want something that looked important. I never even had an oil share.

★

Does college pay? They do if you are a good open-field runner!

★

Is education necessary to football? No, a good coach and good interference is all that's necessary!

★

When should a college athlete turn pro? Not until he has earned all he can in college as an amateur.

★

Are our colleges becoming commercialized? No, no more than U.S. Steel.

★

Instead of giving money to found colleges to promote learning, why don't they pass a constitutional amendment, prohibiting anybody from learning anything. And if it works as good as the prohibition one did, why, in five years we would have the smartest race of people on earth.

30 ECOLOGY

THE FRIGHTENING USE, AND ABUSE, of what nature had provided has concerned some Americans for a long time. "Conservationists" have warned for decades, if not centuries, that our wastefulness and utter disregard for basic laws of nature could but lead to our own destruction.

It seems that certain sections of American society discovered ecology only in the 1960s, but much earlier men like Will Rogers saw the terrible results of man's outrage against the land.

The most horrifying example of misuse of the land in Will's time, was the Dust Bowl. Through Texas, Oklahoma, and into Kansas, the winds carried the topsoil, blotting out the sun at high noon. The strong winds would force the dust through the smallest cracks around windows or doors; breathing was difficult and usually done through a wet cloth. Soil piled up inside farmhouses, inside closets, and even inside iceboxes. Nothing was safe. Cattle were blinded, sometimes smothered. The farmers and ranchers were in a powerless rage against the elements, mostly unleashed by man himself.

Naturally Will Rogers wrote and spoke about the dust storms. It affected his home area. But he could see the futility of it all: "That's another thing, that dust storm. The poor farmer spent a lifetime fixing his farm, then goes out and looks down at it, and it's up above him. But they are going to fix that! The administration is sending a Mr. Tugwell out west to see about stopping that wind out there."

When Betty Rogers and their daughter Mary came back from a trip to Egypt, where they had visited the Pyramids, and Tutankhamun's tomb, which had been buried in sand for thousands of years, Will mused on a radio broadcast:

Now about these dust storms, that's how every civilization since time began has been covered up. It's been this dust. It's a terrible thing to happen to those people in the middle west, but on the other hand, it's a great tribute to know that the Lord feels that you have a civilization that is so advanced over the rest of civilization, that it's the first place to be buried under. I didn't think at first that we was that smart in Oklahoma, in Kansas, in Texas, and eastern Colorado, but our Almighty must know.

Now that He would ever cover up California for the same reason, I've got my doubts.

In March 1935 Will wired: "Flew through these dust storms last night, with the pilot flying entirely by instruments. Where in the world is it going to?"

It would be another twenty years before man had learned to manage the land and to eradicate most of the damage.

I hope my Cherokee blood is not making me prejudiced, I want to be broad-minded. We're always talking about pioneers, and what great folks the old pioneers were. Well, if we stopped and looked history in the face, the pioneer wasn't a thing in the world but a guy that wanted something for nothing. He was a guy that wanted to live off everything that nature had done. He wanted to cut a tree down that didn't cost him anything, but he never did plant one. He wanted to plough up land that should have been left to grass. We are just now learning that we can rob from nature the same way as we can rob from an individual. The pioneer thought it was nature he was living off, but it was really future generations that he was living off of.

★

We are going at top speed and we are using all our natural resources as fast as we can. If we want to build something out of wood, all we got to do is go and cut down a tree and build it. We didn't have to plant the tree, nature did that before we come. Suppose we couldn't build something out of wood till we found a tree that we had purposely planted. Say we never would get it built. Suppose we didn't have any coal and had to ship it in! Now we bore a shaft and get some. But when our resources run out, if we can still be ahead of other nations, then will be the time to brag; then we can show whether we are really superior.

I got a wire from a very influential club in New Orleans, saying that the sewage from Chicago, Kansas City, St. Louis, and Memphis was coming past Canal Street in New Orleans!

I wonder if there ain't a bit of truth in that statement. Even a town where people live on top of a hill, they are not allowed to just throw everything out of their doors, and let it roll down the hill on to people that live at the bottom!

You know, Americans have been getting away pretty soft up to now. Every time we needed anything, why, it was growing right under our noses. Every natural resource in the world, we had it.

But with them getting less, and national debts getting more, there is going to be some work going on in this country some day. Something will happen, and we won't be doing well.

★

You know, the Lord has sure been good to us. Now what are we doing to warrant that good luck any more than any other nation? Just how long is that going to last? Now the way we are acting, the Lord is liable to turn on us any minute; and even if He don't, our good fortune can't possibly last any longer than our natural resources.

31 INDIANS

WILL ROGERS WAS APPROXIMATELY one-quarter Cherokee Indian. There was nothing that he was as proud of as his Indian ancestry. The Cherokees, of course, are one of the Five Civilized Tribes, and considered the most highly advanced. When the Cherokees still lived in the East, before their forceable removal to the West, they had sent their children to schools, and their social and economic structure rivaled that of their "white" counterparts. The Cherokees are the only Indian tribe to have their own written language.

Whenever Will Rogers had an opportunity, he would take the Indians' side. In his radio broadcast of April 7, 1935, Will chided the Pilgrims: "I bet you when the Pilgrims landed on Plymouth Rock, and they had the whole of the American continent, and all they had to do to get an extra 160 acres was to shoot another Indian, I betcha anything, they kicked on the price of ammunition."

The Chamber of Commerce of Provincetown, Massachusetts, took exception, not with the reference to the Pilgrims shooting Indians, but with Will's mistaken statement as to exactly where the Pilgrims landed. So the following week, April 14, 1935, Will fired the second barrel.

On last Sabbath evening I referred to the Pilgrims landing on Plymouth Rock. Well, Boy, you wait till I heard from New England. I split New England just wide open. It seems there is a town up there called Provincetown. They have adopted a slogan which says: Don't be misled by history, or any other unreliable source, here is the place where the

179

Pilgrims landed. This is by unanimous vote of the Chamber of Commerce of Provincetown. Provincetown has been made the official landing place of the Pilgrims. Any Pilgrim landing in any other place, is not official.

Now in the first place, I don't think that this argument I have created up there is so terribly important. The argument that New England has got to settle in order to pacify the rest of America is: Why were the Pilgrims allowed to land anywhere? That's what we want to know. Now I hope my Cherokee blood is not making me prejudiced, I want to be broad-minded. But I am sure it was only the extreme generosity of the Indians that allowed the Pilgrims to land. Suppose we reverse the case. Do you reckon the Pilgrims would ever let the Indians land? What a chance! Why, the Pilgrims wouldent even allow the Indians to live, after the Indians went to the trouble of letting 'em land.

Well, anyhow, the Provincetown officials sent me a lot of official data that when the Pilgrims landed they found some corn that the Indians had stored, and that the Pilgrims were about starved and that they ate the Indians' corn. And they claim that the corn was stored at Provincetown. So then you see, the minute the Pilgrims landed, they got full of the corn, and then they shot the Indians—perhaps because they hadent stored more corn.

Of course the Pilgrims would always pray, mostly for more Indian corn.

There is no indication that either Provincetown, or Plymouth, Massachusetts, ever sent Will any more information.

My ancestors didn't come over on the *Mayflower*—they met the boat.

★

"Memoirs" that's another Cherokee word; means when you put down the good things you ought to have done, and leave out the bad ones you did do.

★

I see where the government ruled that beer couldn't be sold on an Indian reservation. They don't want to take 'em off whisky too quick.

★

Pilgrims would always pray. I bet any one of you have never seen a picture of one of these old Pilgrims praying that he didn't have a gun right by the side of him. That was to see that he got what he was praying for!

But they were very religious people that came over here from the old country. They were very human. They would shoot a couple of Indians on the way to every prayer meeting.

It is certainly gratifying to read about one conference that got somewhere. The Navajo Indians held a conference, and decided that they could get along without the services of about 25 white officeholders that had been appointed to help look after 'em. The Indians said they were doing it to save the white man money.

Who said the Indians didn't have a sense of humor?

You know, Indians used to be the wards of the government, but now we all are. Everybody is an Indian.

I hear the Navajos have struck oil on their reservation. That will give the white man a chance to show his so-called 100 percent Americanism by flocking in and taking it away from the Indians.

Did you read where my hometown of Claremore, Oklahoma, just opened an Indian Hospital? Just think, Columbus discovered America a little over 400 years ago, and here they are building us a hospital.

Just imagine what us Indians got to look forward to in the next 400 years. Why, they might even build us a cemetery.

Lots of people think 'cause the Osages have oil, that all Indians are rich. Why, the Pine Ridge Agency Sioux have eaten so much horsemeat, they are wearing bridles instead of hats.

Let's don't get down in intolerance as far down as the Indians. Because if you monkey around, I'm Cherokee too, and a few of us will get together, and run you all out of this country, that's all, and take it back over again.

To tell you the truth, I am not so sweet on old Andy Jackson. He is the one that run us Cherokees out of Georgia and North Carolina. I ate the Jackson Day Dinner once, but I didn't enjoy it. I also thought that the Democrats were going mighty far back to find some hero that they could worship.

Old Andy Jackson made the White House. The Indians wanted him in there so he would let us alone for awhile. Andy stayed two terms. The Indians were for a third term for Andy.

They sent the Indians to Oklahoma. They had a treaty that said: "You shall have this land as long as the grass grows and the water flows." It was not only a good rhyme, but looked like a good treaty—and it was, till they struck oil. Then the government took it away from us again. They said that the treaty only refers to water and grass; it don't say anything about oil.

So the Indians lost another bet—the first one to Andrew Jackson, and the second to the oil companies.

Every time the government moved the Indians, they gave 'em the same treaty: "You shall have this land as long as the grass grows and the water flows." But finally they settled the whole Indian problem. They put the Indians on land where the grass won't grow, and the water won't flow!

Our California state legislature passed a law the other day, to give the Indians liquor. Well, I don't mean actually give them the liquor, I mean allow them to buy it, if he can. One old California cowpuncher told them: "We ought to give the Indians something back, the land or the liquor," and so they compromised on giving them the liquor.

But it did raise the Indians' social standard up to the white man. He is equal now. The Indian can go out and get drunk according to law.

You can learn a lot from Indians. They say you must never disagree with a man while you are facing him. Go around behind him and look the same way they do; look over his shoulder and get his viewpoint, then go back and face him, and you will have a different idea.

We were out there on Indian land, dedicating a dam to get water for white people to come out and use and gradually take more Indian land away. There is going to be nothing different. It started with Leif Ericsson in 996, then skip over Columbus in 1492, for he couldn't find this country in four trips. Then come the Spanish settlers, then the *Mayflower* was the last straw.

They didn't have any ex-president at the dedicating at their taking land away from the Indians, but they got it just the same, and they kept right on doing it. The more so-called civilized we get the more we kill and take.

★

As you saw all those Indians, you couldn't help but think of the old days. Here was the old warlike Apaches that fought to hold all they had, and most of them wound up in jail, but there was a Washington, that fought for his tribe and wound up with a flock of statues and a title of "Father of his country." And yet, I expect, if the truth were known, the old Apache Chiefs went through more, and fought harder for their country than George did. But George won, that's the whole answer to history; it's not what did you do, but what did you get away with at the finish.

★

Mr. Coolidge asked me about my being part Indian, when he up and said: "I am part Indian. My folks had Indian blood!" He said he didn't know the exact tribe, but he knew that away back, his ancestors had Indian blood. I knew it wasent the Cherokees. If my tribe ever settled in New England, with the rest of North America to pick from, they certainly wouldent be known as the most highly civilized tribe in America! But he really, away back, is some kind of Indian—he told me.

32 LATIN AMERICA

REGARDLESS OF AMERICA'S OFFICIAL, and unofficial, policies, Will practiced the "good-neighbor" policy at all times. The U.S. State Department could ignore our neighbors to the south, or it could court them, but Will's feelings toward them never changed, he liked them. He even learned several words and phrases in Spanish and urged his fellow Americans to do likewise.

It was Will Rogers' attitude throughout his life that if you went into the other man's country, that country was his, and you had no business to tell him how he should run it. You are the guest, and if you don't like it, well, nobody was forcing you to stay. Foreign policy, so often simply a stern note from the State Department, was an extension of dollar diplomacy. What American business needed and wanted, the other country better be willing to supply! If not, America would send cruisers steaming into Venezuela or, as Will wrote: "send valentines shaped like Marines."

Early in 1931 Nicaragua was struck by an earthquake. Strictly as a private citizen, Will immediately flew into Managua, the capital, which had also suffered from a devastating fire in the aftermath of the earthquake. This telegram was sent by Matthew E. Hanna, United States Minister to Nicaragua: "Will Rogers left here this noon by special plane for San José Costa Rica (Period) His visit brought cheer to this saddened community and has given new hope to the despondent (Period) He has snapped us out of our morbidness and he has given us a saner spirit to carry on our work of reconstruction (Period) We all owe him a profound debt of gratitude (Period)."

In March 1939 President Anastasio Somoza of Nicaragua had a

184

set of five stamps issued, honoring Will Rogers. Several sets were sent to Betty Rogers, and in the accompanying letter President Somoza wrote:

At the time of the terrible affliction for Nicaragua, when its capital, Managua, was destroyed by the earthquake and fire of March 31, 1931, your illustrious husband, Will Rogers, paid us an interesting visit we shall never forget.

Mr. Rogers, wanting to know the extent of the disaster, visited all the sections of the ruins, talking to a multitude of victims. Without seeking publicity, he gave to the Red Cross $5,000, so they could continue their aid to the distressed.

Nicaragua, so kindly helped, will never forget Will Rogers.

P.S. Actually the official records of the Red Cross show that Will Rogers raised almost twenty thousand dollars for the victims in Nicaragua.

We are supposed to pay Panama for killing all their mosquitos and putting an irrigation ditch from one ocean to the other through their property. They say we are to pay in gold as they question us on the worth of our 59-cent dollar.

It would be a good joke on 'em if we just picked up our canal, and came home.

★

Say, I've been thinking, why don't we dig a canal from the head of the Columbia River to the head of the Mississippi River? At least there is no Central-American propaganda against that.

★

If we could let Nicaragua alone, they might like us by the time we got ready to build a canal through their country.

★

We have a commission down there now, trying to get Mexico to recognize us. We have changed so in the last few years that very few nations know us now. The way we are trying to make up to Mexico now, they must have struck more oil lately.

★

The difference in our exchange of people with Mexico is: they send workmen here to work, while we send Americans there to work Mexico.

★

There is one thing about a Latin-American country. No matter who is running it, they are always run the same.

★

For a Central-American dictator, he died a natural death—he was shot in the back.

★

You know we got the wrong impression of those Latin-American revolutions. They love 'em. It's their relaxation. Sure, people get killed sometimes, if it's a first-class A revolution. In fact, they may lose about as many as we lose over our weekends by trying to pass somebody on a turn.

★

In Mexico, we speak of ourselves as being from America, as though they were in Asia. You know, Mexico feels—and with some slight justification—that they are in America, too. They don't feel that America ends at the Rio Grande River.

Of course, they may be wrong, but they are just childish enough to feel that way.

★

If you travel to Mexico City, there is not much to see after you leave Laredo. It's mostly level and nothing but mesquite brush. Nature so provided that the worst part of Mexico adjoins us. If it hadn't been, we would have taken any good part long ago.

★

I see where America and Mexico had a joint earthquake. That's the only thing I ever heard we split 50-50 with Mexico.

★

I see where we are starting to pay some attention to our neighbors to the South. We could never understand why Mexico wasent just crazy about us; for we have always had their goodwill, and coffee and minerals and oil at heart.

★

Some of our politicians were just for going down and taking Mexico over. Where did this country down there, with no great chains of Commercial Clubs and Chambers of Commerce, and no advertising radio programs, where did a nation like that come in to have oil, anyway? We should have taken the whole thing before, you know, when we took the part we did.

★

The Pan-American conference is still in session. If we gave fairer

treatment to our sister republics, then we wouldn't need these conferences.

★

Criticism can get us in more trouble than a gun can. I don't want
somebody telling me how to run my country. I want to ruin it myself
without outside aid, and that is especially true of these Latin countries.
The minute there is any trouble in any Latin-American country, that
should be the tip right there for us to crawl in a hole, and not even be
allowed to poke our head out, till it was all over.

Why did the president think we were trusted in South America?
  "He had never been there!"
  "Was you ever in South America?"
  "I was!"
  "Was you trusted?"
  "Yes, as long as I paid in advance, I was!"
  "Do you think America stands very good with those countries there?"
  "We stand alone."
  "Do you think any one of them would help us out?"
  "Well, offhand I can't think of a single one that would, unless it might
be Wisconsin."

33 CANADA

SINCE HE WAS ON THE VAUDEVILLE CIRCUIT for quite a few years, Will Rogers traveled into Canada many times. Cities like Montreal, Ottawa, Toronto, Winnipeg, and Vancouver were on the regular schedule.

It was in Canada that Eddie Cantor first met Will Rogers. This is what Eddie wrote years later about that meeting:

I first met Will Rogers in 1912, when we were on the same vaudeville bill at the Orpheum Theatre, in Winnipeg, Canada. Right away I knew this Oklahoma cowboy was like no other actor I'd ever met. He actually enjoyed listening as much as talking. Before I knew it, I had told him how I'd grown up in a New York tenement, how I'd gotten into show business, and on and on. I think I realized then that the day was to come when I would love him more than any other man I'd ever known, with the kind of deep and admiring love I might have had for a father or older brother.

The two men, actually thirteen years apart in age, met many times again, including the *Ziegfeld Follies* of 1917 and 1918. When Will was unable to keep a certain radio broadcast date, Eddie Cantor stepped in and took his place.

Will again visited Canada repeatedly on his lecture tours during the years between 1925 and 1928. This time, however, he never went farther west than Toronto. His opinions of Canada were strong, and he had the conviction that the United States could not ask for a better neighbor. He thought, in fact, that Canada managed her affairs even better than did the United States. Wrote Will during the Great Depression: "I was a-reading in the papers here lately where Canada was having a sort of a tough time. I hadent been keeping up with their affairs much lately. I have always had such high regard for the way they generally handle their affairs, that I just naturally thought they were doing good."

Been reading a lot of criticism by our papers of what Canada was doing. When it comes to running their own business, they don't need any great advice from us. Canada is a mighty good neighbor and a mighty good customer. That's a combination that is hard to beat. You see, we agreed to buy from each other, and we will—till somebody comes along and sells cheaper.

★

Canada has made a great showing with a few people over a tremendous area. Take the whole of New York City, where 80 percent of our wealthy people are in storage; if you turned 'em loose in Canada on their own resources, it would be fifty years before one would get far enough away from Toronto to discover Lake Erie.

★

Canada, they have truly been a good companion; I won't call 'em neighbors, for they havent borrowed enough from us to be called neighbors; I would prefer to still call 'em friends. They are a fine tribe of people.

They are hardy—they got to be to live next to us and exist.

★

The big boss said he wished, if I had the time, to go up into Canada and see what kind of a deal I could make in the way of annexation. England has kind of lost her hold on them and they are getting out, doing a little thinking of their own. England claimed that on account of them living so near to us, that they are soaking up a lot of our meanness.

Now from what I can see, there don't seem to be any demand up here in Canada to join in and be murdered or run over with us. They strike me as entirely too sane a nation to fit in our scheme of things down home.

★

Now, Canada is principally an agricultural country, and we already raise more than the farmers down home can sell for enough to put in the next year's crop. About the only thing I can think of we could use Canada for would be a skating rink in the winter, and we got such a poor class of skaters that we couldn't hardly afford to maintain it just for that. Unless we could trade in Wisconsin on it in some way, I can't see any reason to annex Canada.

What we need is some good country to annex us.

I am still up here in Canada to see for the boss if this country is worth taking over. Now, I have no doubt that we could make a paying proposition out of them, for that country now is supplying about everything we use in the way of raw materials. But I hate to interrupt a friendship that has been going on now pretty steady since the battle of Lake Erie.

So, if we can just keep from annexing them, and keep from loaning them anything, why, we ought to be friends for years to come.

After looking over Canada in regard to taking it under the auspices of the United States, well, that's off! We don't want more people in this country, what we want is to try and improve the mob we have now. And Canada couldn't help us out, they couldn't even learn us English—they speak it just as bad as we do.

34 RELIGION

THERE ARE NO PICTURES OF WILL ROGERS emerging from a church on a Sunday morning; there are not even accounts of it. He was born into the Methodist church, and attended Sunday School, but in his adult life he never made a show of his personal beliefs—he simply lived his life as an example for all to see.

However, in his writings Will states that he was never a "nonbeliever," and many times he calls on the Lord or, as he sometimes calls Him, the Almighty.

Among his close personal friends were Father Duffy, Rabbi Stephen Wise, and the Reverend J. W. Brougher. Among Will's effects are cancelled checks to numerous religious organizations. Not simply token gifts, but substantial amounts, as for example a $400 check to the Free Synagogue in New York City.

When the Community Church in Beverly Hills needed money for their building fund, Will was among the first and largest contributors. When the church was completed, his children were among the first to attend Sunday School there.

The Solax Club of New York City planned a testimonial dinner for Eddie Cantor. This was a Jewish charitable club, yet Will asked to be the toastmaster. The year was 1925, and Will was the foremost after-dinner speaker in New York. Everyone looked forward to his remarks, but nobody expected what they heard. In the six weeks preceding the dinner Will had studied Yiddish with a rabbinical student, and the notes for his talk—still preserved today—show Will's own typing, reproducing each Yiddish word phonetically.

Will, Jr., recalls the year 1927 especially well. It was the year Will Rogers had a gallstone operation, and for days he was in grave danger. As Will, Jr., then barely sixteen years old, remembers, their mother assembled the three children in the master bedroom, and how for the first time they knelt and prayed as a family. But the family was not alone in its prayer; the country prayed right along with them.

Will believed in charity, whether through organizations or on a personal basis. He always had indigent actors on his payroll, and he paid them so well that Eddie Cantor reported that some refused small parts in pictures or plays, because it would have meant less money than they were getting from Will.

Will was offered $75,000 for a series of radio broadcasts. He accepted with the stipulation that one-half of the fee go directly to the Salvation Army and the other half to the Red Cross. Will never saw a cent of the total.

Eddie Cantor also tells the story of Will when the two of them were in Detroit, in 1917. Rogers walked up to the Good Fellow Fund window and laid down ten $100 bills: "Get some toys for the kids," he said, turning away.

"Wait a minute," the girl called after him. "What's your name?"

"My name won't help the toys any," Will answered and kept going.

Will's father wanted his son to follow in his footsteps and take over the ranch some day. Will's mother wanted her son to become a preacher, a minister.

From all we know about Will Rogers, his mother certainly had her wish answered.

I was raised predominantly a Methodist, but I have traveled so much, mixed with so many people, in all parts of the world, I don't know just what I am. I know I have never been a nonbeliever. But I can honestly tell you that I don't think that any one religion, is *the* religion. Which way you serve your God will never get one word of argument or condemnation out of me.

★

We pray for anything, whether we got any dope on it, or not. The trouble with our praying is, we just do it as a means of last resort.

★

I maintain that it should cost as much to get married as it does to get divorced. Make it look like marriage is worth as much as divorce, even if it ain't. That would make the preachers financially independent, like it has the lawyers.

★

Our Savior had a plan; He left it to us and He knew it would help us, and we know it would help us. He said: "Love thy neighbor as thyself"; but I bet there ain't two people in your block that's speaking to each other.

★

Can you imagine our Savior dying for all of us, yet we have to argue over just whether He didn't die for us personally and not for you. Sometimes you wonder if His lessons of sacrifice and devotion was pretty near lost on a lot of us.

★

There is no argument in the world that carries the hatred that a religious belief one does.

★

It seems the more learned a man is the less consideration he has for another man's belief.

★

Whoever wrote the Ten Commandments made 'em short. They may not always be kept, but they can be understood. They are the same for all men. No industry can come in and say: "Our's is a special and unique business." They apply to the steel men, the oil man, the bankers, the farmers, and even the United States Chamber of Commerce.

★

What would happen to our Savior if He would come to earth today? Why, say! He wouldn't last near as long as He did then. Civilization has got past "truth and poverty and renunciation," and all that junk. Throw those nuts in jail!

★

If there are people who think they come from a monkey, it's not our business to rob them of what little pleasure they may get out of imagining it. What good will it do at this late date to argue over who we came from. The Lord didn't leave any room for doubt when He told you how you should act when you got here. His example and the Commandments are plain enough. So let's just start from there.

★

The church is in politics more than politicians. All our preachers are doing our principal legislation for us now. A preacher just can't save anybody nowadays. He is too busy saving the nation. In the old days those fellows read their Bibles. Now they read the Congressional Record. If congress met Sundays, why, there would be no services anywhere, all the ministers would have their eyes on congress.

★

I read statistics every once in a while, and it shows how church attendance is sorter falling off on Sunday mornings. But it's not lack of religious inclination. It's just that you can't beat Sunday morning to get the old car out and ramble. And no minister can move 'em like a secondhand car. A preacher can have the best sermon in the world, but he will just have to deliver it to folks without any gas.

★

I was just thinking, if it is really religion with these nudist colonies, they sure must turn atheists in the winter time.

★

I have been libeled by my friend Arthur Brisbane. In his editorial he says that at one time I was a Sunday school teacher. Now, he is wrong. I went, but I didn't teach. I didn't even take up the collection. Some banker always did that.

★

No great revival will ever start from an argument over where we come from. The religious revival of the future, when it is started, will be people's fear over where we are going.

★

Missionaries are going to reform the world, whether it wants it, or not.

★

What degree of egotism is it that makes a nation, or a religious organization think, theirs is the very thing for the Chinese or the Zulus? Why, we can't even Christianize our legislators!

★

If the churches want to do something worthwhile with their missionaries, bring them home and put them to work among poor renters or "sharecrop" workers in the cotton and wheat belt. Some of them have a dozen children and never had $20 in the family in their lives. Let them work among them and help 'em and teach 'em! We just got the missionary business turned around—we are the ones that need converting.

★

That's one trouble with our charities; we are always saving somebody away off, when the fellow next to us ain't eating. Same thing wrong with the missionaries. They will save anybody if he is far enough away, and don't speak our language.

35 OIL AND GAS

WHEN THE CHEROKEE INDIANS were forced from their lands in the Carolinas, Tennessee, and Georgia, and driven onto land west of the Mississippi River, thousands died. Those who survived, and those who had gone before the horrible trek, had found the western Ozark mountains reminiscent of the lush, tree-covered mountains of the Smokies. They decided to settle there, in what today are parts of Missouri, Arkansas, and Oklahoma. There was only one thing drastically wrong with this resettlement plan—the land had already been settled by the Osages. Battles followed, with the result that the Cherokees took the land, pushing the Osages to the west, as next-door neighbors.

Years later oil was found under the land now settled by the Osages, while hardly any was found under Cherokee land. Kidded Will:

We Cherokees are supposed to be the most civilized tribe; that means we don't have any oil.

It was our tribe of Cherokees that sold the original old Cherokee Strip. I think the government only gives us about a dollar an acre for it. We had it for hunting grounds, but we never knew enough to hunt oil on it. I can remember as a kid, the payment we had, when the government paid out the money to the Cherokees for it. There was something like three million dollars, as there was that many acres, and we got about $320 a piece, I think it was.

The Cherokees are supposed to be the highest civilized tribe there is, and yet, that's all we got in all our lifetime. We sold a fortune in oil and wonderful agricultural land to get that little $320 a piece. Yet there was the Osages, lived right by us, and they got that much before breakfast every morning, and they are supposed to be uncivilized.

So it shows you, it kinder pays not to know too much. I would trade my so-called superior knowledge right now for an Osage Headright. If you had their payment, you wouldent need to know anything, only where the payment was going to be made.

It's a question what we can convert these 4 billion filling stations into in the years to come when the oil runs out. But it ain't my business to do you folks' worrying for you. I am only tipping you off, and you-all are supposed to act on it.

★

Gasoline was never much higher. But there you have a business that is in the hands of a few men, and they see that the price is kept up. It's not regulated by supply and demand, it's regulated by manipulation.

★

You remember, a few years ago, this country had to pass a special law, called the Anti-Trust Law, aimed primarily at two trusts—the Oil and the Steel.

Now, if you have to pass a law to curb businesses like that, they are not exactly the businesses to inspire confidence to the rest of the nation, in regard to keeping the law.

★

Between our missionaries and our oil men, we are just about in wrong all over the world.

★

I am always writing about politics, or the Supreme Court, or World Court, or disarmament, or Russia, or any and everything. I don't know any more about 'em than a boweevil—and I don't even know how to spell boweevil. But I do have a sprinkling of knowledge on one thing. The difference between good times and bad times, is gasoline, and what goes with it.

★

The idea that a tax on something keeps anybody from buying it, is a lot of hooey! They put it on gasoline all over the country and it hasn't kept a soul home a single night or day. You could put a dollar a gallon on it, and still a pedestrian couldn't cross the street in safety without armor.

★

Every one of us out here in the land of sunshine and second mortgages, is hustling from bank to bank, trying to renew our notes. A man has to be careful nowadays, or he will burn up more gasoline trying to get a loan than the loan is worth.

★

Is this a good tip, or ain't it? No business in the U.S. is as cockeyed as the oil business. If ever a business needed a dictator, it is them. It would be the biggest job held by a single man, outside the president; it must not be an oil man, for he is already linked with one side or the other. It's got to be a man that the whole oil industry knows is on the level, fearless, fair, seeking nothing but justice to thousands that produce oil, and millions that use it.

★

You know that every state has its own Standard Oil Company. You remember how that all came about, don't you? Well, senators got the idea that the Standard Oil Corporation was too big, so they made it split up.

It split up into forty-eight states, with each state corporation bigger than the whole original one. Those senators did an awful fine job with that, they broke up one little one into forty-eight big ones. It's just little things like that, that make the senate a body so well respected.

36 SHOW BUSINESS

WILL'S ENTRY INTO SHOW BUSINESS really began on July 4, 1899 when he won a roping contest in Claremore. His prize money was $18.50, which in those days must have been a small fortune. Will entered other contests, but won few, according to his own reports. But "show business had gotten into my blood, and I was ruined for life as far as any actual work was concerned."

Will's thoughts of rodeos and Wild West shows were even more enhanced in South Africa, when he came across *Texas Jack's Wild West Show*. Will needed a job and he sought out Texas Jack. What could he do, he was asked. Will demonstrated his artistry with the rope, ending up with a giant loop, using the entire fifty-foot length of the rope. This was a most difficult trick, known as the crinoline. Texas Jack hired Will at once, at $20 per week. Only later did Will learn that Texas Jack performed the crinoline nightly as part of his act and then challenged members of the audience to duplicate the trick, with a prize money of fifty sovereigns as the reward. Too late.

Will learned the basics of his trade in South Africa, and later with the Wirth Brothers' Circus in Australia. When he returned to America, he was well qualified to perform at the St. Louis World's Fair in 1904, in New York City in 1905, and on into vaudeville. Broadway shows followed, then the biggest and best of all, the *Ziegfeld Follies*. From Broadway, Will went into motion pictures, back to the *Ziegfeld Follies* for a while, and then, when the films discovered sound, Will became a top motion-picture star.

By 1934 when he was asked to be master of ceremonies at the Academy Awards, he was the number one box-office attraction. In fact, by that time he was also America's foremost radio commentator and America's most widely read newspaper columnist. At the 1934 Academy Awards something happened that some of the old timers still remember. In the category of "Best Director" among those nominated were Frank Borzage and Frank Capra. When the time came to open the fateful envelope, Will peeked into it to announce the best director and began to read: "The winner is Frank. . . ." Capra and Borzage rose out of their seats, ready to rush to the stage. Will continued, without mentioning the last name: "Why Frank, I am so happy for you, but I knew you deserved it . . ." and on, while two embarrassed men just stood there. Finally, Will finished the name—it was Frank Capra.

But as *Photoplay Magazine* of June 1934 wrote on its editorial page: "At the recent Academy Awards dinner, the prophet of Fox Movietone City tossed big executives, stars, artists and whatnot on his griddle and roasted them to a turn. He even took a crack at the industry itself: "It's a racket," said Will; "if it wasn't, we all wouldn't be here in dress clothes."

The editorial ended with: "Will's wit changed the big affair from a customary ceremony of long-winded speeches into a joyous riot."

An actor is a fellow that just has a little more monkey in him than the fellow that can't act.

★

The moving picture theatre owners want to eliminate the sensational and suggestive advertising used for pictures. You can't make a picture as bad as the ads lead you to believe it is.

★

The off-colored, or risqué, pictures haven't been going so good as they used to. It wasn't that tastes were improving, it was that there wasn't anything new that they could shock folks with.

★

A critic's contribution to the success of most theatres is at about the same ratio that a fire would be.

★

They have more workmen in the theatres now than they have audiences.

★

I was called on to speak at the 30th anniversary of the Empire Theatre. I don't know why I should have been there; I had never played the place. I suppose I really contributed more to its success by not playing there.

We try to make moving pictures as good as we can. Bad pictures are not made with a premeditated design. It looks to you sometimes we must have purposely made 'em that way, but honest, we don't. A bad picture is an accident, and a good one is a miracle.

What an education those moving-picture ads are! I thought the underwear ads in the magazines were about the limit in presenting an eyeful, but these movie ads give you the same thing without the underwear.

About the only thing an actor can start, is a fad, or a divorce.

This is the day when the Academy of Motion Picture Arts and Sciences hands out those little statues. They were originally designed for prizes at a nudist colony's bazaar—but they didn't take 'em. They must be terribly artistic for nobody has any idea what it is. It represents the triumph of nothingness over the stupendousness of zero.

This Academy of Motion Picture Arts and Sciences, that's the highest sounding named organization I ever attended. If I didn't know so many of the people who belong to it personally, I would have taken the name serious. But everything that gives pleasure and makes money, is not an Art or a Science. If it were, bootlegging would have been the highest form of artistic endeavor.

An actor has as much right as anyone else to have his political beliefs. He pays his taxes, and is a good citizen. But I don't think he should carry any propaganda into his stage work. He has no right to use his privilege as an actor to drive home his political beliefs.

If he wants to, as a citizen, let him hire a hall and tell 'em what he wants to. He is a citizen then, not an actor.

Producers decided to make fewer and worse pictures. They may make fewer, but they will never make worse ones. The Decency Code people said: "They got to be cleaner!" The exhibitors say: "If you get them too clean, nobody is interested in them!" The novelists say: "What's the use of selling them a story, they don't make the story they buy!" The scenario staff says: "It reads good, but it won't photograph!" The so-called intellectual keeps saying: "Give us something worthwhile in the movies, that we can think about!" The regular movie fans say: "Give us something to see, never mind think about. If we wanted to think, we wouldn't go to the movies!"

37 SPORTS

IN HIS SCHOOL DAYS Will had played some football. "I played what you might call a 'wide end.' I would play out so far that the other twenty-one would be pretty well piled up before I could possibly reach 'em. I would arrive a little late for most of the festivities. I could run pretty fast. In fact, my nickname was, and is to this day among some of the old-timers, 'Rabbit.' I could never figure out if that referred to my speed or my heart."

During the vaudeville years Will would often work out with local professional baseball teams before game time. He would play the outfield and catch fly balls.

As a spectator, Will enjoyed baseball and rodeos the most; as a participant, nothing could beat polo. Will and polo seemed made for each other, for it combined everything Will loved. The only improvement anyone could have possibly made to suit Will would have been to suggest that the wooden ball had to be lassoed. He would take off in hot pursuit of the ball, without the slightest concern for his own safety. He was an excellent player and played with the foremost champion players of his time.

Eddie Dowling, the actor and producer, told about the time Will played at Sands Point, Long Island. With his usual abandon he went into the thick of battle. There, one of the players struck Will with the mallet, splitting his upper lip wide open. Will did not wish to miss the rest of the game, so he let the veterinarian at the stables attend to his lip, and soon he was back on the field, as if nothing had happened. But that evening, at his performance, the stitches gave way, and Will had to speak with a torn lip. For three days, so the story goes, he performed this way.

The rest of the story was told by Dr. Herman Goodman, a physician, who often visited Will backstage. Dr. Goodman saw the lip and suggested a highly competent plastic surgeon; in fact, he made the appointment for the following day. Will showed up at the surgeon's office, but by this time it was no longer a simple matter. While the operation was performed in the doctor's office, it took quite a while to trim the dead tissue and match the cut lip. A week after the stitches were removed, leaving a small permanent scar, the plastic surgeon sent a bill for $10.

The next time Dr. Goodman came backstage, Will cornered him. "What kind of a doctor did you send me to? This must be some honorary doctor, charging only $10. And here I was letting him work on my lip, why, that's how I make my living." Dr. Goodman assured Will that this was a bona-fide medical practitioner, highly respected and qualified, and to just pay the bill, small as it was, and that he would find out if the surgeon had made some mistake.

A few days later Dr. Goodman reported to Will: "No, that was the full bill, just $10. You see, when the surgeon saw you walk into his office in your rumpled and worn blue-serge suit, he just felt that you couldn't afford to pay more."

Obviously, here was a man to whom the name Will Rogers meant little.

How present-day prizefighting ever got mentioned in the category of sports, will always remain a mystery to most people.

★

My idea of an optimist is a nearsighted man in a five-dollar seat at the big prize fight.

★

The deer season just opened. A deer hunter in Ventura county brought in his first man yesterday.

★

In Hollywood you can see things at night that are fast enough to be in the Olympics in the day time.

★

I saw a hockey game here Sunday night, and war is kinder effeminate after that.

After a soccer game in Lima, Peru, five were killed. They only kill ten in a revolution down there, so two games equal one revolution.

Up here we don't kill our football players. We make coaches out of the smartest ones, and send the others to the legislature.

It's open-field running that gets your old college somewhere, and not a pack of spectacled orators, or a mess of civil engineers. It's better to turn out one good coach than ten college presidents.

They threw Iowa out of the Football League for paying too much to their players. Most of the colleges just give 'em board and schooling—if they want to take any schooling.

I went to see one of the modern football games, and the thing that struck an old-timer, was that on every play there would be twenty-two different men facing each other. They could go in and come out, go in and come out—in fact, that's what tired 'em out was going in and out so much.

But I don't want to criticize this system of substituting players all the time. They may be operating under a plan to give shorter hours and more work to more men.

It's no trouble to tell the successful educational institutions these days. It's the one that can afford a new stadium.

The *Daily Princetonian* want an article from me, on any subject that would be of interest to the growing student. So as soon as I get time, I will write one on "Are College Football Players Overpaid?"

The football season is about over. Education never had a better financial year. Successful colleges will start laying plans for larger stadiums; unsuccessful ones will start hunting a new coach.

★

The baseball season opened on Wednesday, matinee day; everything of any importance always happens on a day when we have to work in the theatre. I'll bet that when the world comes to an end, it will be on a matinee day, and I'll miss it.

★

It's a joke to see a home run in some of these ball parks. It does look like as big a game as baseball is, and as much money as they make, they would be able to have a regulation playing field, the same size everywhere. Then if a man got a homer, he would know he deserved it, and everybody would have an equal chance on every field.

You don't see 'em cutting off the end of a tennis court, to put in more stands.

Baseball teams go South every spring to cripple their players. In the old days they only stayed a couple of weeks, and they couldn't get many of them hurt in that time, but, nowadays, they stay till they get 'em all hurt, even if it takes all spring.

They offered Babe Ruth the same salary that President Hoover gets. Babe claims he should have more. He claims he can't appoint a commission to go to home plate and knock the home runs; he has to do it all himself.

Golf is a wonderful exercise. You stand on your feet for hours, watching somebody else putt. It's just the old-fashioned pool hall moved outdoors, but with no chairs around the walls.

★

I guess there is nothing that will get your mind off everything like golf will. I have never been depressed enough to take up the game, but they say you can get so sore at yourself that you forget to hate your enemies.

38 PHILOSOPHY

"I DON'T HAVE A PHILOSOPHY," Will used to say. "I don't even know what the word means. Fourth Grade McGuffey is just as far as I ever got." But he had his own philosophy; he may not have ever put it into words, but then everything he ever said and wrote bespeaks his philosophy. He lived it, for all to see, like his religion. That's why to this day he is often called "The Cowboy Philosopher."

His wit was a combination of humor and philosophy. It contained as much laughter as it required thought. Once, when asked to sum up his humor, Will defined his magic:

I use only one set method in my little gags, and that is to try to keep to the truth. Of course, you can exaggerate it, but what you say must be based on truth. Personally, I don't like the jokes that get the biggest laughs, as they are generally as broad as a house, and require no thought at all. I like one where, if you are with a friend, and hear it, it makes you think, and you nudge your friend and say: "He's right about that!" I would rather have you do that than have you laugh—and then forget the next minute what it was you laughed at.

When Will Durant, the great American philosopher, started to compile his collection of the philosophies of the great men of the world, he contacted Rogers for his statement. Wrote Will:

This doggone Durant wanted me to write him and give him my version of "What Your Philosophy of Life is." And a copy of this same letter was being sent to Hoover, MacDonald, Lloyd George, Mussolini, Marconi, Gandhi, Stalin, Trotsky, Tagore, Einstein, Edison, Ford, Eugene

206

O'Neill, and Bernard Shaw, and three or four others. Now I don't know if this guy Durant is kidding me or not. If I got this kind of letter from somebody else, I would say it's a lot of hooey and wouldent even finish reading it. But putting me in there with that class, why, I figured I better start looking into this Philosophy thing.

I can't tell this guy Durant anything. What all of us know put together don't mean anything. We are just here for a spell and pass on. Any man that thinks that civilization has advanced, is an egotist. Fords and bathtubs have moved you and cleaned you, but you was just as ignorant when you got there. We know lots of things we used to dident know, but we don't know any way to prevent 'em from happening. Confucius perspired out more knowledge than the U.S. Senate has vocalized out in the last 50 years.

We got more toothpaste on the market, and more misery in our courts than at any time in our existence. There ain't nothing to life but satisfaction. Indians and primitives were more satisfied, and they depended less on each other, and took less from each other. We couldent live a day without depending on everybody. So our civilization has given us no Liberty or Independence.

The whole thing is a racket, so get a few laughs, do the best you can, take nothing for serious. Believe in something for another world, but don't be too set on what it is, and then you won't start out that life with a disappointment. Live your life so that whenever you lose, you are ahead.

It's great to be great, but it's greater to be human.

★

People love high ideals, but they got to be about 33 percent plausible.

★

It don't do a fellow much good to be too far ahead of his time. It's better that he be a little dumber, and stay along with the times.

★

Everything worthwhile is a good idea, but did you ever notice there is more bad ideas that will work than there is good ones?

★

Be sure you are right and then go ahead, but don't arbitrate.

★

Whether your parents are good or bad, that's not your business, but stick with 'em when they are in trouble.

★

No man is great if he thinks he is.

Liberty don't work as good in practice as it does in speeches.

Everybody is running around in circles, announcing that somebody's pinched their Liberty! Now the greatest aid that I know of that anyone could give the world today, would be a correct definition of "Liberty."

Now, what might be one class's Liberty, might be another class's Poison. I guess Absolute Liberty couldent mean anything but that anybody can do anything they want to, any time they want to. Well, any half-wit can tell you that wouldent work. So the question arises, How much Liberty can I get and get away with? Well, you can get no more than you give! That's my definition, but you got perfect Liberty to work out your own.

It just looks like everything is doing fine but humans. Animals are having a great year, grass was never higher, flowers were never more in bloom, trees are throwing out an abundance of shade for us to loaf under. Everything the Lord has had a hand in is going great, but the minute you notice anything that is in any way under the supervision of man, why, it's cockeyed.

A fool that knows he is a fool, is one that knows he don't know all about anything. But the fool that don't know he is a fool, is the one that thinks he knows all about anything.

I sometimes wonder if the Lord is going to make the proper distinction between the fellow that means well, and the one that does well. I don't believe he will blackball us just because we don't remember.

There is nothing as easy as denouncing. It don't take much to see that something is wrong, but it does take some eyesight to see what will put it right again.

A remark generally hurts in proportion to its truth.

★

Tradition is nothing more than saying "The Good Old Days," and what you mean by anybody's good old days, is days when they can remember they was having more fun than they are having now.

★

Don't just grab at the first thing that comes along. Have an idea in your head and be willing to wait for it. Know when to refuse something that won't get you anywhere. Struggle along for years, you got to wait for a thing till it is ripe; don't just jump into things just because somebody offers it to you. Look and see if it's going to lead you anywhere.

★

America has millions of people. Now out of all this herd there are about 99 and 9 tenths percent of us that just drag along and what we do or say don't have much effect on any of the rest of the mob. But scattered among these one-tenth percent, every once in a while you run onto some odd individual, some queer bird, that is out of the natural beaten path of human beings. We all go up the main road, while they take the trails.

★

Lead your life so you wouldn't be ashamed to sell the family parrot to the town gossip.

39 LAWYERS

LAWYERS WERE A FAVORITE SUBJECT for Will's jokes. Listeners could usually identify with these jokes because many of them had had their own experiences with the law. There was, however, one time when Will was his own lawyer, and an excellent one at that, since he settled his case out of court, and made some friends in the bargain.

In the early part of 1920 Will syndicated a strip, "The Illiterate Digest," that appeared in many motion-picture theatres throughout the country. It was not long before he received a letter from a William Beverly Winslow, Lawyer, 55 Liberty Street, New York, N.Y. The letter read in part:

"My client, the Funk & Wagnalls Company, publishers of the *Literary Digest*, has requested me to write to you in regard to your use of the phrase, "The Illiterate Digest," as a title to a moving picture subject gotten up by you, the consequence of which may have escaped your consideration.

For more than two years past my client has placed upon the moving picture screen a short reel subject carrying the title "Topics of the Day," selected from the Press of the World by *The Literary Digest*. *The Literary Digest* is a publication nearly thirty years old, and from a small beginning has become probably the most influential weekly publication in the world.

I have advised the publishers that they may proceed against you through the Federal Trade Commission in Washington, calling upon you to there defend yourself against the charges of "unfair competition."

Unless I hear favorably from you on or before the first of December,

210

I shall conclude that you are not willing to accede to this suggestion and will take such steps as I may deem advisable.

Yours truly,
[signed] William Beverly Winslow.

On November 15, 1920, Will Rogers wrote the following reply:

Your letter in regard to my competition with the *Literary Digest* received and I never felt as swelled up in my life. And am glad you wrote directly to me instead of communicating with my lawyers, as I have not yet reached the stage of prominence where I was committing unlawful acts and requiring a lawyer. Now if the *Literary Digest* feels that the competition is too keen for them—to show you my good sportsmanship—I will withdraw. In fact I had already quit as the gentlemen who put it out were behind in their payments and my humor kinder waned, in fact after a few weeks of no payments I couldent think of a single joke.

And now I want to inform you truly that this is the first that I knew my title of the "Illiterate Digest" was an infringement on yours, as it means the direct opposite. If a magazine was published called *Yes* and another bird put one out called *No*, I suppose he would be infringing. But you are a lawyer and it's your business to change the meaning of words, so I lose before I start.

Now I have not written for these people in months and they havent put any gags out, unless it is some of the old ones still playing. If they are using gags that I wrote on topical things 6 months ago, then I must admit that they would be in competition with the ones the *Literary Digest Screen* uses now. I will gladly furnish you with their address, in case you want to enter suit. And as I have no lawyer, you can take my case too, and whatever we get out of them we will split at the usual lawyer rates of 80-20, the client of course getting the 20.

Now you inform your editors at once that their most dangerous rival has withdrawn, and that they can go ahead and resume publication. But you inform your clients that if they ever take up Rope Throwing or Gum Chewing, that I will consider it a direct infringement of my rights and will protect it with one of the best lawyers in Oklahoma.

So long Beverly, if you ever come to California come out to Beverly where I live and see me.

Illiterately yours,
[signed] Will Rogers

When Will told this story as part of the foreward to a book called *Illiterate Digest*, he continued with subsequent events:

When I sent him my answer I read it to some of the movie company I was working with at the time and they kept asking me afterwards if I had received an answer. I did not, and I just thought, oh well, there I go and waste a letter on some high-brow lawyer with no sense of humor. I was sore at myself for writing it.

About 6 months later I came back to join the *Follies* and who should come to call on me but the nicest old gentleman I had ever met, especially in the law profession. He was the one I had written to, and he had had photographic copies made of my letter and had given them around to all his lawyer friends. So it is to him and his sense of humor that I dedicate this volume of deep thought.

I might also state that the *Literary Digest* was broad-minded enough to realize that there was room for both, and I want to thank them for allowing me to announce my illiteracy publicly.

P.S. The *Literary Digest* ceased publication in February 1938. Its name, good-will, and subscription list were purchased three months later by Time, Inc.

Any time a man can't come and settle with you without bringing his lawyer, why, look out for him.

Law is complications and complications is Law. If everything was just plain, there wouldn't be any lawyers.

I know cows better than I do lawyers. There is a way of studying a cow and learning all about her, but a lawyer? There has never yet been a course at college devised in "What makes a lawyer like he is?"

A jury should decide a case the minute they are sworn in, before the lawyers have had a chance to mislead 'em.

The minute you read something and you can't understand it, you can almost be sure that it was drawn up by a lawyer. You see, every time a lawyer writes something, he is not writing for posterity, he is writing so that endless others of his craft can make a living out of trying to figure out just what he said.

★

Thousands of students just graduated all over the country in Law. Going to take an awful lot of crime to support that bunch. A man naturally pulls for the business that brings him in his living. That's human nature, so look what a new gang we got to assist devilment. All trained to get a guilty man out on a technicality, and an innocent one in on their opposing lawyer's mistake.

★

Lawyers are like a lot of the crafts that many of us live by, great, but useless. One level-headed man could interpret every law there is. If you commit a crime, you either did, or you didn't, without habeas corpus, change of venue, or any other legal shindig.

But Lord, if we go into things that are useless, why, two-thirds of the world would have to turn to manual labor. That's really the only essential thing there is.

★

Thirty-five hundred lawyers are in Chicago for their annual convention. They are there, they say, to save the Constitution and to preserve States' Rights. What they ought to be there for, and that would make their convention immortal, is to kick the crooks out of their profession.

★

Went down and spoke at the lawyers' convention last night. They didn't think much of the remark I had made about driving the shysters out of their profession.

They seemed to be kinder in doubt just who would have to leave.

★

Just addressed the California State Legislature and helped 'em pass a bill to form a lawyers' association to regulate their conduct.

Personally I don't think you can make a lawyer honest by an act of the legislature. You've got to work on his conscience—and his lack of conscience is what makes him a lawyer.

40 BANKERS

AMONG WILL'S THREE FAVORITE TARGETS for his jibes were bankers—the other two were lawyers and politicians. It is easy to understand why Will would josh about bankers. Practically everyone in the twenties and thirties knew cases involving bankers or had some personal contact with bankers. The Teapot Dome scandal involved bankers and financiers and huge sums of cash. The congressional investigation of superbanker J. P. Morgan—who Will said held a secured mortgage on the world at 7 percent—made headlines in every newspaper in America.

Many farmers, small businessmen, and home owners fought losing battles in an effort to save their mortgages. And in the early thirties, millions of depositors lost their small savings when banks failed all across the country. Will had his own experiences with bankers, but he was one of the very few who had an opportunity to get even with them—naturally in his own way.

In the early twenties Will produced three motion pictures with his own capital. Knowing next to nothing about the intricacies of film distribution, he found himself in debt and forced to mortgage, or sell, his assets to satisfy creditors—mostly banks. To raise additional cash, he accepted after-dinner speaking engagements, usually for a fee of $1,000. But instead of the time-honored archaic style usually inflicted on such captive audiences, Will would—to the listeners' delight—poke fun at them. Of course, there was as much truth as there was humor in his remarks. One of the few such after-dinner speeches preserved in its entirety was Will's address to the national convention of bankers.

Looking innocent, and flashing his disarming grin, he began:

214

Loan Sharks and Interest Hounds, I have addressed every form of organized graft in the United States—excepting Congress—so it's naturally a pleasure for me to appear before the biggest. You are without a doubt the most disgustingly rich audience I ever talked to—with the possible exception of the bootleggers' union, Local 1, combined with the enforcement officers. I understand that you hold this convention every year to announce what the annual gyp will be. I have often wondered where the depositors hold their convention. . . . I see where your convention was opened by a prayer. You had to send outside your ranks to get somebody that knew how to pray. You should have had one creditor here; he would have shown you how to pray. I see by your speeches that you are very optimistic of business conditions for the coming year. Boy, I don't blame you. If I had your dough, I'd be optimistic, too. Will you please tell me what you do with all those vice-presidents that a bank has? The United States is the biggest business institution in the world, and they only got one vice-president, and nobody has ever found anything for him to do. You have a wonderful organization. I understand you have ten thousand members here, and with what you have in various federal prisons, it brings your membership up to around thirty thousand. . . . Goodby, you are the finest bunch that ever foreclosed a mortgage on a widow's home.

Will continued to quip about bankers, but he never mentioned that his father, Clem Vann Rogers, whom he loved and respected, founded the bank in Claremore, Oklahoma, and was for years one of its officers.

All these big moneyed people, they are just like the underworld—they all know each other and kinder work together.

★

Borrowing money on what's called "easy terms" is a one-way ticket to the poorhouse.

★

If you think banking ain't a sucker game, why is your banker the richest man in town?

★

You can't break a man that don't borrow.

★

Banking and after-dinner speaking are two of the most nonessential industries we have in this country. I am ready to reform, if they are.

Branch banks are all the go now. They realize they have got to bring the bank nearer the robber. He won't be annoyed by driving through traffic, just to rob one bank. The branch bank is the robber's only salvation.

The Banker, the lawyer, and the politician are still our best bets for a laugh. Audiences haven't changed at all—and neither have the three above professions.

The American Bankers' Association are holding their annual benefit. It's their biggest benefit year yet. The government has contributed permission for them to consolidate and freeze out the little fellow, and the public will contribute everything else. So really, the only problem before the convention is: What percentage will we make 'em pay above the legal rate of interest?

See where congress passed a 2 billion dollar bill to relieve bankers' mistakes and loans to new industries. You can always count on us helping those who have lost part of their fortune, but our whole history records nary a case where the loan was for the man who had absolutely nothing. The theory is to help those who can get along, even if they don't get it.

If you notice, they are always trying to put through some kind of bill in congress, but nobody ever puts through one to do something about bank interest. No, Sir, you couldn't do that, because then you are getting into the business of the boys that really hold the hoops while the jumping is going on.

They limit a Savings Bank from paying you more than a few percent, but anything is legal if you are the one to do the borrowing.

It's not from a personal view that I am for abolishing banks. It's just that I don't think these boys realize what a menace they are. As far as being good fellows, personally, well, I have heard old-timers talk down home in the Indian Territory, and they say that Jesse James or the Dalton Boys, were the most congenial men of their day, too.

41 AUTOMOBILE

IF WILL ROGERS HAD A SHORTCOMING, it probably was his complete lack of any mechanical ability. In his youth, of course, there were few machines; besides, Will cared little about anything but his pony and his lariat. As an adult, any engine remained an enigma to Will. Said he about a plane's engine: "If they raised up the hood and a rabbit jumped out, I would just figure he belonged in there." If his car had enough gasoline in the tank and still refused to start, Will would simply leave it stranded. There was nothing, absolutely nothing, he could do to get it going, beyond possibly pushing it. Betty doubted that Will even knew how to change a tire.

But all this does not mean that Will Rogers did not like automobiles. On the contrary, he loved them. Perhaps to Will cars were the nearest thing to piloting your own plane—an accomplishment he never even attempted to learn. The comparison is quite valid, because Will drove cars with utter abandon. He amassed an unenviable number of speeding tickets, and he paid the attendant fines as if they were part of the maintenance cost of the car.

Will bought his first car in 1915. That was the summer the family rented a house in Amityville, Long Island. Will had vaudeville bookings in and around New York City, and to make commuting easier, he bought a magnificent secondhand Overland touring car. Nightly, usually around 2:30 A.M., the neighborhood awoke to the explosions, backfiring, and sputtering of the old car. Finally the law stepped in to protect the innocent. "Rogers," Will reported the policeman's monologue, "Rogers, I can't stop you from going down these quiet roads, you live here. But this car is not going to wake up another resident. It will have to stay up on the main road and you'll just have to walk in!" And so it was.

Once Will bought a truck to help around the ranch in Santa Monica. Expecting it to perform like a horse, he got behind the steering wheel and drove it up and down the slopes, across ditches, never bothering to avoid natural hazards such as roots or boulders. He probably felt that the truck would sidestep them as cleverly as a horse would. On the very first day, Will bent the drive shaft and the truck stalled. He had it towed back to the dealer, paid for the repair, and gave the truck to a circus that was in financial difficulties and needed it badly.

Though he was given the very first Model-A car by Henry Ford, Will preferred a large Buick. Predating the current "mobile home," Will would drive his car on to the motion-picture set. He would park it as close to the cameras as possible, and for the rest of the day it was home. It was his dressing room where he could change his costume; it was his study where he would sit with his typewriter on his knees, pecking out the daily columns; between takes he would stretch out on the fender and catch up on his newspaper reading; and if he felt a little tired, he would curl up on the back seat and catch forty winks.

And, best of all, when the clock struck 4:30, he would jump behind the wheel, yell "Santa Monica Canyon!" and would be off to join the family and do a little roping before the sun set.

I see by today's statistics that a big item is secondhand cars. I am sorry to hear it. We haven't got twenty men in America that are rich enough to support one.

★

I have a solution to the problem of traffic and that is to raise the speed limit to 75 miles an hour, and make everybody go that fast, or be arrested. That would eliminate the slow, and kill off the fast.

★

Another way to solve the traffic problems of this country is to pass a law that only paid-for cars be allowed to use the highways. That would turn our boulevards into children's playgrounds overnight.

★

Why do they call it traffic? When it ceases to move it's not traffic.

Has somebody with a knack for statistics kept track of how many times they have told the joke of a "certain small-make car" catching up with a big car, going seventy miles an hour, and asking: "Say, how do you get this 'certain small-make car' out of second gear?"

In 1918 motorless Sundays were invented, not to save gasoline but to save lives. Undertakers made a strenuous objection.

I unconsciously broke an American record of five years' standing yesterday. I bought a new car and didn't trade an old one in.

I told you about breaking a record by buying a new car and not trading one in. Well, if I just had paid cash for it, I would have broken a real record, but I didn't.

A backseat driver can do more harm with their voice, than the one in front can do with a steering wheel.

Automobile manufacturers say that in ten years there will be an auto to every man, woman, and child in the U.S. Now all they got to do is control the birthrate.

★

It was National Automobile Show week. You never saw as many cars alike in your life. The cheap cars have imitated the high-priced ones, and the high-priced ones have made cheaper models that are almost like their expensive ones. The only distinguishable feature of the whole show, is that there is no distinguishable feature.

★

Headline says: "Five Autos Held Up." Didn't say whether it was a bandit, or a garage.

★

The big thing about automobiles is still accessories. You price a car nowadays, and he gives you a figure. It sounds pretty reasonable. Then you say: "That includes everything?"

"Well, no. If you want wheels on it, that will come extra; you can get either wheels or runners, most people prefer wheels. But on account of us not knowing just what they might like, why, we make 'em extra. Then the bumpers, front, rear, and side, and the lights. Of course, you will want lights, in case you might want to use the car at night. And the mirrors are extra, in case you want to see what's going on in the back seat."

"Well, just what does go with the car at the original price you quoted me?"

"Well, the name and the goodwill."

P. T. Barnum came nearer having a true slogan than anybody. He said: "There is a sucker born every minute," and the car manufacturers are right there to take care of him the minute he comes of age.

I represent what is left of a vanishing race, and that is the pedestrian. While traffic officers have been directing traffic, I know more about it than they do. I have been dodging it. That I am able to be still here, I owe to a keen eye, and a nimble pair of legs. But I know they'll get me someday. I am not as young as I used to be, and they are missing me closer every day.

Mr. Henry Ford is a good friend of mine, and I was at his home. I happened to ask him: "In case of stiff competition, how cheap he could sell his car." He said: "Will, by controlling the selling of the parts, I could give the cars away. Why, those things would shake off enough bolts in a year to pay for themselves, and the second year, that's just pure profit."

In 1914, the Ford Company passed its first 1,000-cars-a-day production. So Americans woke up and said: "We got to have somewhere to put these things"; and somebody thought of the idea of building roads to store them on. And as fast as they would make roads, these things would clutter them up. I don't care where you try to hide a road, one of those road fillers will find it.

Americans are getting like Ford cars—they all have the same parts, the same upholstering, and they all make exactly the same noises.

I see where one automobile manufacturer announced that his car was going to be four inches wider. Now how many times have you missed someone by less than four inches?

Well, from now on you will hit him.

Been reading in the papers what Lord Cecil said about aerial disarmament. What about the auto? They kill more than all the wars. Their warfare is going on all the time. A war is started by somebody agreeing to fight, but the old auto just keeps on reaping 'em down with no previous agreement.

Now right here in the paper is the following: "Annual Auto Bill of U.S. is 14 billion dollars." In another part of the paper it tells that 22,000 met their death last year by auto. 14 billion dollars we paid to kill 22,000. About $635,000 apiece, with no charge at all for the wounded. They will run at least two or three times as many as the killed, and for what? Why, just to get somewhere a little quicker—if you get there at all. If cholera or smallpox or some disease killed, or left affected that many, why, congress and every agency of the government would be appropriating money and doing every mortal thing necessary to do something about it. But, as it is, we go right on.

Too bad.

America has been just muscle-bound from holding a steering wheel. The only callous place on an American is the bottom of his driving toe.

42 BUSINESS

WHILE WILL ROGERS WAS SUCCESSFUL in everything else he ever attempted, business was not on his list of accomplishments.

Time and time again he tried in his earlier years to enter business as a producer of shows, and every time he ended up either even or, worse yet, with a loss.

His first attempt as a producer was in Memphis, in May 1901. Will was just twenty-one years old, and he had persuaded the organizers of a big Confederate veterans' reunion to let him put on a riding and roping contest. He began to organize a group of forty riders and on May 25 they left for Memphis. The show lasted four days, a tremendous success as an entertainment, except that Will returned home completely broke.

Six years later Will tried producing again. He had been successful in Europe with his act; how much better to have a larger act. He hired two more riders and horses and shipped them all to England. They had bookings, but Will found that all of them together were paid no more than he had been paid as a "single" act. As quickly as he could he shipped the two riders back with their horses—broke again. He had to stay behind to earn enough to pay for his own passage.

By 1912 Will Rogers had a wife and a baby son. Vaudeville was a livelihood, but he did not seem to advance any further. Will again wanted to stage his own shows. He envisioned the largest Wild West show ever produced on a stage. He also engaged a large number of cowgirls, feeling that the public would be most interested in seeing girls doing barrel racing and trick riding. The show was so huge that few stages could have handled it, even if

222

Will could have afforded the payroll. The effort failed.

Once more, Will tried his hand at business. He had been in Hollywood three years, made over a dozen feature films for Sam Goldwyn, and he thought that he could produce his own films. The films were good, but Will had no distribution, and he failed once more. It was the last time Will Rogers entered the strange world of commerce. It was not that anyone took advantage of him; it was simply a case of Will being unfamiliar with the intricacies and pitfalls of business.

There was one field of commercial enterprise where the country boy from the Indian Territory could show those city slickers a thing or two—and that was real estate. Will knew land, and whatever he chose was the best available. Some land he acquired trying to help others. Even there he succeeded beyond expectation. Take the 300-acre lot in far-out Santa Monica.

A fellow actor came to Will, imploring him to take a piece of land off his hands. It seemed that the actor had hoped to purchase the land and had put a rather large amount down as a deposit. He now found himself unable to pick up the option and would therefore also lose the deposit. Will promised to take Betty and look the land over. The following Sunday both drove out to Santa Monica, which seemed to be at the end of the world. They liked what they could see from the car (much of the 300 acres was hilly and there was no way to get to it). Will decided to buy. He not only repaid the actor's deposit, but gave him a handsome profit as well.

That was the land on which Will Rogers eventually built his ranch.

A Holding Company is a thing where you hand an accomplice the goods, while the policeman searches you.

★

If the other fellow sells cheaper than you, it is called "dumping." 'Course, if you sell cheaper than him, that's "mass production."

There is two things that can disrupt business in this country. One is war, and the other is a meeting of the Federal Reserve Bank.

We will never have any prosperity that is free from speculation, till we pass a law that every time a broker, or a person, sells anything, he has got to have it sitting there in a bucket, or a bag, or a jug, or a cage, or a rattrap, or something, depending on what he is selling.

As it is now, we are continually buying something that we never get, from a man that never had it.

This current investigation is going to be very educational of all big business. It's going to show just how Big Business got Big. It got Big according to law, but not according to Hoyle.

The latest census reports show that the small town is passing. We not only ought to regret it, we ought to do something to remedy it. It was the incubator that hatched all our big men, and that's why we haven't got as many big men today as we used to have. Take every small-town-raised man out of business, and you would have nobody left running it but vice-presidents.

Real estate is quite a business. You know you buy a lot in Los Angeles with the same frequency you would a newspaper in any other town. After buying it, you put it back in the hands of the agent again, for don't think you're going to get away with that lot.

Every lot in Los Angeles has its own agent. If an agent handles two lots, he opens a branch office and has an assistant. And you try and call one a real estate agent, and he won't sell you anything. He is a "Realtor"—it's the same as what the old-fashioned real estate agent used to be, only the commission is different.

If a business thrives under a protective tariff, that don't mean that it has been a good thing. It may have thrived because it made the people of America pay more for the object than they should have, so a few got rich at the cost of the many.

★

The day of the little guy working for himself is passing. We are living in an age of mergers and combines. The poor little fellow, he can't combine with anything, except the sheriff in case he goes broke, which he generally is.

★

There's talk of a ship subsidy, which, of course, we should have. If you don't think so, just go around to the docks and see how few American flags you see on all the ships that are there.

But, of course, it's too sensible to ever get by.

★

Big business went to see the president and they said: "Quit trying to reform us, and just give us a chance to recover." The President says: "Can't you reform and recover, too?"

But Big Business answered: "No! We can't do anything with a cop on every corner watching everything we do. Give us a chance to recover first, and honest, when we are able, we will reform."

43 PERSONAL

WILL ROGERS' TRAGIC DEATH in an airplane crash in Alaska was a calamity to America. He had been a most reassuring and calming voice, like that of a father, or favorite uncle. And now that voice was stilled—so suddenly, without a warning, or even a moment's preparation. He had been the man who had personified all that can be right, at a time when all seemed wrong. And now he was gone.

Few, even among those who knew him well, were aware of the many times before that Will Rogers had barely escaped a violent death. The year was 1896, Will was sixteen years old. Always adventuresome, he had struck out on his own, as far east as Buffalo, New York. The day was May 21. Will needed a haircut, and he finally saw a barbershop in the Brown Building, at the corner of Main and Seneca streets, just three blocks from the waterfront. Will was about to cross the street toward the barbershop, which was on the ground floor, at the very corner of the building. As he was about to step off the curb, a beggar accosted him, and as Will usually did, he reached into his pocket for some money while he talked to the man. A dollar bill and some conversation having been exchanged, the beggar was on his way, and Will once more started out to cross the street. There was an excavation right next to the Brown Building, partly cutting under it. And as Will approached it, there was a deafening roar, like an explosion, and the building collapsed. In the building there had been nine barbers working at the time, as well as a cashier, a bootblack, and several customers. Three of the barbers were killed and every patron was either hurt or killed. If Will had not stopped to talk to the beggar, he would have been in the shop.

Will was now eighteen and home from the Kemper Military School in Boonville, Missouri. He looked strange walking around in his form-fitting military uniform, brass buttons gleaming, with that little cap on his head. Some of his friends gathered around and wanted to know all about life at a military school; none of them had ever attended one. Will was happy to show off; he was going to perform the cadet's manual of arms for them. Since he did not have his school rifle with him, he went into his house and took his father's. Then, shouting orders, as the officers did at Kemper, Will went through the ritual. At the very end of the performance, when he let the rifle butt hit the ground, the gun went off, firing straight up. The bullet grazed Will's forehead and went right through the cap. Blood streamed down Will's face, but the wound was only superficial. However, it left a permanent scar, both on the boy's face and on his psyche. He never bought a gun, or went hunting.

In the fall of 1898 Will was on a roundup. Riding a black pony, Will had raced up and down, keeping the herd together while roping everything in sight, whether it moved or not. Finally he stopped under a tree for a rest. He loosened the saddle cinch to give the horse a chance to cool off too. Suddenly, one of the steers made a run away from the herd. Forgetting to tighten the saddle girth, Will jumped on his horse, and tore after the runaway. He threw his lasso and caught the animal squarely around the neck. That was a mistake, because things began to happen. The horse dug in its feet—as it had been trained to do—to tighten the lariat. Will's saddle, to which the other end of the rope was fastened, was jerked halfway under the horse, and Will went flying through the air. He lay stunned for several minutes. When he was finally brought around, it was found that his right arm was broken. He was driven to town, where a doctor set it.

In the fall of 1900 a trainload of cattle had to be taken west, and after they had been delivered, Will and another man decided to go on and see San Francisco. They stayed in an inexpensive rooming house, which was, of course, lighted by gas. Here the story is a little unclear, though not the result. Either Will, or his companion, forgetting that this was gas and not kerosene, simply blew out the flame before going to sleep. Naturally the gas kept on escaping, filling the room. Hours later someone passed the door, smelled the

gas, and called for help. Will and his companion were rushed to
the hospital, both unconscious. The doctors worked feverishly
over both, and after three days Will was released. He was put on a
train and sent home. When he arrived at the Claremore railway
station he was so weak he had to be helped into the buggy. When
his father saw him he sent him immediately to Hot Springs,
Arkansas, to rest and to let the hot baths steam out the gas. For
many months thereafter Will was still weak and tired easily.

Fred Stone, who was Will's best friend, had a summer place
near Amityville. In the summer of 1915 Stone suggested that Will
rent a nearby house and have the family spend the sweltering days
in the relative coolness of Long Island. Betty was expecting their
third child, and Will rented a house on Clocks Boulevard,
diagonally across from Fred's home. Will and Fred, together with
Rex Beach, the famous author and Fred's brother-in-law, would
ride together, play polo, go sailing on Great South Bay, or swim in
Fred's private ocean inlet. One morning, as the three men
approached the inlet for another swim, Will raced ahead of the
others and, without waiting for them, dived headlong into it. His
head hit a submerged rock and, unconscious, he had to be dragged
ashore. Examining Will's head wound, Rex Beach asked, "Didn't
you see that the tide was out?"

"Tide?" Will began to come to. "We didn't have no tide on the
Verdigris River where I learned to swim."

The wound proved superficial, but when Will tried to move he
found that his right arm was completely paralyzed; he could not
even control his fingers. Stunned, he shuffled back to his house.
He had some vaudeville commitments, but his arm hung useless.
How was he going to twirl a rope? A lifetime of practice had been
lost in a split second. Was this the end of his career?

The next day, with no improvement in his right arm, Will began
a strict regimen: hour after hour, from early morning till long after
dark, he would practice, teaching himself to do rope tricks with his
left hand. Since he could not possibly learn to use it in time, he
relied much more on his gags. "I sho' did me a mess of tall gabbing
on anything I could think of, and you know, they never missed the
big rope tricks."

Will became almost as proficient with his left hand as he had
been with his right. Eventually, when the full use of his right arm

had returned, he would astonish audiences by throwing ropes with both hands. He could toss three lariats at once, catching a galloping horse by the neck while the other two ropes would hobble the horses rear and fore feet. He had become the world's greatest roper—except by this time the rope was merely a trademark, and the world came to listen to the man.

Will Rogers was involved in a number of airplane crashes, many not even known to his family. On his first cross-country trip, in 1927, the small plane with Will aboard crash-landed in the hills of Pennsylvania. On his way to the 1928 Republican National Convention in Kansas City, Will was in two separate plane crashes: he was shaken up in Las Vegas, Nevada, when his plane flipped over on landing; later, near Cheyenne, Wyoming, he was bruised when his plane's undercarriage collapsed on takeoff.

On his way to attend a dinner given by Henry Ford for Thomas Alva Edison, Will seemed stuck in Chicago because the regular airline to Detroit had cancelled its flights due to inclement weather. At last Will found a pilot who was willing to fly him to Detroit. Arriving over Detroit in a storm, the pilot refused to land and informed Will that they would have to return to Chicago. Just a few miles from the Chicago airport, the plane ran out of fuel. The pilot handed Will a note and instructed him to brace himself for the crash landing. Will admitted later that looking down on the city below him, he was sure they could not survive. Miraculously the pilot landed in a vacant lot. Will heaved a deep sigh of relief and relaxed—and at that moment the plane flipped over. Dazed and in pain, Will crawled out from under the plane, with a number of ribs either broken or cracked.

Dorothy Stone remembered the time, in the suburbs of New York City, when Will came to their house one morning, his clothing torn, his skin scraped. He had been in an airplane crash and wanted to clean up before going to his home. Said Will: "If Betty sees me like this, she'll never let me fly again." Who can tell how many other crashes there were, on either landing or takeoff, that Will never mentioned, so "Betty would let him fly again."

In 1934 Will, now fifty-four years old, was in a polo game in Los Angeles. At the time he was appearing in the stage version of Eugene O'Neill's *Ah! Wilderness*. Jimmy Rogers, Will's younger son, played on the opposing team. In one encounter, as Jim recalled, "I bumped him so hard I knocked his horse down and he landed on the sideboards. He lay there motionless, and as I jumped from my horse and ran to him, all I could think of was that I had killed him. As I got to his side, he moved and tried to sit up. Still stunned and groggy, his first words were: 'Is the horse all right?'"

Will seemed to recover and insisted on going to the theatre that evening, even though Betty wanted him to rest. During the performance, Will suddenly forgot the script and did a ten-minute monologue on current affairs, until his costar, Anne Shoemaker, slowly guided him back to O'Neill's script. At last Will picked up his cue, and the rest of the show proceeded without further incident. The audience roared at Will's monologue, simply thinking that it was part of the show.

The next day, Will could not even remember having gone to the theatre. There was no aftereffect of the concussion.

Will had several polo accidents. As he described some:

We were playing the Eleventh Cavalry from Monterey. Things were going along pretty good until along about the third chukker. I was on a new pony that suddenly reared up and fell back on me. There he was, lying across my intermission. My head was out on one side and my feet on the other. That was all you could see. Next day, in another game, I'm on my horse, coming lickety-split down the field, when for no reason at all the horse crossed his front legs and starts turning somersaults. They picked me up just south of Santa Barbara. The crowd all said: "Oh, that's Will Rogers; he just does that for laughs."

In August 1935 Will Rogers took a tiny plane to Alaska, and America's luck ran out.

Once a month I answer telegrams marked "Urgent," once a year I answer letters marked "Important."

★

I have been putting what little money I have in ocean frontage, for the sole reason that there was only so much of it and no more, and they wasn't making any more.

Here is a queer streak in me, I'm no hunting man—or fishing, either. I wish I was, for there must be a lot of pleasure in it, but I just don't want to be shooting at any animal, and even a fish, I haven't got the heart to pull the hook out of him.

I get all my quiet amusement talking politics and making them think that I am taking it all serious.

I never could see much percentage in that mountain-climbing thing. Any time I want to do any cliff hopping, I'm going to let a goat do it for me. Any time I go up a mountainside, I'm not going to follow some guide. I'm going to go up after the surveyors have built a two-way road.

★

I sure used to envy General Grant and Jesse James when they had cigars named after 'em, but here I am sitting in the brand new, most up-to-date hotel in the Southwest, the Will Rogers Hotel in Claremore. It's six stories high. I know now how proud Christopher Columbus must have felt when he heard they had named Columbus, Ohio, after him.

★

Early in the autumn Mrs. Rogers and I sent two sons away, supposedly to schools. We got tired trying to get 'em up in the morning. One went to Arizona, the other to New Mexico. Since then we have received no word or letter. Any news from any source will be welcome.

We finally found one of our boys in Rosewell, New Mexico. He has learned to play polo, but hasn't learned to write. We asked him why we never heard from him and he said he had forgot our address.

★

Today is my wife's and my twenty-fifth wedding anniversary. It kind of sneaked up on me. I, of course, being just an ordinary husband, didn't know it was coming. Why is it that wives want to keep those things secret, and then, when you don't notice it, they tell you afterwards and make you feel bad. I just got the news in time, late in the afternoon yesterday, so I bought her a pretty present.

★

Well, all I know is just what I read in the papers. The old paper in the morning is my breakfast. Course, I don't entirely depend on it. I like it accompanied by some ham and eggs, and a few biscuits, a series of cups of coffee, a few wheat cakes to help get your mind off the editorials. So, with my California grapefruit, raised in Laredo, Texas, I like a paper.

A breakfast without a newspaper is a horse without a saddle. You are just riding bareback. Take away my ham, take away my eggs, even my chili, but leave me my newspaper.

When I visited Mexico, they kidded me about not associating with their bull in the ring. I have never become quite half-witted enough to enter the arena with any man's male ox. No sir, I have been butted enough in a branding corral by snorty old calves to know that Clem Rogers' boy Willie, of Oologah, Oklahoma, wasent carved out to meet any bull in combat.

We are always drilling into our children: When I was a boy we dident do that! But we forget that we are not doing those same old things today. We are always telling 'em what we used to not do, but we dident do it because we didn't think of it. We did everything we could think of. I tell you, they got to do some to keep up with us. If any one of us had a child that we thought was as bad as we know we are, we would have cause to start to worry.

With the morning papers stating that we have 11,000 miles of lighted airways, a Zeppelin with sixty people going around the world in less time than a congressman can make a speech, with twenty more-or-less beautiful air-headed women who have exchanged their kimonos for helmets and goggles, with our great navy flier Williams tuning up to go 350 miles an hour, and me feeding two Fords and a Buick and twenty-five head of horses, it looks like I am out of tune with progress.

★

I endorsed chewing gum one time and almost like to had to take up chewing tobacco, to win my "fans" back again. Nothing can get you in wrong quicker than an endorsement.

★

I sure hate to admit it, but there is no use trying to bull it through that I have done much book reading, for I haven't. But with the senate operating 6 hours a day, and the House the same, all the investigations, and the robbers getting out of jails, the million and one things going on, and I read it all, I just got started in wrong. I seemed to have gone from Frank Merriwell, and Nick Carter, right to the Congressional Record, just from one set of low fiction to another.

I tell you, I'm going to read more. I'm at least going to read the titles of some of these books, anyhow. So many books are being published, that you couldn't possibly remember 'em, so you just got to read the titles. Then books nowadays are not written to be remembered, anyhow; they are written just to be sold, not even to be read.

These Irish, you got to watch 'em. There was a few of 'em sneaked into Oklahoma and got mixed up with the Rogerses and the Cherokees, and I am a sort of an offshoot—an Irish Indian.

Darkies raised me. I wasn't only raised among Darkies down in the Indian Territory, but I was raised by them. And Lord, I was five years old out at the ranch before I ever knew there was a white child. There wasn't any other around there. The first one showed up when I was about five years old. You see, I was raised with the Darky children. Now, one of these white children showed up about the same time that Hereford cattle come in. I thought for sure this white child and this bald-face Hereford was the same breed.

I did everything in the circus, Wild West show, rodeo, the *Follies*, and now I've done the play *Ah! Wilderness* by O'Neill; you know, a real play where you had to remember lines, and everything. Oh well, there is only one other amusement line I haven't been in, and that's go to the senate. But I ain't going to try that—I've got some pride left.

I traveled a good deal all over the world, and I got along pretty good in all these foreign countries, for I have a theory that it's their country and they got a right to run it like they want to.

After all, you never heard of the Republicans trying to send a lot of dough to try and carry Alabama, have you? And the Baptists are not rushing any money into Rome to swing it their way, either.

Rex Beach was responsible for my little toe hold in the movies, this eighth science. I played by request of Mrs. Rex Beach in one of his stories, called "Laughing Bill Hyde." The part was that of a crook, who received money under false pretenses. Mrs. Beach had seen my little act in the *Follies*, so naturally she decided that I was the one to do this crook who obtained money under false pretenses.

The whole family is sad, very sad. Dopey had lived with us for nineteen years, and now he left us. He was a little round-bellied coal black pony with glass eyes, the gentlest, greatest pony. I don't know why we called him Dopey, we meant no disrespect.

When nineteen years of your and your children's life is linked so closely with a horse, you can sorter imagine our feelings. He was one of the family; he raised our children and learned them to ride. He never hurt one in his life. He did everything right—and that is a reputation that no human can die with.

★

In London, five years ago, old Lord Dewar, a great humorist and character and the biggest whiskey maker in the world, gave the children a little, white Sealyham, saying: "If this dog knew how well bred he was, he wouldn't speak to any of us."

We have petted him, complained at him, called him a nuisance, but when we buried him yesterday, we couldn't think of a wrong thing he had ever done.

★

Will you do me a favor? If you see or hear of anybody proposing my name humorously, or semiseriously, for any political office, will you maim said party, and send me the bill. I not only don't *choose* to run, I will say I won't run! No matter how bad the country will need a comedian by that time.

★

The *Fourth Reader* McGuffey is as far as I ever got in school. I am not bragging on it, I am thoroughly ashamed of it, for I had every opportunity. Everything I have done has been by luck; no move was premeditated. I just stumbled from one thing to another. I might have been down. I didn't know at the time, for I don't know what "up" is.

★

I have often said in answer to inquiries as to how I got away with kidding some of our public men, that it was because I liked all of them personally, and if there was no malice in your heart, there could be none in your gags; and I have always said I never met a man I didn't like.

44 MISCELLANEA

I don't care how poor and inefficient a little country is, they like to run their own business. Sure America and England can run countries perhaps better than China, Korea, or India, but that don't mean they ought to. I know men that would make my wife a better husband than I am, but, darn it, I'm not going to give her to 'em.

No matter how you built anything and how you painted anything, if it accidentally through lack of wars or rain happened to live a few hundred years, why, it's art now.

★

Weddings are always the same, but no divorces are alike.

★

A young man, he just thinks. But an old man, when he thinks, he is supposed to be pondering.

★

Ah, for the good old days; then you lived until you died, and not until you were just run over.

★

I see where one young boy has just passed 500 hours sitting in a treetop. There is a good deal of discussion as to what to do with a civilization that produces prodigies like that.

Wouldn't it be a good idea to take his ladder away from him and leave him up there?

★

There is nothing impresses "common folks" like somebody that ain't common.

★

Nobody wants to be called "common folks," especially common folks.

★

It's the old gag: people that pay for things never complain. It's the guy you give something to that you can't please.

★

Chewing gum is the only ingredient of our national life of which no one knows of what it is made. We know that sawdust makes our breakfast food, we know that tomato cans constitute automobile bodies, we know that old secondhand newspapers make our 15-dollar shoes, we know that cotton makes our all-wool suits, but no one knows yet what constitutes a mouthful of chewing gum. Maybe it's better that way.

★

We live in an age of "urge." We do nothing till somebody shoves us.

★

The Lord so constituted everybody that no matter what color you are, you require about the same amount of nourishment.

★

I wonder if it ain't just cowardice, instead of generosity, that makes us give most of our tips.

★

What's the matter with the world? Why, there ain't nothing but one word wrong with everyone of us, and that's selfishness.

★

Humanity is not yet ready for either real truth, or real harmony.

★

You know, I truly believe that our public men in high office want to do something worthwhile for us, but they just can't think of anything to do.

★

There is nothing that makes a disreputable nation look respectable as quick as to have it give you a fat war contract. When Judgment Day comes, civilization will have an alibi: I never took a human life, I only sold the gun to take it with.

★

We have had statues built to every person who had a good press agent during their lives.

CHRONOLOGY

1879

November 4, Will Rogers born on his father's ranch, near Oologah, I.T. (Indian Territory), now Oklahoma.

1887

[–1892] Attends schools (Drumgoole, near Chelsea; Presbyterian Mission School, Tahlequah, I.T.; Harrell Institute, Muskogee, I.T.).

1890

Mary America Rogers (mother) dies.

1892

Willie Halsell College, Vinita, I.T. (approximately four years).

1896

Scarritt College Institute, Neosho, Missouri.

1897

[–1898] Kemper Military School, Boonville, Missouri.

1898

Begins work as cowboy on the Ewing Ranch, Higgins, Texas.

1899

[–1902] Manages Rogers ranch; attends roping contests.

1902

Leaves for South America, via England; works for about five months with gauchos, then leaves for South Africa.

1903

South Africa. Joins *Texas Jack's Wild West Show*, billed as the Cherokee Kid. Leaves to tour Australia and New Zealand with Wirth Brothers' Circus.

1904

With *Colonel Zach Mulhall's Wild West Show* at St. Louis, Missouri (World's Fair). A few vaudeville bookings in Chicago.

1905

With Mulhall show at New York's Madison Square Garden as part of Horse Fair. First New York vaudeville appearance. Vaudeville career begins, lasts to 1915, including three trips to Europe.

1908

November 25, marries Betty Blake, at Rogers, Arkansas.

1911

Clem Vann Rogers (father) dies. Birth of first son, Will, Jr., in New York City.

1912

[–1913] Specialty act in Broadway show *The Wall Street Girl*, starring Blanche Ring.

1913

Birth of only daughter, Mary Amelia, at Rogers, Arkansas.

1914

London, England. In show *Merry-Go-Round*. Vaudeville in America.

1915

First airplane flight at Atlantic City, N.J. Appears in musical *Hands Up*, Ned Wayburn's *Town Topics*, and Ziegfeld's *Midnight Frolic*. Birth of second son, James Blake, on Long Island, N.Y.

1916

[–1925] *Ziegfeld Follies*.

1918

Birth of third son, Fred Stone Rogers. While working in *Follies* at night, makes first motion picture (made at Fort Lee, N.J.) *Laughing Bill Hyde.*

1919

Published *The Cowboy Philosopher on the Peace Conference* and *The Cowboy Philosopher on Prohibition.* Moves to California to begin two-year contract with Goldwyn Studio.

1920

Fred Stone Rogers, age twenty months, dies during diphtheria epidemic.

1922

First radio broadcast (Pittsburgh, Pa.). Produces and stars in his own motion pictures. Begins series of weekly syndicated articles (McNaught Syndicate), which continue to 1935.

1923

[–1924] Stars in two-reel comedies for Hal Roach. Publishes *Illiterate Digest.*

1925

[–1928]Travels all over America on lecture tour.
[–1927] Writes daily article "Worst Story I've Heard Today."

1926

London, England. Appears for four weeks in the Charles Cochran *Revue.* Writes *Letters of a Self-Made Diplomat to His President.* Benefit for Florida hurricane victims. Made honorary Mayor of Beverly Hills. Trip to Russia.
[–1935] Begins series of "Daily Telegrams," syndicated in over four hundred newspapers.

1927

First civilian to fly from coast to coast with mail pilots. Publishes *There's Not a Bathing Suit in Russia.* Made "Congressman-at-Large" by National Press Club, Washington, D.C. Visits Mexico with Charles A. Lindbergh, as guest of Ambassador Dwight Morrow. Benefit tour for Mississippi flood sufferers.

1928

[–1929] Substitutes for friend Fred Stone in musical comedy *Three Cheers*, with Dorothy Stone.

929

First sound film for Fox Film Corporation *They Had To See Paris*, with Irene Rich. Publishes *Ether and Me*.
[–1935] Twenty-one films for Fox.

1930

Radio broadcasts for E. R. Squibb & Sons.

1931

To London to observe Disarmament Conference. Benefit for drought victims in Southwest. Appears on national radio broadcast on unemployment with President Hoover, Calvin Coolidge, Al Smith, and others. To Managua, Nicaragua for benefit of earthquake and fire victims.
[–1932] To the Orient.

1932

Central and South America tour.

1933

[–1935] Radio broadcasts for Gulf Oil.

1934

Trip around the world. Stars in Eugene O'Neill's stage play *Ah! Wilderness* in San Francisco and Los Angeles, California.

1935

August 15, dies in plane crash with Wiley Post, famous pilot, near Point Barrow, Alaska.

INDEX